Cybersecurity: The Beginner's Guide

A comprehensive guide to getting started in cybersecurity

Dr. Erdal Ozkaya

BIRMINGHAM - MUMBAI

Cybersecurity: The Beginner's Guide

Commissioning Editor: Vijin Boricha
Acquisition Editor: Heramb Bhavsar
Content Development Editor: Shubham Bhattacharya, Deepti Thore
Technical Editor: Rudolph Almeida
Copy Editor: Safis Editing
Project Coordinator: Nusaiba Ansari
Proofreader: Safis Editing
Indexer: Tejal Daruwale Soni
Graphics: Jisha Chirayil
Production Coordinator: Nilesh Mohite

First published: May 2019

Production reference: 2100619

Published by Packt Publishing Ltd.
Livery Place
35 Livery Street
Birmingham
B3 2PB, UK.

ISBN 978-1-78961-619-4

www.packtpub.com

To my family, my real friends, my mentors, I cannot thank you enough. Yes, I am a doctor and yes I lead a big team and yes, I have a career; but none of those would be the case without YOU. I would like to thank everyone who gave me feedback for being honest, allowing me to focus on my goals; to ignore people who gave negative vibes; to work hard with a positive attitude and always look forward.

– Dr. Erdal Ozkaya

`mapt.io`

Mapt is an online digital library that gives you full access to over 5,000 books and videos, as well as industry leading tools to help you plan your personal development and advance your career. For more information, please visit our website.

Why subscribe?

- Spend less time learning and more time coding with practical eBooks and Videos from over 4,000 industry professionals

- Improve your learning with Skill Plans built especially for you

- Get a free eBook or video every month

- Mapt is fully searchable

- Copy and paste, print, and bookmark content

Packt.com

Did you know that Packt offers eBook versions of every book published, with PDF and ePub files available? You can upgrade to the eBook version at `www.packt.com` and as a print book customer, you are entitled to a discount on the eBook copy. Get in touch with us at `customercare@packtpub.com` for more details.

At `www.packt.com`, you can also read a collection of free technical articles, sign up for a range of free newsletters, and receive exclusive discounts and offers on Packt books and eBooks.

Contributors

About the author

Dr. Erdal Ozkaya is a leading cybersecurity professional with business development, management, and academic skills, who focuses on securing cyberspace and sharing his real-life skills as a security adviser, speaker, lecturer, and author.

He is passionate about reaching communities, creating cyber-awareness campaigns, leveraging new and innovative approaches, technologies that holistically address the information security, and privacy needs for people and organizations worldwide. He has authored many cybersecurity books, security certification courseware, and exams for different vendors.

He is an award-winning technical expert and speaker. His recent awards are as follows: Microsoft Circle of Excellence Platinum Club (2017), NATO Centers of Excellence (2016), Security Professional of the Year by MEA Channel Magazine (2015), Professional of the Year, Sydney (2014), and many Speaker of the Year awards awarded at conferences.

He holds Global Instructor of the Year awards from the EC-Council and Microsoft. He is also a part-time lecturer at the Charles Sturt University in Australia.

The following are Erdal's social media accounts for anyone who would like to stay in touch:

Twitter: https://twitter.com/Erdal_Ozkaya

LinkedIn: https://www.linkedin.com/in/erdalozkaya/

Facebook: https://www.facebook.com/CyberSec.Advisor

Instagram: https://www.instagram.com/learncybersecurity/

About the reviewers

Steve Hailey is President/CEO of the CyberSecurity Academy and an IT veteran of 36 years. He has 33 years of data recovery experience, and has been providing cybersecurity and digital forensics services professionally for 22 years. He is the founder and former President of the Washington State High Technology Crime Investigation Association, and has also held the office of Vice President of the Digital Forensics Certification Board. Steve is a trusted consultant to Fortune 500 companies, law firms, the Department of Defense (DoD), and law enforcement agencies worldwide. He is a cyberterrorism subject matter expert and has trained DoD and federal law enforcement personnel to protect some of the most aggressively targeted information systems in the world.

John Webb is an IT manager who holds both the CISSP and CEH certifications. He has over 15 years of IT experience and has been a student of cybersecurity for the entire time. He is a Linux expert and has been supporting enterprise RHEL systems for the past six years.

Packt is searching for authors like you

If you're interested in becoming an author for Packt, please visit `authors.packtpub.com` and apply today. We have worked with thousands of developers and tech professionals, just like you, to help them share their insight with the global tech community. You can make a general application, apply for a specific hot topic that we are recruiting an author for, or submit your own idea.

Table of Contents

Preface

There are two types of organizations: those who know they have been hacked and those who don't. Nearly every day there is news about a hacked company, regardless of their size.

On the other hand, independent research firms, such as Gartner; Fortune companies, such as Microsoft and Cisco; respected magazines, such as Forbes; global non-profit organizations, such as ISACA; governments; and recruiters are talking about the cybersecurity skill shortage today, and they estimate that the talent gap is in the millions. There are many organizations and individuals that are passionate about closing this gap. There are also possibly endless resources, although very fragmented, on the internet. You will find many books and videos that have the essentials to get you started in cybersecurity, but none of them provide guidance from A to Z on what beginners need to know, what core technology they need to focus on, why they need to have a mentor, how they can network, which certifications they can take, how they can find the resources they need, and finally, how they can find a job.

Again, none of the resources have very well-known industry experts, or hiring managers' advice and suggestions on what a beginner needs to do.

This beginner's guide explores deep technical content pertaining to cybersecurity; however, it also provides real guidance on how to become a cybersecurity expert.

While this book is called a beginner's guide, it also offers a ton of information for professionals who want to switch their careers to cybersecurity.

Who this book is for

This book is targeted at anyone who is looking to venture in to the world of cybersecurity and explore its various nuances. With real-life recommendations from the field, this book is beneficial for everyone from beginners to career switchers.

What this book covers

Chapter 1, *Importance of Cybersecurity*, focuses on the importance of cybersecurity, and will help anyone who wants to become a cybersecurity professional to understand what is expected of them.

Chapter 2, *Security Evolution – From Legacy to Advanced, to ML and AI*, discusses the evolution of cybersecurity and the future of the integration of cybersecurity with machine learning and artificial intelligence integration.

Chapter 3, *Learning Cybersecurity Technologies*, covers what you need to learn to be a cybersecurity professional, with all the paths that are available in the job market today.

Chapter 4, *Skills We Need for a Cybersecurity Career*, looks at the job market to find the cybersecurity roles that organizations are advertising and the in-demand skills that you can learn in order to change to or build your career in cybersecurity.

Chapter 5, *Attacker Mindset*, explores attackers, traits and their way of thinking to find out what drives a hacker.

Chapter 6, *Understanding Reactive, Proactive, and Operational Security*, covers what reactive, proactive, and operational cyber defenses are, what job the pillars of security are, and how you can position yourself to choose the optimal skills for you and your company.

Chapter 7, *Networking, Mentoring, and Shadowing*, discusses the importance of these three essentials to your career.

Chapter 8, *Cybersecurity Labs*, covers self-assessment and learning skills, ways to help you skill up fast, and some key resources to help you build your own practice lab.

Chapter 9, *Knowledge Check and Certifications*, looks at the need to be certified and how you can choose the right places and certifications to study, as there are far too many options based on the real-life experiences of the author and the experts who have contributed to the book.

Chapter 10, *Security Intelligence Resources*, focuses on existing security intelligence resources that can be publicly and commercially consumed to achieve higher standards of security for organizations. As a beginner in security, this information will always come in very handy from a ramp-up perspective.

Chapter 11, *Expert Opinions on Getting Started with Cybersecurity*, contains contributions by academics from universities, such as Oxford and Charles Sturt, and also experts from the field, such as Microsoft, FireEye, SAP, and Keepnet Labs, as well as training institutes, such as the Rochester Institute of Technology, and the privately owned Cqure and Dimension Data. In this chapter, they share their own journeys into cybersecurity, the steps they took, the training they had, and recommendations on how to keep your skills sharp. Besides this, some of them also share what skills they look at when they hire talent.

Chapter 12, *How to Get Hired in Cybersecurity, Regardless of Your Background*, covers tips and tricks on how to get a job in cybersecurity. This includes tips and tricks for interviews, how recruiters work, and how Fortune companies hire. This is the chapter that puts the book into practice.

To get the most out of this book

Read it carefully, decide which path you want to choose, and take the advice from the experts. Regardless of whether you are new to the cyber industry or you have some experience in IT, this book has everything that you need to be successful in the cybersecurity industry.

Download the color images

We also provide a PDF file that has color images of the screenshots/diagrams used in this book. You can download it here: https://www.packtpub.com/sites/default/files/downloads/9781789616194_ColorImages.pdf.

Conventions used

There are a number of text conventions used throughout this book.

CodeInText: Indicates code words in text, database table names, folder names, filenames, file extensions, pathnames, dummy URLs, user input, and Twitter handles. Here is an example: "In order to calculate how much MB your x bit data is, you use four basic operations, and in order to classify your log data, you can use a discriminant function."

Bold: Indicates a new term, an important word, or words that you see onscreen. For example, words in menus or dialog boxes appear in the text like this. Here is an example: "You can then click on the **Start SSL test** button to begin the test."

 Warnings or important notes appear like this.

 Tips and tricks appear like this.

Get in touch

Feedback from our readers is always welcome.

General feedback: If you have questions about any aspect of this book, mention the book title in the subject of your message and email us at customercare@packtpub.com.

Errata: Although we have taken every care to ensure the accuracy of our content, mistakes do happen. If you have found a mistake in this book, we would be grateful if you would report this to us. Please visit www.packt.com/submit-errata, selecting your book, clicking on the Errata Submission Form link, and entering the details.

Piracy: If you come across any illegal copies of our works in any form on the Internet, we would be grateful if you would provide us with the location address or website name. Please contact us at copyright@packt.com with a link to the material.

If you are interested in becoming an author: If there is a topic that you have expertise in and you are interested in either writing or contributing to a book, please visit authors.packtpub.com.

Reviews

Please leave a review. Once you have read and used this book, why not leave a review on the site that you purchased it from? Potential readers can then see and use your unbiased opinion to make purchase decisions, we at Packt can understand what you think about our products, and our authors can see your feedback on their book. Thank you!

For more information about Packt, please visit packt.com.

Disclaimer

The information within this book is intended to be used only in an ethical manner. Do not use any information from the book if you do not have written permission from the owner of the equipment. If you perform illegal actions, you are likely to be arrested and prosecuted to the full extent of the law. Packt Publishing does not take any responsibility if you misuse any of the information contained within the book. The information herein must only be used while testing environments with proper written authorizations from appropriate persons responsible.

Importance of Cybersecurity

In this fast-paced industry, digitization and staying connected are playing a vital role. This is further coupled with the proliferation of cloud-based and mobile technologies. *"Why focus on security?"* is a question that has moved from mere security team discussions to board room discussions, and it doesn't stop there either. This, now, is the talk of the industry today. Everyone we know around us, in our work places or otherwise, is talking about security, one way or the other. Security is no longer just a requirement of an IT administrator, or security administrators in an IT organization. It is now the requirement of all those entities who are connected in one way or the other with any type of data.

The importance of cybersecurity, as the name suggests, will be the crux of the discussion in this chapter, and we will closely look into the following:

- The history of breaches
- The importance of securing networks and applications
- The threat landscape
- How security helps

The history of data breaches

The general notion encircling hacking is that it started a few decades ago. However, in reality, hacking was in practice even before that. it goes as far back as 1834, yes almost two centuries back. Historically, it came to light in the year 1836 when two persons involved in the act were caught. During the last decade of 1700, France implemented its national data network to transfer data between Paris and Bordeaux, which was one of its kind at the time. It was built on top of a mechanical telegraph system, which was a network of physical towers. Each tower was equipped with a unique system of movable arms on the tower top.

The tower operators would use different combinations of these arms to form numbers and characters that could be read from a similar distant tower using a telescope. This combination of numbers and characters was relayed from tower to tower until it reached the far end. As a result, the government achieved a much more efficient mechanism of data transfer, which resulted in greater time saving. Interestingly, all this happened in the open. Even though the combinations were encrypted, and would've required an experienced telegraph operator to decode the message at the far end to bring up the original message, the risks were just around the corner. The following image is one such tower:

Figure 1: Replica of Claude Chappe's optical telegraph on the Litermont near Nalbach, Germany (Photo by Lokilech CC BY-SA 3.0)

This operation was observed by two bankers, Francois and Joseph Blanc. They used to trade government bonds at the exchange in Bordeaux, and it was they who figured out a hack to poison the data transfer in between, and include an indicator of current market status, by bribing a couple of telegraph operators. Usually it took several days before the information related to Bond performance reached Bordeaux by normal mail, now, due to this hack, they had an advantage to get that same information well before the exchange in Bordeaux received it. In a normal transmission, the operator included a *Backspace* symbol to indicate to the other operator that he needed to avoid the previous character and consider it as mistake. The bankers paid one of the operators to include a deliberate mistake with a predefined character, to indicate the previous day's exchange performance, so that they could assume the market movement and plan to buy or sell bonds. This additional character did not affect the original message sent by the government, because it was meant to be ignored by the far end telegraph operator. But this extra character would be observed by another former telegraph operator who was paid by the bankers to decode it by observing through a telescope. Also, the Blanc brothers did not care about the entire message either; all they needed was the information related to market movement, which was well achieved through this extra piece of inert information. The Blanc brothers had an advantage over the market movement and continued to do this for another two years, until their hack was discovered and they were caught in 1836. You can read more about such attacks at https://www.thevintagenews.com/2018/08/26/cyberattacks-in-the-1830s/.

The modern equivalent of this attack would perhaps be data poisoning, man-in-the middle attack, misuse of the network, attacking, or social engineering. However, the striking similarity is that these attacks often go unnoticed for days or years before they get caught. This was true then, and it's true today. Unfortunately, the Blanc brothers could not be convicted as there were no laws under which they could be prosecuted at that time.

Maybe the Blanc brothers' hack was not so innovative compared to today's cyber attacks, but it did indicate that data was always at risk. And, with the digitization of data in all shapes and forms, operations, and transport mechanisms (networks), the attack surface is huge now. It is now the responsibility of the organization and the individuals to keep the data, network, and computer infrastructure safe.

Let's fast forward another 150 years, to the late 1980s. This is when the world witnessed the first ever computer virus—**Morris worm**. Even though the creator of the worm, Robert Tappan Morris, denied the allegation that it was intended to cause harm to computers, it did, indeed, affect millions of them. With an intention to measure the vastness of the cyber world, Tappan wrote an experimental program that was self-replicating and hopped from one computer to another on its own.

This was injected to the internet by Morris, but, to his surprise, this so-called worm spread at a much faster rate than he would have imagined. Soon, within the next 24 hours, at least 10% of the internet connected machines were affected. This was then targeted to ARPANET, and some reports suggested that the of connected computers at the time was around 60,000. The worm was using a flaw in the Unix email program, `sendmail`, which typically waits for other systems to connect to the mail program and deliver the email, and a bug in the `fingerd` daemon. This worm infected many sites, which included universities, military, and other research facilities. It took a team of programmers from various US universities to work non-stop for hours to get to a fix. It took a few more days to get back to a normal state. A few years later, in 1990, Morris was convicted by the court, for violating the *Computer Fraud and Abuse Act*; unlike at the time of Blanc brothers when there was no law to prosecute, this time there was.

Fast forward another two decades to 2010, and the world saw what it never imagined could happen: an extremely coordinated effort to create a specifically crafted piece of software, **Yes Software**, which was purpose-built to target the Iranian nuclear facility. It was targeting **Industrial Control Systems**, otherwise known as **ICS**. This was designed only to target a specific brand and make of ICS by Siemens, which controls centrifuges in a nuclear facility to manage their speed. It is presumed that it was designed to deliver onsite, as per some reports, because the Iranian facility that it was targeting was air-gapped. This was one of its kind industrial cyber espionage.The malware was purpose-built so that it would never leave the facility of the nuclear plant. However, somehow, it still made its way out to the internet, and there is still speculation as to how. It took researchers many months after its discovery to figure out the working principle of the malware. It's speculated that it took at least a few years to develop to a fully functional working model. After the Stuxnet, we have witnessed many similar attack patterns in forms of Duqu, and Flame, and it's believed by some experts in this field, that malware similar to these are apparently still active.

Currently, we are seeing extremely new variants of attack with new modus operandi. This is to earn money by using ransomware, or to steal data and then try to sell it or destroy it. Alternatively, they use victim infrastructure to run crypto miner malwares to mine cryptocurrencies. Today, security has taken center stage, not only because the attack surface has increased for each entity, or the number of successful high profile and mass attacks are a norm, but because of the fact that each one of us now knows that the need for securing data is paramount, irrespective of whether you are a target or not.

Scenarios for security

To make it more intuitive and simpler, let's look into a few scenarios as we proceed further with this chapter to discuss the need for security:

- **Scenario (organizations in general)**: Try to visualize an organization with standard digital and IT functions that caters to their business needs. As an organization, it is important that the digital and IT infrastructure that you use is always up and running. Also, the organization has the responsibility to secure the identity, data, network, equipment, and products that you deal with. Digitization is the norm today for all businesses and organizations. Digitization brings in connectivity and a mixture of all the various different technologies working together to achieve the set business goals for the organization. With the increase in digitization, the level of connectivity also increases, within the boundary and outside the boundary of the organization. This connectivity also poses a risk to the security of the organization (we will discuss this further in the following chapters).

  Digitization and connectivity largely fits into three macro aspects, namely: identity (by which we allow the users to interact), data (individual, business, personal, or system), and network (the connection part). Furthermore, we should not forget the factors that bring them all together, namely: equipment, solutions, and various business processes and applications. Any organization today controls the level of access needed to view, modify or process data, or access a business application/system through identity. It is the de-facto requirement for the organization to secure these identities. You also need proper measures to secure the data you are handling, be it at rest, motion, or during compute. And it is an obvious fact that the network perimeter, be it physical or in the cloud, has to be secured with proper measures and controls. This scenario is to set the context; we will talk more about these aspects in the following chapters.

- **Scenario (everything is moving to cloud)**: As most organizations are moving to cloud at a rapid speed, the need for higher processing capability and reduced operating cost benefit is increasing. Cloud, as a technology, provides more scalability for businesses when it is required. Also, as the global footprint of each business is now increasing, the need for collaboration is important and cloud makes it possible. Employees nowadays prefer working remotely, thereby eliminating the need for office infrastructure. The other important benefit of cloud computing is that it takes away the burden from IT about constantly keeping track of new updates and upgrades of software and hardware components.

But, as it is true that technological advancements bring in more control, speed, power, accuracy, resiliency, and availability, they also bring in security concerns and risks. Cloud is no different when it comes to security concerns and the risks that are exposed if it is not properly implemented or used. The biggest boon of cloud is that the organizations are reaping the benefit of not owning any infrastructure or operations of their own. This boon also brings in security risks and concerns, such as who has access to the data that is positioned in the cloud, how do you maintain and manage security regulatory requirements, and how do you keep up with compliance mandates such as GDPR and others? Cloud computing also complicates the **disaster recovery** (**DR**) scenario for each organization because it depends on the service provider's terms and conditions and their business model around data recovery. Moreover, organizations have no control where the cloud provider will bring up their data center and operate from, which raises concerns around data sovereignty. There are many other challenges and risks around operating from cloud, which will be discussed in relevant portions of this book.

Understanding the attack surface

I am sure, by now, that you have a grasp of security and its importance to some extent. So, let's take a look at what **attack surface** is, and how we define it, as it's important to understand the attack surface so that we can plan well for our security. In very simple terms, attack surface is the collection of all potential vulnerabilities which, if exploited, can allow unauthorized access to the system, data, or network. These vulnerabilities are often also called **attack vectors**, and they can span from software, to hardware, to network,and the users (which is the human factor). The risk of being attacked or compromised is directly proportional to the extent of attack surface exposure. The higher the number of attack vectors, the larger the attack surface, and the higher the risk of compromise. So, to reduce the risk of attack, one needs to reduce the attack surface by reducing the number of attack vectors.

We witness all the time that attacks target applications, network infrastructure, and even individuals. Just to give you an extent of attack surface and the exposure, let's look into the **Common Vulnerabilities and Exposure** (**CVE**) database (https://cve.mitre.org/cve/). It has 108,915 CVE entries (at the time of writing this chapter), which are all those that have been identified so far over the past few decades. Certainly many of these are now fixed, but some may still exist. This huge number indicates how big the risk of exposure is.

Any software that is running in a system can potentially be exploited using vulnerabilities in the software, remotely or locally. This applies particularly to software which is web facing, as it is more exposed, and the attack surface is much larger. Often, these vulnerable applications and software can lead to the compromise of the entire network, and also pose a risk to the data it is managing. Apart from these, there is another risk that these applications or software are exposed to all the time: insider threat, where any authenticated user can gain access to the data that is unprotected due to badly implemented access controls.

On the other hand, an attack surface that exposes network attacks can be passive or active. These attack surfaces can allow the network services to collapse, make it temporarily unavailable, allow unauthorized access of the data flowing through the network, and so on.

In the event of a passive attack, the network can be monitored by the adversary to capture passwords, or to capture information that is sensitive in nature. During a passive attack, one can leverage the network traffic to intercept the communications between sensitive systems and steal the information. This can be done without the user even knowing about it. Alternatively, during an active attack, the adversary will try to bypass the protection systems by using malware or other forms of network-based vulnerabilities to break into the network assets; active attacks can lead to exposure of data and sensitive files. Active attacks can also lead to Denial-of-Service type attacks. Some common types of attack vectors are:

- Social engineering, scams, and so on
- Drive-by-downloads
- Malicious URLs and scripts
- Browser-based attacks
- Attacks on the supply chain (which is rising day by day)
- Network-based attack vectors

The threat landscape

The attack surface also brings in another term, **threat landscape**. We, in the cybersecurity community, talk about it every day. Threat landscape can be defined as the collection of threats that are observed, information about threat agents, and the current trends of threats. It is important that every security professional keeps track of the threat landscape. Usually, many different agencies and security vendors will release such threat landscape reports, for example, **ENISA (European Union Agency for Network and Information Security)**, and **NIST (National Institute of Standards and Technology)**, along with some of the big security corporations.

Moreover, the threat landscape is an extremely dynamic space; it changes very frequently, and is driven by many factors, such as available tools to exploit vulnerabilities, the knowledge base of available resources and vulnerabilities, and the skill requirements to place an attack. (This is becoming increasingly easy due to the freely available tools on the internet.) We will talk more about the threat landscape resources in following chapters in this book. The following is a list of different threats in 2016-2017 and their relative rankings:

Top Threats 2016	Assessed Trends 2016	Top Threats 2017	Assessed Trends 2017	Change in ranking
1. Malware	⬆	1. Malware		→
2. Web based attacks	⬆	2. Web based attacks		→
3. Web application attacks	⬆	3. Web application attacks		→
4. Denial of service	⬆	4. Phishing		↑
5. Botnets	⬆	5. Spam		↑
6. Phishing	⮃	6. Denial of service		↓
7. Spam	⬇	7. Ransomware		↑
8. Ransomware	⮃	8. Botnets		↓
9. Insider threat	⮃	9. Insider threat		→
10. Physical manipulation/damage/ theft/loss	⬆	10. Physical manipulation/damage/ theft/loss		→
11. Exploit kits	⬆	11. Data breaches		↑
12. Data breaches	⬆	12. Identity theft		↑
13. Identity theft	⬇	13. Information leakage		↑
14. Information leakage	⬆	14. Exploit kits		↓
15. Cyber espionage	⬇	15. Cyber espionage		→

Legend: Trends: ⬇ Declining, ⮃ Stable, ⬆ Increasing
Ranking: ↑ Going up, → Same, ↓ Going down

Figure 2: ENISA Threat Landscape Report 2017

The preceding image is the threat landscape for 2017 based on a report from EN brings us to a point where it is important to know a little bit about some comm attacks:

- **Unstructured attacks**: These are one of those attacks where the adversary has no prior knowledge of the environment they are launching an attack on. Mostly, in such scenarios, they rely on all the freely available tools. Unstructured attacks are often targeted en masse, based on any common vulnerability and available exploitation.

- **Structured attacks**: In the case of a structured attack, unlike an unstructured one, the adversary is much more prepared and well planned in carrying out the attack. In most of the cases of structured attacks we notice that the attackers demonstrate their advanced skills of programming, and knowledge about the IT systems and applications they are targeting. These attacks can be highly organized in nature and mostly targeted towards an individual entity or industry vertical.

- **Social engineering (phishing, spear phishing, and so on)**: This attack is targeted towards one of the weakest links, humans. In this attack, the user is exploited in various ways. Often these attacks are successful because of a lack of knowledge or ignorance. Information is extracted from the user by tricking them one way or the other. The most common way is by phishing and spear phishing. In a phishing and spear phishing attack, data is extracted by impersonating something that looks authentic to the user, such as, posing as an administrator helping the user to reset their password, and other account details, via a web portal. These portals are specially crafted to suit the purpose of extracting data which the attacker wishes to collect. Users fall prey to those, and share sensitive information.

- **Eavesdropping**: This attack can be performed by gaining unauthorized access to the network and listening to the network communications. Commonly, all the traffic that is not encrypted can be easily targeted by the attacker.

- **Denial of Service (DoS and DDoS)**: This is one of the oldest forms of network-based attacks, where the attacker will attempt to overwhelm the processing or computing capacity of the application or device by sending such a flood of data that it is more than the application or the device can handle, thereby disrupting the system. On the other hand, **distributed denial of service (DDoS)**, is launched from multiple sources towards a single victim application or system on a very large scale, more than the amount that can be handled. This is one of the hardest to mitigate without proper technologies in place.

- **Man-in-the-middle attack (MITM)**: In this attack form, the session or the network is hijacked in between by manipulating the communication between server and client, and acting as a proxy server, often without the knowledge of the victim.

- **Malware**: Malware can be defined as disruptive software, which is intentionally designed to cause damage or achieve any other malicious intent by its creator. Most of the time, this access is gained by exploiting the computing system's security, or any vulnerabilities, with help from the malware. Worms and Trojans are different forms of malware, and these have a very specific capability to spread from computer to computer and replicate themselves. Malware can cause theft of data, mass destruction of computer systems, disruption of network activities, and also can help in corporate espionage. Most of the latest malware may have unique capabilities to hide itself extremely well from the security systems and detection mechanisms, and stay active for weeks to years.

- **Botnets**: When computer systems are infected with malware, or any other malicious remote tools, and these infected computer systems are controlled by the attacker remotely, it is known as a bot. Furthermore, when there are many computers which are compromised by this malware, and controlled by the attacker, this network, or collection of compromised computers, is called a **botnet**. The remote mechanism and the control method are also termed as *"Command and Control"*. Botnets can be used for various other purposes by the adversary, and, to achieve these, the botnet master will keep updating the malicious program's binary. Botnets used to be single-focused in terms of their mission. However, in the recent past, they have changed to become multiple-purpose malicious applications.

- **Cross-site scripting**: Cross-site scripting, commonly known as **XSS** attack, is an exploitation of flaws in web applications, which allows the adversary to inject malicious client-side script and compromise the user, without their knowledge in most cases. In general, these flaws exist due to poor input validation of web-based applications. Once the XSS is sent to the user, the browser will process it because the browsers have no mechanism to stop XSS based attacks. There are multiple forms of XSS attacks. **Stored** and **reflected** types of XSS are very common. Stored XSS allows the attacker to leave permanent malicious scripts in the victim's server, while reflected XSS usually takes place when the attacker sends a specially crafted link with a malicious query in the URL to the user, and the unsuspecting user clicks on the link, which then takes the user to a malicious site and captures the user's sensitive data, which is then sent to the attacker. Reflected XSS is possible only if the user clicks on the link. Or, another method is if the attacker tricks the user into clicking it.

- **Drive-by download attack**: This form of attack is very commonly seen over the internet. It has been one of the top threats in the past couple of years. In practice, attackers will compromise a well-known benign website and host their malware there, by embedding malicious links. Once users visit these non-suspecting websites, they get compromised by automatically being redirected to the malware download locations. Often, the links of compromised websites could be spread via spam or phishing emails, where a user might click a link out of curiosity, or unknowingly, and get the malware downloaded into the system.

- **SQL injection attack**: SQL injection attack is usually targeted towards the database exposed via the web. An attacker would execute malicious queries via poorly configured web applications, mostly in the data input mechanism to run SQL commands. The attacker, if successful, can gain access to the database, manipulate sensitive data, or, at times, also modify data. SQL injection can also allow arbitrary commands to manage the operating system remotely. This vulnerability is successful mostly due to the poor input sanitization at the web application, rather than at the database end, because databases are designed to execute queries as they receive them and return results accordingly. So, the developers must take care about input sanitization and only accept data input as desired, and check for any malicious inputs, before sending it to a database for query execution.

- **Advanced persistent threat (APT)**: This attack has been on the rise over many years. The modus operandi of these attacks is mostly to launch highly targeted attacks against specific individual organizations, industry segments, or even a nation. These threats are called *"advanced persistent"* because the attacker, or the group of attackers, will use many advanced and stealthy techniques to stay undetected for a very long time. Often, it is found that the attack and persistent methods are specifically crafted for the particular attack and have never been used in any other attacks. APT based attacks are mostly well funded and they are mostly a team driven activity. APT is used to target intellectual property, any form of sensitive information, disruptive activities, or may even be for corporate espionage, or sabotage of data, and/or the infrastructure. APT attacks are entirely different from the other forms of attack; the adversary/adversaries take a very organized approach to know their target and the mission they want to achieve, and they do not rush to attack. The attack infrastructure is very complex at times. The main goal of the attacker/attackers is to stay in the compromised network as long as possible and stay hidden from security detection. One of the significant natures of APT, is that it can only impact certain parts of the network, or certain persons in the company, or just a few systems in the network that are the point of interest. This, therefore, makes it more challenging to detect APT activities by security monitoring systems.

- **Web-based attacks**: In these attacks, as the name suggests, the target systems are mostly those which are internet facing devices, applications, services, and so on. Practically, we can say that the majority of internet applications are exposed to web attacks. These can be attacked via flaws and vulnerabilities, not only in the applications, but, also, in the medium by which we access those applications, such as web browsers. Web browser exploits have been on the rise for many years. Web servers are always a very lucrative target for the adversary/adversaries. Some of the famous attack forms are drive-by downloads or watering hole attacks (where a legitimate web application, used by the target/targeted organizations, is compromised and then the attacker waits for the employees/users to visit the website and, thus, it becomes compromised).

- **Insider attacks**: Insider attacks are the human element of cybersecurity that are extremely vulnerable and very difficult to track, monitor, and mitigate. This threat indicates that the users with authorized access to the information assets will cause harm to the entity/business, or the organization. This is sometimes done unknowingly by becoming prey, or, sometimes, they are the ones conducting the attack. In general, there are no definitive ways to detect or monitor insider threat proactively; it can only be found when the damage has already been done in most cases. It's been a rising trend over many years, as the advanced attackers try to exploit insiders to gain access to the organization or businesses. This has been a major threat to governments and it's increasing day by day. Even if the organizations have a bullet proof network with a lock down environment, and strong perimeter defenses, insider attacks are considered to be the most effective. The mitigation of an insider threat is beyond the technical implementation. The organization also needs to include the social culture and education of its own users about how to treat security and stay vigilant.

- **Ransomware**: Ransomware has done a lot of damage recently and has come up as a prominent threat. The modus operandi of ransomware is mostly to gain monetary profit by holding the user's data/system in ransom by making it unusable. This is achieved by compromising the system with one or other form of existing exploits and vulnerabilities and then encrypting the data in the user's system. Once encrypted the attacker would demand money in exchange for the decryption key. The following screenshot shows an example of a ransomware message:

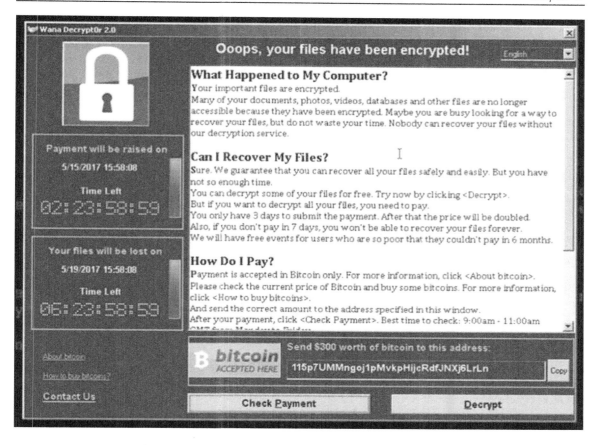

Figure 3: Example of Ransomware message, https://digitalguardian.com/sites/default/files/zdnet.jpg

Ransomware attacks are extremely dangerous because of their mechanism. Anyone with a little knowledge and access to freely available exploitation tools can use them to gain access and encrypt data. This is mostly done on a wide scale to generate more profit by volume, and the process is entirely automated. There are dark net groups that have created ransomware-as-a-service to offer the infrastructure and tools needed to generate such a campaign. Ransomware attacks are now being targeted more at organizations, such as banks and other financial institutions, to generate huge profits by disrupting their business and asking for ransom. **WannaCry** and **NotPetya** are the two most disrupting examples of ransomware that we have seen recently.

One of the notorious examples of ransomware even had the modus operandi to make the system unusable, which implied that it not only encrypted the data on the systems, but also had overwritten the master boot record that makes the computer unusable if rebooted. The impact of ransomware is unimaginable when it comes to attack against infrastructure like airlines, hospitals, governments, and emergency services.

- **Espionage**: This is one of those serious issues that has always been there since the beginning of human warfare. Today, this is taking place between corporate, governments, and various other entities, and the battleground is cyberspace. It's beneficial, in a sense, because no one is directly coming in front to perform this espionage; they are all behind the hidden cyberspace, and the attackers can stay anonymous. We have already seen in the news in the past couple of years how one government is trying to damage or disrupt the other by using a cyber form of espionage, by compromising sensitive information, and then leaking it to the public, to cause chaos and disruption. Even corporations are not far behind. They do it to gain access to each other's intellectual property to stay ahead of the competition. Cyberspace is way more interesting and dangerous when we think from this perspective of cybersecurity.

The importance of securing the network and applications

With every passing day, the network of connected devices is increasing, and, while this growth of connectivity continues to grow bigger, the risk of exposure is also increasing. Furthermore, it is no longer dependent on how big or small the businesses are. In today's cyberspace it is hard to establish if any network of application is not prone to attacks, but it has become extremely important to have a sustainable, dependable, and efficient network system, as well as applications. Properly configured systems and applications will help reduce the risk of attack. But it might not ever be able to eliminate the risk of attack completely.

A modern IT security system is a layered system, as a single layer approach to security is not enough anymore. In the event of a network breach, the victim can sustain a huge impact, including financial, disruptions to operations, and loss of trust factors. In the recent past, the number of breaches has increased for various reasons. The attack vectors for these breaches could be many, such as viruses, Trojans, custom malware for targeted attacks, zero-day-based attacks, or even insider threats. The following table shows the biggest data breaches of the 21st century:

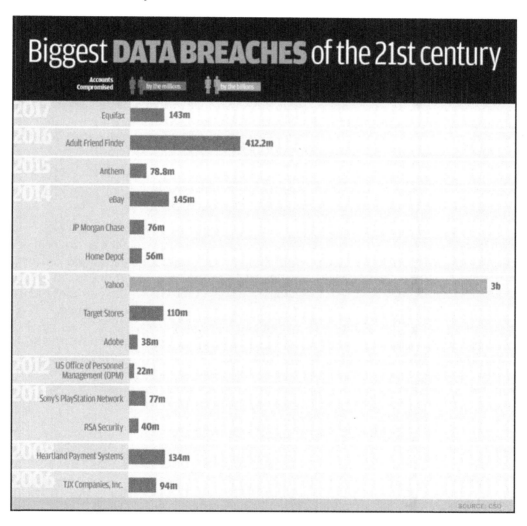

Figure 4: https://images.idgesg.net/images/article/2017/10/biggest-data-breaches-by-year-and-accounts-compromised-1-100738435-large.jpg

For instance, one of the biggest data breaches that happened with Target Stores in December 2013, was planned during the Thanksgiving holidays and the organization did not discover it until a few weeks after the actual attack. The attack was started from an internet enabled air conditioning system and then to the point of sale systems. Eventually this attack led to the theft of about $110 million in credit and debit card data. The after-effect of the attack led to the resignation of the, then, Target CEO and the cost impact to Target was in the region of $162 million. (For readers, a more detailed report can be found here: https://www.csoonline.com/article/2134248/data-protection/target-customers--39--card-data-said-to-be-at-risk-after-store-thefts.html)

The history of breaches

Attacks on computers, as we see today, may have evolved in terms of the techniques and sophistication of the attack itself, but one thing that has not changed is the reason for the breaches—**data**. Data has always been the center of attraction for all the hackers, both past and present.

1984 – The TRW data breach

Looking into the past for data breaches, one cannot miss the incident that was one of the most critical at the time, in 1984, which exposed personal and financial information of about 90 million users. TRW (today known as Experian), at the time, was hosting one of the largest databases of confidential records of about 90 million users and their credit history. TRW was responsible for providing information on users' credit history, employment details, banking and loan details, and, most importantly, social security numbers. These were transmitted over a telephone line to their many subscribers, who were mostly banks and department stores in remote locations. The following screenshot shows some online news coverage that this incident received:

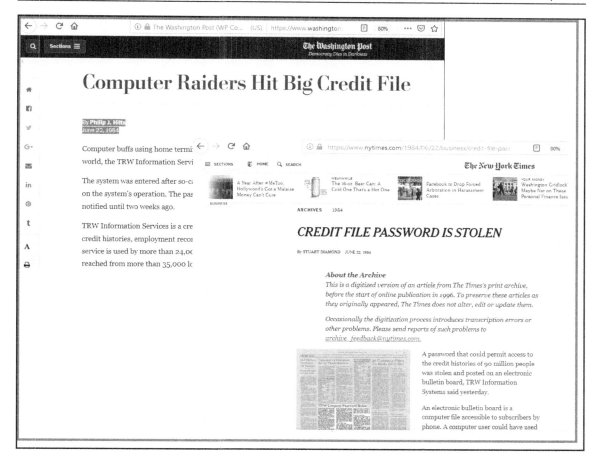

Figure 5: Washington Post and NY Times coverage of the incident in 1984

Quite interestingly, the access to these databases was not so secured, and the subscribers could log in to the TRW database as needed to query the required information about a user. These details were confidential in nature, and only to be accessed by the bank officials or the department store operators. Even though the data accessed was read-only and no one could change any data, one could still expose it and misuse it, which is exactly what happened. The password and the manual on how to operate the TRW system and access the database was leaked from a department store in one location, and, once the adversaries got hold of the login and access information, they posted it in bulletin boards, (something equivalent of today's social media). Now, not only did the attackers have the login information, but also a whole profile of those who were connected and had access to the bulletin board.

Surprisingly, the incident was not detected by TRW officials for many months (it's not clear how long). The breach was reported to TRW by an external party. As per the investigation reports at the time, it was believed that the database was accessed via the store line, and TRW had no clue about how many times it had been accessed. Experts said during that time that a proper monitoring and detection could have flagged this activity (note that this is true even in today's environment). Investigators at that time also suggested that, if TRW had implemented a system to call back the telephone number via which access was requested, and verified before the information was transmitted (today we can compare this with our two-factor authentication), and rotated the user password frequently in conjunction with a few other methods, the attack could have been averted.

The points that we need to focus on in this incident of 1984, and compare with today's attack scenarios, are that the attack vectors, methods, and the mitigation that could have averted this, are quite unchanged. Firstly, one is that the attacker used some sort of social engineering to get hold of login credentials, which is still a very common method today. Secondly, they had full and complete information about the TRW systems by getting access to the manual, which might have helped them stay undetected for a very long time. Thirdly, they targeted user data not to damage or tarnish the company. It's the same as today, attackers get silent access to the systems with various methods, and try to stay undetected as long as possible, and make use of the stolen data.

1990s – Beginning of computer viruses and worms

At the beginning of the last decade of the 20th century, the world witnessed the start of a new challenging problem—computer viruses and worms. This changed the course of computer security in the years to come. In 1989, Robert Morris created a program to measure the size of the internet by counting the number of connected devices. He developed a program that would self-propagate using a vulnerability (we discussed this at the beginning of this chapter). But this incident did not get fixed or barred there, and there was more to come. The early 90s saw the rise of another virus, which was dubbed the *"Michelangelo virus"*, designed to attack DOS systems at the time and modify the boot sector of the disk to stay put. This virus infected any media that was attached to it, such as hard disks or floppy disks, during that time. The Michelangelo virus was designed to stay dormant all the time, except for a particular date, 6 March, which is when it would come alive and act. (It was this date because, the researchers believed, it is the birthday of the famous Renaissance artist Michelangelo, but it's a mere coincidence.)

It was during these years that we saw the rise of antivirus companies too. Viruses and worms gave birth to a whole new industry, which became mainstream business in the computer security industry in the forthcoming years. The last decade of the 20th century continued to witness more viruses and worms, which moved into the new millennium with increased sophistication.

The years 2000-2010

This was the decade which saw the rise of computer attack sophistication and was much more targeted towards its motive and mission.

In early 2000s, the world was devastated with a new form of virus and the way it spread. The virus was dubbed the *"ILOVEYOU"* virus, which infected millions of computers, and caused the email systems across the world to collapse. The virus started spreading by email attachment with a VBScript code. Anyone who opened that file executed the VBScript. The VBScript was designed to download another payload, which then created various persistence methods by including entries in a registry, and the malware started itself whenever the system was rebooted. This executable also installed other malware to steal passwords, and, at a later stage, sent all the captured password from the system to the attacker via email.

Another subroutine in the malware that helped it to spread across the world was designed in such a way that, the moment the malware was executed, it captured all the email addresses in the mail client address book and sent a copy of itself as an attachment with the subject like ILOVEYOU from the user's address. All the unsuspecting users, thinking it came from a known source, did the same mistake and tried to open the attachment, repeating the whole process. In the days that followed, there were many other variants of this similar modus operandi.

This decade also saw the rise of worms, viruses, and attacks by exploitation of software, OS, and other system vulnerabilities. One of the famous was the **SQL Slammer** worm that eventually became the fastest spreading worm of that time; it was active for many years, causing massive internet disruption. This worm exploited a vulnerability in the Microsoft SQL Server. This worm was so agile that it spread over close to 100,000 hosts (maybe even more; the exact count is not available) over the first hour of its infection. It used a buffer overflow bug in the **SQL Server and Desktop Engine (MSDE)** products. This worm generated random IP addresses and then tried to communicate to those IPs over a destination port UDP/1434 (SQL port).

Once it found the host, it exploited the vulnerable SQL server or the MSDE, and sent a copy of itself to the same host, thereby infecting the host. Once this new host was infected, it repeated the same process. Even though the patch to this bug was made available by Microsoft six months before the attack was launched, most of the systems over the internet were not patched. This indicates how important it is to keep the systems updated with the latest patches.

In November 2008, we witnessed yet another massive attack by another worm, which targeted Windows machines (ranging from Win 2000 to Win 7). This worm eventually impacted 10-15 million servers worldwide in over 190 countries, as a rough estimate. The worm impacted governments, military bases and fleets, corporate and home users, and, in fact, practically everyone in its path. Between November 2008 and April 2009, there were five variants that were found, **Conficker A**, **B**, **C**, **D**, and **E**. This worm not only created a massive infection around the globe, but it also created one of the biggest botnets of the era. Maybe the motive behind the worm was to create a large botnet to do more serious attacks, but nothing was made conclusive regarding the actual motive to generate an attack of this scale. This worm also used many new techniques that had never been used before this time. This included methods to block disinfection, infections of USB and other removable devices to spread further, along with a few other propagation methods, including files shares, and admins shares. The most innovative was the method to *"call home"* to the botnet controller via a communication framework based on random domain generation algorithms, later famously known as DGA algorithms, and these became the norm for other malware infections and botnet commands and control infrastructure. This method allowed the worm to generate hundreds and thousands of random domain names every day by a pre-determined algorithm and seed value (usually the date and time).The same algorithm was used proactively by the attacker to register one, or a few, of the domains from the random list for each day. This domain name was used by the malware on the particular day for command and control activities.

By the end of the decade, the industry was taken by surprise with the discovery of a major espionage activity by using a carefully and meticulously created malware, named **Stuxnet**. This was specially targeted towards a nuclear plant in Iran, with a single purpose of creating disruption in their nuclear programs. To a major extent, this attempt was successful in damaging the nuclear plan in target. This malware brought up some serious issues and concerns within the security fraternity regarding the safety of operational technologies controlling industrial systems, such as SCADA systems, and other similar ones.

In the days to come, the attack sophistication will not only increase but will also be highly targeted, as we have seen in the case of the Bangladesh bank heist where approximately $81 million was siphoned out of the bank in an extremely well-coordinated and planned activity.

How security helps to build trust

With the rise of technologies, most corporations and business houses are moving towards adapting newer and newer technologies to be in the race to keep their businesses ahead of the competition, and enhancing customer experience. With this also comes the potential risk of cybersecurity.

Customers trust corporations and business houses with their data. Making sure that the data is secure is the sole responsibility of the corporations, governments, and businesses. If the data is breached, then the business loses trust from the customer and ultimately loses business and brand value.

It is extremely important for customer-facing businesses to maintain trust and progress towards digitization to ensure smooth business operations. As in today's scenarios of mobile first approach, and IoT approach, connectivity is paramount to stay in business and give customers a richer experience. The only binding factor is trust. And trust can only be achieved by making sure that the data is secured, avoiding breach situations, and, if there is a breach, then recovering as quickly as possible from a breach situation without causing much impact to customers and their data. In other words: to minimize the impact.

Companies must build security into their products and services from the beginning. This will decrease the risk of compromise or any breach, thereby strengthening the trust factor. As no business today can run alone, they have to partner with third parties. It is the responsibility of both the company and the third party to ensure the safety and security of consumer data and intellectual properties. So, as the enhancement of technologies are important for businesses to become profitable and sustain growth, building a security-first culture is also paramount to maintain consumer trust.

Summary

In this chapter, we explored the various aspects of the internet and how digitization has brought in a new era of cyber crimes and attacks. We also learned about the history of cyber attacks, which broke our usual belief that cyber crimes started a few decades ago. As we progressed, we learned about the various aspects of cloud computing and how it brings data under threat.

By reading this chapter, you will clearly have understood the importance of security in the current technological landscape, gained visibility of the cybersecurity landscape, and how organizations, as well as individuals, can protect data from being stolen. This knowledge is useful in identifying potential threat areas and designing a defensive game plan.

As we continue the discussion, we will explore the evolution of security from legacy systems to machine learning, AI, and other turnkey technologies. This will help us gain an insight about the past, present, and future of cybersecurity.

2
Security Evolution — From Legacy to Advanced, to ML and AI

Security has evolved over the last few decades. It started off with antivirus systems that were for a long time referred to as the ultimate cybersecurity tools. These were then joined by an array of other tools.

Before 1971, cybersecurity was unheard of. That is unsurprising, since computers were still being developed, were too pricey for hackers, and only a few people knew how to write code to do basic input/output functions. A researcher called Bob Thomas then discovered that it was possible to create a malicious program that could propagate from one computer to another and leave an annoying message. Following this discovery, another researcher modified the program so that it could become self-replicating. Essentially, he created the first computer worm. He then decided to build another program that could catch the malicious one and delete it from a computer, thus stopping it from replicating and spreading further. This was the world's first antivirus software.

However, the cybersecurity space has dramatically changed since the 1970s. Threats have become more complex and this necessitated the development of more complex security systems. Advancements in technology have offered hackers more tools and techniques with which to build threats. In addition to this, security systems are having to cover for technologies that were built without security in mind. Such technologies include the internet, which is relied on by billions of people. Therefore, cybersecurity has had to do more than evolve to respond to the cyber threats landscape; it has had to foresee and future-proof systems, users, and networks from attacks. This chapter discusses the evolution of cybersecurity and the future of the integration of cybersecurity with machine learning and artificial intelligence, and will cover the following topics:

- Legacy cybersecurity systems
- Transformations in cybersecurity
- Advancements in security technology, and the future
- How **machine learning** (**ML**) and **artificial intelligence** (**AI**) will play a larger role in cybersecurity

Legacy cybersecurity systems

As noted in our discussion of the creation of the first worm and the first antivirus, cybersecurity was initially designed as a response to a cyber threat. Legacy systems were built to secure organizations from known threats. After the discovery of a cyber threat, security experts would learn its unique execution or coding patterns. This information would be used to enable security systems to detect and stop the identified cyber threat. This tradition still continues up to the present day. There is a famed database known as **Common Vulnerabilities and Exposures** (**CVE**), where all the discovered threats are explained and a unique identification number is given to them.

Signature-based security systems

During the age of legacy security systems, security tools were built with the attack signatures of the many threats that had been discovered. Since the know-how for creating new malware was limited to a few, this security approach was initially effective. Individuals and organizations were meant to believe that having a single security system on a computer was good enough. These security systems were then improved to receive updates to their database where new malware signatures would be added. Therefore, users could get new updates after a certain duration or when security companies made them available.

The signature-based creation of cybersecurity products was applied across a whole array of defense systems, which were principally antivirus systems. Therefore, all these systems had a single point of failure: the reliance on databases of signatures. This left a vulnerability of organizations being attacked using malware or attack techniques that were not already known by their security systems. In addition, the security systems were mostly designed to prevent attacks from malware. Therefore, the threats that were covered were viruses and worms. Hackers decided to pounce on this chance and made several notable attacks.

Network cyber attacks

By the end of the 1970s, a sixteen-year-old called Kevin Mitnick had learned how to get unauthorized access into a network. He used this knowledge to breach the network of Digital Equipment Corp. His aim was to copy its operating system, and he was able to do just that while in the network. He was later arrested and put in solitary confinement as authorities tried to understand how he was able to gain access to one of Digital Equipment Corp's computers. The following image is a photograph from an article on Kevin Mitnick:

To find out what Kevin Mitnick is doing now and learn about his past, you can read this article at https://www.mitnicksecurity.com/site/news_item/hacker-the-first-the-best-and-the-most-feared-hackers-of-all-time.

In the 1990s, the biggest hack on the US military and NASA was conducted by a tech-savvy individual called Gary McKinnon. He reportedly broke into 97 computers remotely. He then deleted critical files and the OSes of the computers, causing them to become inoperable. The computers were so important that the hack caused a shutdown of the army's network, and the cost implications of the hack reached a devastating $700,000 USD. The following is a screenshot of Gary McKinnon's Wikipedia page summary:

Gary McKinnon

System administrator

Gary McKinnon is a Scottish systems administrator and hacker who was accused in 2002 of perpetrating the "biggest military computer hack of all time," although McKinnon himself states that he was merely ... Wikipedia

Born: February 10, 1966 (age 53 years), Glasgow, United Kingdom

Education: Highgate Wood School (1977–1982)

Known for: Security hacker

You can read more about Gary McKinnon on Wikipedia at `https://en.wikipedia.org/wiki/Gary_McKinnon`.

Many other hackers were gaining and improving on their skills. Even worse, new tools were discovered that could be used by non-expert hackers. They were known as **exploit kits**, and hackers would either buy or rent them to attack their targets. This caused a lot of pressure on the cybersecurity industry to evolve. It was clear that the initial design of tools that could detect malicious software based on attack signatures did not foresee many hackers coming up with new ways to beat such security systems. With the introduction of exploit tools that could generate malware that could change its attack patterns to avoid detection, it was clear that the cybersecurity industry had been beaten by the hackers. In addition, hackers were exploiting the weaknesses in networks to gain access to remote computers and carry out malicious actions.

Network security tools

Owing to the increased breaches facilitated through the network, the cybersecurity industry finally responded with more specialized tools that could prevent attacks that were coming from the network. They, therefore, came up with intrusion detection and prevention systems and major improvements to the rudimentary firewalls that were in use. However, these were still signature-based systems. Initially, they were effective in stopping the network breaches, since hackers did not know many workarounds. They were able to block malicious traffic and keep away hackers from carrying out malicious activities on networks. However, hackers would soon discover ways to beat the network security tools. Therefore, network intrusions came back and the tools designed to prevent them were unable to keep up with newer attack techniques. This caused the cybersecurity industry to respond in the 2000s with more additions to cybersecurity.

Transformations in cybersecurity

Hackers in the early 2000s began experimenting with many security evasion tactics to beat the existing security tools. They had already come up with techniques to evade security tools on networks. They had also come up with a new attack method called a **buffer overflow**. A buffer overflow is conducted mostly on client/server apps, where payloads are delivered with data specifically aimed to fill and write outside memory buffers. For instance, hackers would supply scripts to log in input fields in a client app, which would cause the server to import files. Since the server would be expecting just a few characters in the input field, the excess data would cause a buffer overflow, causing it to fail or function erroneously. Exploit toolkits were also being modified to include security evasion tactics.

Layered security

Since having antivirus or firewall programs didn't provide enough security, the cybersecurity industry took a new turn where organizations were advised to have layered security. Therefore, they had to extend their budgets to purchase cybersecurity tools for different types of threats on different attack landscapes. The move was aimed at creating a hardened security shield against organizations. This strategy came to be referred to as **defense in depth**. At the minimum, organizations had to have a firewall, an antivirus program, intrusion-detection systems, strong authentication on login platforms, and encryption of data. The strategy worked well against single-vectored attacks. Hackers who had bought exploit kits would fail to go through all layers of protection so as to breach an organization's security. Hackers who had been relying on using network vulnerabilities were finding an extra layer of security that they could not go through.

The problem with layered security was the cost; it was too expensive. Cybersecurity became a significant expense for many organizations. Company executives were having a hard time authorizing IT departments to spend so much on the tools. Nonetheless, the layered security strategy also pushed hackers to go back and come up with better ways of breaching organizations' security measures. The following diagram shows the different layers of security and their components:

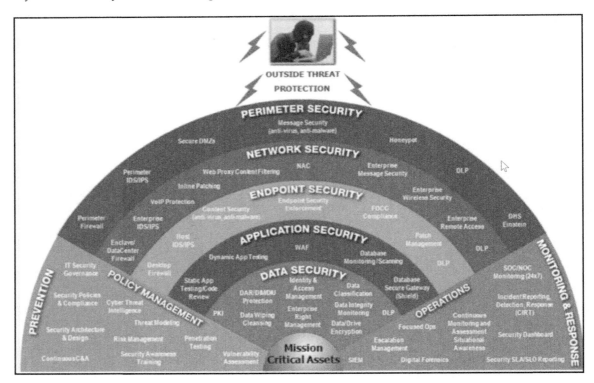

New security threats

By 2010, a new pattern of cyber criminal activity had been detected. Attackers could breach a network and stay hidden in the network for a long period without detection. Such types of attacks were referred to as **advanced persistent threats**. Hacking became a profession and cyber criminals were taking the time to study targeted systems and acquire the tools needed to attack them. Once an attack was successful, the attackers would maintain access to it as they stole or modified data. One of these incidences was the Stuxnet attack against a nuclear fuel enrichment facility in Iran. The attackers, believed to have been state-sponsored, breached the security systems of the facility and stayed hidden in their networks for a long time. The malware collected enough information to determine how to carry out the attack that caused the destruction of the facility. This attack was most significant due to the zero-day vulnerabilities it used and the fact that the attacked computers were not even connected to the internet.

In addition to advanced persistent attacks, **phishing** also made a comeback. Phishing was initially popular when members of the public were just getting computers and access to the internet for the first time. However, the phishing attacks of that time were quite rudimentary. The most common one was called the **Nigerian Prince scam**. It was an email sent to many people highlighting the tribulations of a purported Nigerian prince trying to get his inheritance money, but who needed some assistance to do so. Mostly, the targets were being asked to send some money to help clear the money. The scam gained popularity, before becoming less effective after it was publicized. However, 2011 saw a new wave of phishing attacks that were more sophisticated. The attempts shifted from simply trying to trick internet users into sending small amounts of money. Hackers started cloning legitimate company websites and email templates and informing them that there was a problem with the user accounts created with these companies. Users were being offered to rectify the issue by logging into given links. On the cloned websites, users would give out their real credentials and the hackers would use these credentials to steal data or money or gain access to sensitive systems.

After this, **Denial of Service (DoS)** attacks also came into the spotlight. The increased number of personal computers on the internet that did not have sufficient security systems was a blessing to hackers. They would install malware in such computers that would recruit them into a network of zombie computers, called a **botnet**. These zombie computers would be commanded by the hackers to send illegitimate traffic at specified targets, thus causing DoS and DDoS attacks.

Responses to the new threats

It became apparent in the industry that stopping the known attacks was not enough. Hackers were increasingly becoming successful in beating the security tools that relied on signatures to stop attacks. They were also targeting users instead of having to try to breach the multiple layers of security, and they had come up with attack techniques such as DoS that were hard to stop. There were two responses to the new developments: **cyber resilience** and **user training**. Cyber resilience was adopted to keep business operations going during and after cyber attacks. The end goal of having security changed from simply protecting the organization from attacks, to ensuring that business functions would not be severely interrupted by attacks. Businesses paid more attention to having ready backups, alternative hot sites to take over operations during cyber attacks, and faster incident-response measures to ensure that organizations could mitigate and recover from attacks more quickly.

Secondly, organizations started paying more attention to training their users against cybersecurity threats. This was because employees had become easier targets for cyber criminals. Social engineering was becoming a more successful way of breaching into many organizations. This has remained true for many years. Statistics provided in 2016 by the Anti-Phishing Working Group showed that, of all malware infections recorded, 95% were enabled by humans. The report showed that less than 5% of attacks are targeted at technical flaws in software. Most attacks are targeted at employees.

Therefore, organizations added employees to the cybersecurity chain and became more focused on teaching them about phishing and other common types of cybersecurity threats. The knowledge gained was intended to enable them to avoid falling into traps such as providing login credentials or clicking on malicious links.

Advancements in security technology to security 2.0

The cybersecurity industry was under immense pressure to move from signature-based detection techniques to other, more efficient alternatives. The old ways of hardening the security infrastructures in organizations increasingly failed. Despite having many layers of security, organizations were still being breached. Zero-day vulnerabilities and social engineering were major contributors to these attacks. The cost of cyber attacks also increased. In 2018, IBM published that the global average cost of a cyber attack was $3,860,000 USD. This cost factored in expenses such as lawsuits and loss of customers.

Anomaly-based security systems

Finally, cybersecurity tools got a major update, allowing them to do active scans of traffic and program execution, and determine any deviations from the normal patterns. Cybersecurity moved from signature-based detection to anomaly-based detection. For instance, firewalls were made to detect when servers were accepting multiple outside connections from new clients and at a higher rate than normal. This would be a sign that the connections were illegitimate and coming from a botnet. Therefore, such connections would be dropped. Many cybersecurity vendors came up with tools that could allow organizations to do real-time threat analysis, thus preventing attacks from unknown attack vectors.

Anomaly-based security tools also solved a significant problem that the cybersecurity industry was facing. This was the reporting of false positives. Initially, cybersecurity tools were just made to be more thorough in checking malicious programs and activities. It reached a point that they were so thorough, they were reporting harmless programs and activities as security threats. This was most common in network security tools, which were becoming highly inefficient in determining and separating actual threats from activities that had a small resemblance to threats. False positives were making the security tools unreliable. Network and security admins had to ignore many would-be threats, and sometimes, they would ignore legitimate threats in the process. The introduction of anomaly-based security tools ensured that the detected threats were real threats and needed to be stopped.

Anomaly-based security systems also led to growing ease of detection. Initially, cybersecurity tools had to check with many signatures, and this slowed down the performance of networks and systems. Anomaly-based tools did not have to refer to a signatures database. Instead, they did real-time analysis to check whether traffic or apps had abnormal behavior. Lastly, anomaly-based threats countered many social engineering attacks. On the network, these tools were capturing the packet headers to read origin and destination IP addresses and thus allow in traffic from known sources. Traffic from unknown sources was being subjected to thorough checks to find more details, such as whether the origin had been blacklisted or reported by other security tools to be malicious.

The main limitation of anomaly-based detection was that humans had to be involved in making key decisions. Therefore, tools with these capabilities were more hands-on than autonomous. Enterprises did not have enough workers to tend to all the alerts that these systems were sending that needed human intervention. Therefore, the cybersecurity industry decided to further improve these solutions to make them more accurate and autonomous. A lot of research was done on ML and AI. Today, cybersecurity companies are increasingly considering adding ML and AI into their cybersecurity products. The future is expected to be dominated by such products.

How ML and AI will play a larger role in cybersecurity

AI and ML present a new dawn in the cybersecurity industry. AI is not a new concept to computing. It was defined in 1956 as the ability of computers to perform tasks that were characteristic of human intelligence. Such tasks included learning, making decisions, solving problems, and understanding and recognizing speech. ML is a broad term referring to the ability of computers to acquire new knowledge without human intervention. ML is a subset of AI and can take many forms, such as deep learning, reinforcement learning, and Bayesian networks. AI is poised to disrupt the cybersecurity space in many ways in what might be the ultimate win for the cybersecurity industry against cyber criminals.

AI/ML in cybersecurity involves deploying self-sufficient tools that can detect, stop, or prevent threats without any human intervention. The detection of threats is done based on the training that the algorithm in the security tool will have undertaken on its own, and the data already supplied by the developers. Therefore, throughout its life cycle, an AI-powered security tool will become better at detecting threats. The original dataset of threats provided by developers will provide reference base that it can use to know what is normal and what is malicious. The security tool will then be exposed to insecure environments before final deployment. In the environments filled with threats, the system will continually learn based on the threats that it detects or stops. Hacking attempts will also be directed at it. These attempts will involve hacking or attempts to overwhelm its processing capabilities with lots of malicious traffic. The tool will learn the most commonly used hacking techniques for breaching systems or networks. For instance, it will detect the use of password-cracking tools such as **Aircrack-ng** on wireless networks. Similarly, it will detect brute-force attacks on login interfaces. The main role that will be played by humans in cybersecurity will be to update the algorithms of the AI tools with more capabilities.

AI security systems will possibly contain all threats. Conventional security systems are usually unable to detect threats that exploit zero-day vulnerabilities. With AI, even after evolving and adapting new attack patterns, malware will not be able to penetrate the AI system. The system will check the code being run by the malware and predict the outcome. Outcomes that are deemed to be harmful will cause the AI system to prevent the program from executing. Even if the malware obfuscates its code, the AI system will keep tabs on the execution pattern. It will be able to stop the program from executing once it attempts to carry out malicious functions such as making modifications to sensitive data or the operating system.

It is already projected that AI will overtake human intelligence. Therefore, a foreseeable point in the future will see all cybersecurity roles moved from humans to AI systems. This is both advantageous and disadvantageous. Today, when an AI system fails, the results are normally tolerable. This is because the scope of operations played by AI systems is still limited. However, when AI finally overtakes human intelligence, the results of a failure in the systems might be intolerable. Since the security systems will be better than humans, it is possible that they will be in a position to refuse input from humans. A malfunctioning system might, therefore, continue operating without any interventions. The perfectionist nature of AI will be both good and bad. Current security systems work toward reducing the number of attacks that can succeed against a system. However, AI systems work toward eliminating all threats. Therefore, false-positive detection might not be considered as such; they might be treated as positive detection and thus cause disruptions in the affected harmless systems that are stopped from executing.

Lastly, there are fears that the integration of ML and AI into cybersecurity might lead to more harm than good. As has been observed over the years, attackers are resilient. They will always try to find ways to beat a cybersecurity system. Normal cybersecurity tools are beaten using more sophisticated methods than the tools are aware of. However, the only way to beat AI will be to confuse it. Therefore, threat actors might infiltrate AI training systems and provide bad datasets, thus affecting the knowledge acquired by the AI-backed security systems. The actors might also create their own adversarial AI system to even the playing field. This would result in an AI versus AI battle.

Lastly, hackers might still use methods that circumvent AI security systems. Social engineering can still be carried out physically. In such cases, AI systems will not be able to help the target. **Shoulder surfing**—the simple act of looking over someone's shoulder as they enter crucial details—is also conducted without the use of hacking tools. This also circumvents the security system. Therefore, AI and ML might not be the ultimate answer to cyber crime.

Summary

This chapter has looked at the evolution of cybersecurity from legacy to advanced and then on to futuristic technologies such as AI and ML. It has been explained that the first cybersecurity system was an antivirus system that was created to stop the first worm. Cybersecurity then followed this example, where security tools were created as responses to threats. Legacy security systems started the approach of using signature-based detection. This is where security tools would be loaded with signatures of common malware and use this knowledge base to detect and stop any program that matched the signature. However, the security systems were focused on malware, and thus, hackers focused on breaching organizations through the network. In 1970, an OS company was breached via its network and a copy of an OS was stolen. In 1990, the US military suffered a similar attack where a hacker broke into 97 computers and corrupted them. Therefore, the cybersecurity industry came up with stronger network security tools. However, these tools still used the signature-based approach and thus could not be trusted to keep all attacks at bay.

In the 2000s, the cybersecurity industry came up with a new concept of security where it advised organizations to have layered security. Therefore, they had to have security systems for securing networks, computers, and data. However, layered security was quite expensive, yet some threat vectors were still infiltrating computers and networks. By 2010, cyber criminals started using threats called **advanced persistent threats**. Attackers were no longer doing hit-and-run attacks; they were infiltrating networks and staying hidden in the networks while carrying out malicious activities. In addition to this, phishing was revolutionized and made more effective. Lastly, there was another development where attackers were using DoS attacks to overwhelm the capabilities of servers and firewalls. Since many companies were being forced out of business by these attacks, the cybersecurity industry developed a new approach to security, known as **cyber resilience**. Instead of focusing on how to secure the organization during attacks, they ensured that organizations could survive the attacks. In addition to this, users became more involved in cybersecurity where organizations started focusing on training them to avoid common threats. This marked the end of security 1.0.

The cybersecurity industry then moved to the current *"security 2.0"*, where it finally created an alternative to signature-based security systems. Anomaly-based security systems were introduced and they came with more efficiencies and capabilities than signature-based systems. Anomaly-based systems detect attacks by checking normal patterns or behaviors against anomalies. Apps and traffic that conform to the normal patterns and behaviors are allowed to execute or pass, while those that do not are stopped. While anomaly-based tools are effective, they rely on decisions from humans. Therefore, a lot of work still comes back to IT security admins. The answer to this has been to leverage AI with the hopes that such security systems will become self-sufficient.

AI sounds promising, though many doubts have been cast against it. AI and ML security tools will operate by detecting threats based on anomalies and taking informed decisions on how to handle these threats. The AI-security tools will have a learning module that will ensure that they only get better with time. Before deployment, these systems will be extensively trained using datasets and real environments that have real threats. Once the learning module is able to provide sufficient information to protect an organization from common threats, it will be deployed. One of the main advantages of AI security systems is that they will evolve along with the threats. Any new threats will be studied and thwarted. Despite the advantages of AI-powered security systems, there are worries that they may ultimately become harmful. As AI overtakes human intelligence, there might come a point where such tools will not accept any human input. There are also worries that attackers might poison the algorithms to make them harmful. Therefore, the future of AI in cyber security is not easy to foretell, but there should be two main outcomes: either AI-backed security systems will finally contain cyber crime, or AI systems will go rogue, or be made to go rogue, and become cyber threats.

Further reading

The following are resources that can be used to gain more knowledge of the subjects covered in this chapter:

- *The Evolution of Phishing*: https://www.tripwire.com/state-of-security/featured/evolution-phishing/
- *Social Engineering: an IT Security problem doomed to get worse*: https://medium.com/our-insights/social-engineering-an-it-security-problem-doomed-to-get-worst-c9429ccf3330
- *Cost of a Data Breach Study*: https://www.ibm.com/security/data-breach
- *The Evolution of Cyber Threat and Defence*: https://www.infosecurityeurope.com/__novadocuments/96072?v=635742858995000000

- *What's Lurking Back There: Cybersecurity Risks in Legacy Systems*: https://businesslawtoday.org/2018/03/whats-lurking-back-there-cybersecurity-risks-in-legacy-systems/
- *Legacy cybersecurity products failed to protect 97% of organizations*: https://www.helpnetsecurity.com/2014/05/21/legacy-cybersecurity-products-failed-to-protect-97-of-organizations/
- *Signature-Based or Anomaly-Based Intrusion Detection: The Practice and Pitfalls*: https://www.scmagazine.com/home/security-news/features/signature-based-or-anomaly-based-intrusion-detection-the-practice-and-pitfalls/
- *Five questions on the evolution of cyber security*: https://www2.deloitte.com/content/dam/Deloitte/global/Documents/Governance-Risk-Compliance/gx_grc_Deloitte%20Risk%20Angles-Evolution%20of%20cyber%20security.pdf

3
Learning Cybersecurity Technologies

There is a unique trend that is being witnessed world over in the job market. While the overall number of jobs in different industries is rising, the technology industry is seeing one of the highest rates of job growth. In some countries, it is expected that by 2020, the number of IT jobs will outweigh the supply of people with skills to take them up. It is evident that the world is leaning more toward technology and that this is opening up opportunities for those skilled in different technologies. This is why the future is more promising for those that invest time to learn IT skills today.

There are different paths that someone can take in their IT career. While most careers in IT are good, there are some that are limited or might face sudden death in the near future as well. Therefore, caution must be taken when choosing the right path in the tech industry.

One of the most assuring paths to take is that of a cybersecurity career. The demand for cybersecurity professionals will only get higher. According to previous reports and future projections, cyber attacks are on the rise. The losses from cyber attacks are growing each year. Most organizations are planning on how to defend their systems, networks, and data from cyber attacks, so they have created a demand for cybersecurity professionals.

Cybersecurity is emerging as a rewarding career for professionals that master the skills needed to help protect organizations against cyber attacks. Cybersecurity is also a wide-scoped career. There are many technologies to be covered, all of which are built on different systems, and a cybersecurity professional needs to be knowledgeable about this.

This chapter will take you through the most vital security technologies to take to kick-start your cybersecurity career. We will cover the following topics:

- Mobile security
- Advanced data security
- Cloud security
- Modern day regulations
- Incidence response and forensics
- Enterprise security at scale
- Penetration testing
- DevSecOps
- IoT security
- User behavior analytics
- **Endpoint detection and response (EDR)**

Mobile security

Mobile security is a cybersecurity field that deals with the protection of portable computing devices from threats and vulnerabilities. In this section, we will discover what mobile computing devices are normally more exposed to.

Loss or theft

Devices such as phones and laptops can be easily lost or stolen in public places, cabs, and offices, among other places. From a cybersecurity perspective, what is more worrying is the amount of sensitive data that can be recovered from the lost or stolen devices. Users tend to keep lots of personal information in mobile devices. Passwords, bank information, social security numbers, and even confidential information belonging to corporations can be stolen from these devices. Alongside these, mobile devices are normally logged in to several email accounts, social media accounts, and sensitive systems. When the device is accessed by unauthorized people, sensitive data could be stolen and the logged-in accounts could be used for theft, extortion, or social engineering.

Below are some recent newspaper articles which highlights the dangers of losing your mobile phone. And based on Kensington the average cost of a loss or theft of a mobile device can be exceeding US $49.000

Tips you should apply before you lose your mobile device:

- Turn on remote tracking:
  - **In iOS:** Find my iPhone
  - **In Android**: Find My Device
  - **For Windows**: Sign in to `http://account.microsoft.com/devices` with your Microsoft account, and follow the steps in Lost My Device to register your laptop

Software-related security issues

Most smartphone operating systems use a permission-based system to allow apps to do certain functions or access certain data from the phone. However, this is not a guarantee that the apps will not request too many privileges. The approval part still lies with the user, but not all users are tech-savvy enough to know when apps are requesting unnecessary permissions. According to Appthority Inc., many free apps have ties with advertising networks. Therefore, the apps are used to collect data such as contacts, browser records, and location, which is then shared with the advertisers.

By using the Appthority Platform™, the security team at Appthority analyzed the top 50 free apps from Apple's App Store and Google Play Store for risky app behavior. The findings are recorded in the *App Reputation Report*. You can read the *App Reputation Report* at `https://www.appthority.com/company/press/press-releases/appthority-reveals-security-risks-of-free-mobile-apps/`.

Malware attacks are also increasingly becoming a mobile security concern. There has been a rise in the number of threats that can be used against phones across several operating systems. This is a big threat, since many users do not install antivirus systems on their phones.

The number of threats and vulnerabilities keeps rising, and this has opened up a career for mobile security professionals. Individuals and corporations that want to have all-around security want professionals that can protect their mobile devices so that they cannot be easily compromised when on the go. Also, there is an increasing demand for smartphone forensic experts that can track back a mobile security attack to find its root cause and mitigation. Therefore, studying mobile security technologies and mobile forensic technologies could open up a long-term career in cybersecurity.

Advanced data security

Data has become a prime target in cyber attacks, and, consequently, individuals and corporations are opting to spend more resources to secure their confidential data. There have been many reports of data breaches where user data is stolen by hackers, trade secrets are stolen by competitors, enemy states steal each other's military records, and prototypes for sensitive products are continually stolen.

The threat landscape surrounding data is continually changing. To prevent attacks and comply with all data security regulations, organizations are going to be looking for experts to offer advanced data security. This will prevent data breaches, ensure that sensitive data is not accessed by unauthorized people, and prevent an event that will lead to non-compliance with data regulations. A cybersecurity career in advanced data security is, therefore, a guarantee of never-ending career opportunities in the future. As an expert in this field, you will mainly be in charge of installing data security products, configuring existing security software in the most secure way, and drafting security policies to ensure data protection in organizations.

There are several e-Learning websites that offer training courses on data security. One of them is Udemy, which offers introductory courses to data security and then allows a learner to specialize with one of many advanced data security courses. The introductory course lays a good foundation from which you can advance to specific aspects of data security. Some of the advancement options in data security are cloud data security and encryption. Taking these courses allows you to build a career in the general data security field or in specific niches, such as data stored in the cloud.

 Please Google `advanced data security` and read the recommendations from Microsoft, IBM, and Oracle to learn more what those tech giants offer in terms of advanced data security.

Cloud security

The cloud technology has come with benefits that are valuable to many organizations. Today, organizations do not need to own computing resources to deploy software and systems. The cost benefits that have been realized from cloud computing have seen quite a number of organizations adopting it. However, there have been several fears about the technology that have possibly held back organizations from fully adopting it. Organizations are not quite ready to trust third-party cloud vendors with sensitive data. The organizations that have put out their data on the cloud want to ensure that it is safe and cannot be accessed by unauthorized parties, and this includes the cloud platform vendors.

Many of the organizations that have adopted, or are contemplating adopting, the cloud technology undoubtedly need a cybersecurity expert to guide them. As a cloud security expert, you will have the skills to ensure that data and systems are secure on the cloud platform. You will ensure that apps running from the cloud cannot be manipulated by third parties. You will also ensure that the data stored on the cloud is secure and cannot be accessed by unauthorized parties. You will ensure that authentication and authorization to databases and systems are strict, so that stolen credentials cannot be used to access it. Lastly, you will have to devise ways to prevent the cloud platform owner or vendor from accessing data on the cloud. Since many organizations will eventually adopt cloud technologies, job opportunities in this field will gradually increase.

The learning options in cloud security are many, as most e-Learning academies offer the course. Some of the trusted platforms that you can learn about this include Coursera and edX. edX in particular offers cloud security as a micro masters program and delves deeply into the cloud, its associated security challenges, and how they can be mitigated. At the end of the course, a student is able to handle virtually all security challenges affecting the cloud.

We will discuss more about this in `Chapter 9`, *Knowledge Check and Certifications*.

Secure your Azure resources with conditional access

26 min • Module • 6 Units

There's a tradeoff between security and ease-of-access. The conditional-access feature of Azure Active Directory helps you

Introduction to Microsoft 365 unified endpoint management

15 min • Module • 5 Units

Unified endpoint management helps users be productive wherever they are while keeping

Data warehouse security

35 min • Module • 4 Units

Learn about the security controls that Azure SQL Data Warehouse provides to help secure your data warehouse infrastructure and the data that's stored in it.

Large Scale Data Processing with Azure Data Lake Storage Gen2

2 hr 5 min • Learning Path
• 3 Modules

In this learning path, you will see how Azure Data Lake Storage can

Microsoft runs on trust

30 min • Module • 7 Units

Organizations today are moving beyond the early promise of the cloud to digitally transform their businesses through faster innovation, flexible resources, and

Secure your Azure Storage account

45 min • Module • 8 Units

Learn how Azure Storage provides multilayered security to protect your data. Find out how to use access keys, to secure networks.

An example from Microsoft Learn web site on Free Cloud Security training

If you would like to learn more about Amazon cloud security, check out this web site: `https://aws.amazon.com/security/security-resources/`.

For IBM cloud security resources check this web site: `https://www.ibm.com/security/solutions/secure-hybrid-cloud`.

If you would like to learn vendor-neutral cloud security, then check the SANS website out: `https://www.sans.org/reading-room/whitepapers/cloud/`.

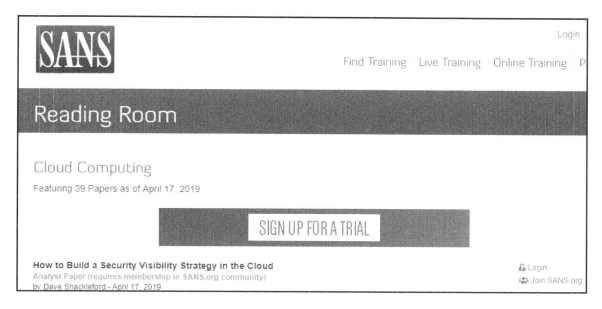

You can find up to date free white papers at SANS **Reading Room**. And of course you can find resources about cloud from Cisco as well at `https://www.cisco.com/c/en_sg/solutions/cloud/overview.html`.

Modern day regulations

Tough regulations have already been put in place to punish companies that fail to safeguard user data. The most recent regulation touching on this was the **General Data Protection Regulation (GDPR)**, which is quite demanding for organizations that want to be fully compliant with its requirements. The consequence of non-compliance with GDPR is that organizations found culpable will be heavily fined. GDPR is just one of the many regulations in cyberspace that have been designed to protect privacy and ensure security. There are many other regulations that apply to different jurisdictions. In the US, there is the **HIPAA Act**, the **Gramm-Leach-Bliley Act**, and the **Federal Information Security Act**, which regulate the collection, use, and protection of data in healthcare, financial, and federal agencies. There are more laws that are coming up in countries such as the US, with more bills still in the queue to become future laws.

The regulatory space can, therefore, drastically change in months. Organizations do not always have the resources to stay abreast with the regulatory changes. The problem with data is that it can move across several regions and be subject to different regulations. For instance, while the GDPR only affects the data belonging to EU citizens, organizations world over have to comply with it, since they cannot foretell when they will interact with data from EU citizens. Many data regulations have to be followed, regardless of the geographical region they are passed in.

It would take a lot of resources for organizations to research all of the regulations that they are supposed to follow, and this is why they mostly outsource this function. You can create a career out of being a consultant for data regulations. You have to be conversant with all applicable data regulations to a company and help the company in complying with the regulations. You have to keep updated with all the changes in these regulations and advise organizations accordingly when changes are made. The cyberspace is soon going to face major challenges for regulatory compliance. It is estimated that there is an average of 200 regulatory changes globally. While many of these do not currently affect the cybersecurity industry, soon they will. It is, therefore, best to start learning to become a regulatory compliance consultant for organizations today.

Incidence response and forensics

Statistics released each year from credible sources show a startling fact that cybersecurity incidences are going up at a fast rate. In July 2018, Positive Technologies released a report showing that cyber attacks had increased by 32% in 2018's first quarter compared to the previous year's statistics. Malware attacks alone had increased by 75% since 2017 and had been targeted at individuals, government agencies, and businesses.

You can read more about this at https://www.ptsecurity.com/ww-en/about/news/293941/.

What is common in many cybersecurity incidences is that the targets try to respond to minimize the impacts and then do thorough investigations to find out the cause of the incident. However, there are not many professionals skilled enough to do this. With the frequency of attacks only going up, organizations are finding the need to hire competent personnel that can respond to and mitigate cybersecurity incidences as they happen. Individuals and organizations that have already fallen victim to cyber attacks will be looking for professionals that can trace back the attack in order to prevent future similar attacks.

The problem is that the cybersecurity industry is playing catch-up with cybercriminals, since today's attackers are increasingly becoming sophisticated. Organizations are finding hope in skilled incidence response personnel that have the capabilities to stop attacks as they happen, or drastically reduce the impact. If you train to be an incident response expert, you will hardly be free given the trend that's been observed in the cybersecurity industry. Coupled with this, digital forensics is also now coming into play.

Some organizations that lost money to attackers have been able to track and find part of it due to digital forensics. For instance, Ubiquiti Networks lost $44 million to attackers, and, due to efforts from digital forensic experts, $8 million was recovered shortly afterwards. Therefore, you will also find demand in the digital forensics job market. Incidence response and digital forensics go hand-in-hand and it is best that you learn the two together. If you pursue these two, you will first learn about the techniques used to respond to cybersecurity incidences at different stages. You will also learn about the tools and techniques used in digital forensic investigations. Once equipped with these skills, you will be ready for a promising career in the cybersecurity industry.

Enterprise security at scale

Security has become a broad and challenging issue for enterprises. It is wide-scoped and includes ensuring the security of systems and networks, understanding the motive of attackers, understanding different types of attacks, understanding the users and targets, and also planning on how to respond to attacks. The scope keeps getting wider as organizations adopt new technologies, deploy new systems, or get new personnel. Internal staff working in IT departments are not always able to comb through the wide scope and ensure that the organization is safe. This is why there has been an increase in the demand for enterprise security specialists.

To venture into this career, you need to have vast experience in IT. This is because clients will expect you to be knowledgeable in all of the seven domains of an IT infrastructure. You will also need to have up-to-date information on the most prevalent cyber attacks and how they can be prevented or mitigated. You might also need some soft skills, as you will be expected to train users on security threats and how they can reduce their exposure or act during an attack.

There are several courses for this career being offered by reputable institutions. Microsoft has 39 courses on enterprise security, which touch upon the whole scope of today's IT infrastructure. One of these is the **Microsoft Professional Program for Cybersecurity**, which is fully inclusive of all that you need to know to be an enterprise security specialist for organizations that use Microsoft operating systems. Taking such courses is an investment, since job opportunities are already there and others will continually present themselves. Besides this, there is less competition in this line of work, as it requires a specialist that has undergone long-term training and is conversant with all the enterprise security needs.

Penetration testing

Most organizations are opting to have white hats search for vulnerabilities in different systems, networks, and even users to identify the weak points that can be used to attack. Penetration testing entails the legal attempts to hack an organization with the purpose of finding all possible avenues that can be exploited by real hackers during attacks. Learning to be a penetration tester takes you through the same concepts of hacking that black hats use. Black hats only use these hacking skills for their own malicious purposes, while white hats use the hacking skills they have to help organizations protect themselves. In a penetration testing course, the tools and techniques that are used during real attacks are the ones that get taught. This ensures that white hats are at par with black hats as far as skills and techniques are concerned.

Leading universities and online learning academies have warmed up to the idea of teaching this course. A comprehensive outline of what the course covers can be obtained from SANS, and it outlines the following:

The initial training introduces a learner to cybersecurity and ethical hacking in general. The learner then progresses and learns the categories of learning tools, techniques, and exploits that are used during hacks. The real ethical hacking then begins where learners are taught about web-based systems penetration testing using tools and techniques that hackers rely on to compromise such systems. From web-apps, learners are taught about network penetration where different tools that can compromise networks and devices connected to the networks are taught. At this point, the learner is able to scout for networks, steal network passwords, observe the traffic flowing in a network, and target devices connected to the network.

The stage of penetration testing involves learning social engineering techniques that can be used to hack the users. Users are often referred to as the weakest links in the cybersecurity chain because they can be easily manipulated. White hats are taught the techniques and tools that they can use to dig up background information about a user, target them with a social engineering attack, and take advantage of the user when he or she has fallen prey to the attack. Commonly, social engineering allows hackers to steal login credentials to highly secure systems, or directly steal data and funds by ordering the users to make unauthorized transactions. Lastly, the penetration testing course trains students on how to steal data from mobile devices. It might seem as though the course might lead to more malicious hackers, but, in the real sense, it produces white hats that protect organizations from black hats. Penetration testing courses are also neatly structured so that they promote ethical values in the IT world.

Learning penetration testing thrusts you into a lucrative career of being a vulnerability assessment consultant or a penetration tester. As the number of malicious actors continues to rise, organizations are going to be in demand of experts that can find vulnerabilities in their systems before the hackers can. Statistics show that organizations are continually increasing their IT spending on cybersecurity, and hiring a pen tester is one of the best investments that they can make. Therefore, it is worthwhile to learn penetration testing as it can guarantee a stable and well-paying career in the cybersecurity industry.

 If you do not want to sign to a course which is standard worldwide, and you want to learn from worldwide known experts directly, companies like TrueSec, Cqure can help you as well.

TruSec training

The website for TruSec training can be found at `https://www.truesec.com/training/`.

I would highly recommend training from Marcus Murray and Hasain Alshakarti:

CQURE Academy

Good as TruSec, with many customized cybersecurity training options. Their website can be found at `https://cqureacademy.com/`.

Training with Troy Hunt

Troy Hunt is an Australian web security expert who is known for public education and outreach on various security topics. He created **Have I Been Pwned?**, which is a data breach search website that allows non-technical users to see if their personal information has been compromised. The website was launched in late 2013. You can follow the link to get access to his workshops at `https://www.troyhunt.com/workshops/`.

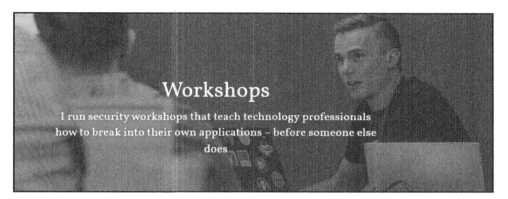

Have I Been Pwned ?

This website by Troy Hunt, will allow you to see if your personal data or password has been compromised. The service is totally for free and highly recommend you to visit the web site and subscribe to get alert if you get hacked. The website can be found at `https://haveibeenpwned.com/`.

DevSecOps

Learning institutions are continually releasing developers into the world. However, most of these institutions only focus on teaching developers how to actualize functionalities in application systems. Very few developers join the market with the aspect of security in development. As the IT environment is continually becoming less secure and more unpredictable, a new approach is required when developing apps and systems.

DevSecOps is a premise that states that anyone involved in software development is responsible for bringing together development and security. Initially, security used to be an after-thought. The development team would build the software first and then integrate security into it.

DevSecOps discourages this, and instead enforces a new development approach where security is tightly coupled with all other software development phases. Security is thus embedded in all development processes rather than coming in as an addition at the end of a development project.

DevSecOps ensures that the responsibility of security is equally shared in a software development project and that security is continually integrated from start to end. With the integrated approach, security is not built around the perimeter of systems—it is built within every part of the system. This makes it hard for malicious persons to compromise the system. During software development, developers have security in mind and they continually share their insights on security threats and how they can make their software resistant to the threats. For instance, if the known threat takes advantage of a one-time authentication procedure, the developers can implement authentication at every module of a software so that an unauthorized person is not able to carry out any significant transactions in a system, even after bypassing the initial authentication process.

When learning DevSecOps, you will develop a new perspective on development. It will not just be about functionalities, but the security of the software as well. You will learn how to determine the risk tolerance of a software and how to improve it. You will also learn how to do a risk/benefit analysis. At times, too much security might hinder some essential services or make the software needlessly slow. Therefore, DevSecOps ensures that security is not at either extreme so that it makes a software unusable due to the inclusion of too many security controls, or insecure to use due to few security controls. DevSecOps is fast gaining popularity in the market and organizations are looking for system developers that use this approach of building software. The benefits of DevSecOps are as follows:

- **Speed and agility**: Software development is done in small iterations in which security is continually added. Also, security teams do not have to wait until a piece of software is completed to integrate security controls.
- **Response to changes**: There are many changes that occur in the IT environment and they may, at times, affect the way security is integrated into software. For instance, new threats may emerge during software development and the developers have to respond by making their system resistant to the threat. For instance, older systems were built to check where login credentials matched those in a database. However, when hackers began using password dictionaries, software developers responded by including a counter to prevent a certain number of login trials from being exceeded. DevSecOps prepares developers to react in such ways.
- **Quality assurance testing**: Systems built with the DevSecOps approach are easier to test, since all components are tightly coupled. Security is not a module; rather, it is built into the software and can be thoroughly tested when other functionalities of the software are being tested.

- **Early identification of vulnerabilities**: With DevSecOps, software does not have to get to bug testers for vulnerabilities to be identified. All developers have the mindset of ensuring the security of a system, so they are always on the lookout for vulnerabilities that can be exploited. With many eyes sweeping through the code just to find out vulnerabilities, nearly all possible vulnerabilities are identified and resolved during development.

DevSecOps training is focused on a technical shift where you learn how to prioritize security during development. You also learn how to collaborate with other developers or security teams to ensure that the end deliverable is highly secure. DevSecOps is also focused on agility and fast responses to change. When taking the training, you will mostly learn code analysis, change management, compliance monitoring, threat investigation, and vulnerability assessment. In the future, other software development approaches will slowly be abandoned and companies will be looking for developers who are well-versed in DevSecOps. Therefore, take the course today and reserve yourself a guaranteed space in software development in tomorrow's job market.

IoT security

In the first two quarters of 2018, IoT devices grew at an unprecedented rate to hit a total of 7 billion devices. It has been projected that there may be 20.8 billion IoT devices in active use by 2020.

You can find more about this at https://iot-analytics.com/state-of-the-iot-update-q1-q2-2018-number-of-iot-devices-now-7b/.

Going by the numbers from the first two quarters of 2018, the numbers are going to grow quickly. However, there has been a major challenge with IoT devices regarding their security. These devices have been flooded into the market by different manufacturers while lacking the bare minimum security requirements. As a result, many botnets are being formed using these devices.

Botnets are malicious networks of internet-connected devices that are used for performing denial-of-service attacks, or spamming. One of the most powerful botnets today is called Mirai, which is purely made up of IoT devices. These are the repercussions of having so many insecure devices in use.

IoT devices are being targeted by hackers and are being used as points of entry into organizations or homes. Since the devices are normally connected to a network, hackers are breaching the devices and navigating through the network to attack other devices.

For instance, a hacker might breach an IoT device and get into the network to spread malware to all computers sharing the same network with the device. Such attacks have been happening, and there are bound to be more attacks like this in the future.

Since many organizations are prioritizing their security, they will be looking for experts to secure their IoT devices so that they cannot be manipulated by hackers. Apart from organizations, governments that are using IoT devices to implement systems such as smart grids are also going to be looking for experts to secure such systems from attacks. This, therefore, opens the opportunities for an IoT security expert.

IoT security is a fast growing area that is seeking to add a layer of reliable security to the IoT technology. It aims at eradicating the currently existing security flaws in the IoT technology so that they can be more resistant to cyber attacks. IoT security is performed in four steps:

1. **Understanding the IoT process**: IoT devices play different roles, such as collecting data or actualizing some functionalities in a system. You need to learn how to identify the process that needs to be protected. Some processes are more sensitive than others, and a good example is an IoT that controls a life-critical system.

2. **Understanding the engineering of the product**: There are many IoT device manufacturers and they have engineered their devices in different ways due to the absence of industry-wide standards. Of importance from a security point of view is understanding how some access controls such as login have been implemented. It is also important to identify the backdoors and other poor security practices that may lead the device to being compromised.

3. **Securing the device**: With a good understanding of the engineering of an IoT device, you can make the appropriate changes to secure it. These changes involve the implementation of security best practices to ensure that the device is secured. Default passwords can be changed, backdoors could be removed, cryptography could be enabled, the device could be reset to free it from any botnet, and all IoT devices could be connected to an isolated and highly secured network. The changes made need to be well-thought out to prevent potential damage or disruption of service to the IoT device itself.

4. **Implementation of security policies**: To ensure standardized security for all IoT devices, it is important to set up security policies to be followed wherever IoT devices are concerned. Due to the interconnected nature of these devices, it only takes one insecure IoT device to compromise the whole organization. Therefore, there should be strict compliance with security policies.

It is already expected that there will be more IoT devices in the market, so it is not a question of whether or not there will be IoT security jobs. With the trend of quick adoption of IoT devices and increased cyber attacks, many organizations will seek IoT security services. Therefore, this could be a secure career path to start today.

 You can get free IoT training online from University of California at https://www.classcentral.com/tag/internet-of-things.

CLASS CENTRAL   Courses ∨   MOOC Report ∨   Search online courses   Q   My Classes ∨

Free Online Courses in
Internet Of Things

Study free online *Internet of things* courses and MOOCs from top universities and colleges.
Read reviews to decide if a class is right for you.

User behavior analytics (UBA)

Users have contributed to some of the worst cyber attacks that have happened in the world. For instance, the worst attack on Yahoo, an email service provider, was caused by just one click from a user. The FBI investigated the cause of the breach that led to the compromise of millions of user accounts and discovered that there were spear-phishing emails that were targeted at specific Yahoo employees. It is said that one of those targeted clicked on a malicious link that led to hackers compromising the employee's computer and using it to gain access to the network.

Once in the network, the hackers installed a backdoor that allowed them to connect to and steal Yahoo's user database. Investigations revealed that the hacker responsible for these operations handed over the stolen database to other commercial hackers. Soon, the hackers started breaching individual accounts to a point where Yahoo came open with news about the hack.

The hack can, therefore, be traced back to a single user that did not follow security policies and clicked on a malicious link. There might have been impenetrable defenses in the network, but once a logged in user was compromised, it was easy for the hackers to complete their mission. This type of scenario can happen to any organization. Users are known to be careless and their mistakes can lead to devastating cyber attacks.

Cybercriminals will take advantage of a compromised computer to achieve certain functionalities. For instance, they could use a compromised computer of a finance department employee to initiate financial transactions.

UBA is a new technology aimed at averting disasters when users are compromised. With UBA, big data analytics is used to map the normal user behaviors. For instance, finance department employees could be recorded to transact certain amounts of money to specific accounts and at certain dates. When an anomalous behavior is recorded from a certain user, a red flag is triggered by the system. For instance, if the account of a finance department employee makes abnormally large transactions or transacts at abnormal times, the UBA will send an alert and prevent the transaction from going through. This, therefore, stops an attack from being actualized.

UBA has already been adopted by big organizations that cannot tolerate huge losses. For instance, the SWIFT global payment network, which is used globally by banks to send huge amounts of money, uses such a system. In 2016, there was a hack of the Bangladeshi central bank and hackers initiated huge transactions, some of which SWIFT declined.

The hackers stole $81 million via sending fraudulent messages, and malware which allowed them to hack in to the bank's **SWIFT (Society for Worldwide Interbank Financial Telecommunication)**, ostensibly from the central bank in Dhaka, Bangladesh. Despite blocking most of the transfer, about $81 million was sent to a Fillipino bank. Following this, the money was further moved to casinos and casino agents and much of it is still missing.

According to SWIFT, hackers obtained valid credentials of the banks employees and then used those credentials to initiate money transactions as if they were legitimate bank employees.

UBA is only getting better with the advancements in artificial intelligence and big data analytics. In the future, many organizations will be adopting such UBA systems. Therefore, there is huge potential in consultancy services for this technology. There are online learning academies that are offering training in several UBA programs that can be used to fight cyber attacks. Such courses teach you how to install and configure the UBA system in organizations, collect normal user data, and define the actions to be taken when a threat is detected. Since most of the actions are taken by the UBA system, most of the hard work will be during installation, configuration, and learning processes. With this information, you could be an established consultant for the installation of UBA systems, user training, and troubleshooting. Since many organizations are going to implement these systems to help them deal with hacking attempts, spam, the spread of malware, and leaks from employees, any trained professional in UBA will find lots of work opportunities in the future.

Learn how credentials work, what **Pass the Hash** (**PtH**) is as of April 2019, those kind attacks are still very active and effective.

PtH is an attack technique where an attacker captures a password or hash and then simply uses the passwords or hash for authentication.

 April 2019, Microsoft has confirmed that their free email service (Outlook/Hotmail /MSN) has been compromised. A support agents credential was stolen, which gave hackers unauthorized access to some accounts where they could view account email address, folder names, and some emails.

You can learn how to mitigate PtH attacks and other credential theft attacks via a white paper which Microsoft has published. You can download and read the white paper from this URL: `https://www.microsoft.com/en-us/download/details.aspx?id=36036`

Also having **Privileged Access Workstations** (**PAWs**) can help you to minimize the potential internet attacks and threat vectors. You can learn more about PAW here: `https://docs.microsoft.com/en-us/windows-server/identity/securing-privileged-access/privileged-access-workstations`

To learn more about cybersecurity attack and defense strategies, you can read a book which is published by Packt and authored by Yuri Diogenes and myself:

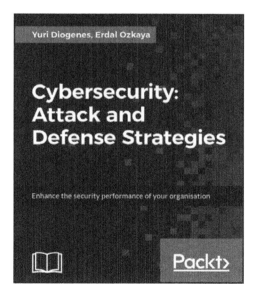

Endpoint detection and response (EDR)

EDR has been predicted to be the future of incidence response. Normal incidence response teams are not always well-informed about an attack to be able to quickly identify the cause, mitigate it to prevent adverse impacts, and to remediate the situation. Even after an attack has ended, the normal incidence response personnel cannot assure that they can prevent a future similar attack from happening. EDR is a term that's used to refer to the combination of tools that are used to detect and investigate incidences on endpoints.

This emerging technology is redefining what incidence response is by providing more reliable and timely incidence responses during attacks. EDR is not just one tool—it is composed of different tools that continually monitor endpoints, networks, and users regarding where they centrally store all important information.

EDR is powered by powerful analytics systems that run from a central point to identify any peculiar data recorded by the monitoring agents running in different systems. When a security incident is about to happen, the EDR will give an early warning to system and network admins about a potential attack. For instance, the EDR could detect that a server's internal firewall has continually blocked suspicious traffic streaming from a certain source. The EDR will warn of an imminent attack on the specific server so that preventative measures can be taken. Some EDRs can integrate with other security software, such as antivirus programs that can be used to intervene in cases where malware is detected to have been passed to an endpoint.

EDR is going to receive adoption in the near future by organizations that want continuous monitoring to deter attacks and assist with incidence response. The technology has been marked as an essential component of today's cybersecurity infrastructure. Since attacks are going to keep increasing, organizations will want to have a tool that can help incidence response teams during attacks to quickly identify the cause and mitigate it. They will, therefore, be looking for professionals that can deploy EDR to their IT infrastructure. Also, knowledge of the EDR technology will give you an advantage in IT jobs. It is, therefore, worthwhile to learn about the technology.

Summary

There are inevitable changes happening today in the cyberspace. Cyber attacks are on the rise and they are becoming more sophisticated. These changes are also shaping careers in cybersecurity. The old approaches to cybersecurity are slowly being phased out and new technologies are being adopted. The future job market in the cybersecurity industry will be significantly impacted by these technologies.

This chapter has gone through some of the most promising technologies to learn today. The analysis of the technologies to learn has been guided by their applicability and job outlook in the near future. The technologies that we discussed are the ones that are going to be predominant in the cybersecurity space in the near future. With knowledge of these technologies, it will be easy to pursue different careers in IT, and, specifically, in the cybersecurity industry. They will also give you added advantages should you choose to go into a normal IT career.

Further reading

The following are resources can be used to gain more knowledge about what was covered in this chapter:

- *Penetration Testing*: https://www.sans.org/curricula/penetration-testing
- *What is DevSecOps? Developing more secure applications*: https://www.csoonline.com/article/3245748/devops/what-is-devsecops-developing-more-secure-applications.html
- *What is DevSecOps?*: https://www.redhat.com/en/topics/devops/what-is-devsecops
- *State of the IoT 2018: Number of IoT devices now at 7B – Market accelerating*: https://iot-analytics.com/state-of-the-iot-update-q1-q2-2018-number-of-iot-devices-now-7b/
- *IoT security (internet of things security)*: https://internetofthingsagenda.techtarget.com/definition/IoT-security-Internet-of-Things-security
- *5 emerging security technologies set to level the battlefield*: https://techbeacon.com/5-emerging-security-technologies-set-level-battlefield

4
Skills We Need for a Cybersecurity Career

The increased concerns about cybercrime in organizations have opened up stable careers in the cybersecurity industry. Unlike a decade ago, organizations today no longer rely on network admins or IT admins to take care of the burden of cybersecurity. They have been onboarding experts that are knowledgeable in different attacks or threats, and improving the security architecture of the organization. This chapter looks at the job market so that we can find cybersecurity roles that organizations are advertising and the in-demand skills that you can learn to transit to, change to, or build your career in cybersecurity.

In this chapter, we will cover the following topics:

- General cybersecurity roles
- Skills to acquire in cybersecurity
- Choosing skills to acquire based on current professional experience and skills

General cybersecurity roles

The cybersecurity industry is currently flooding with jobs. It has been reported that there are fewer people than required to fill all the roles in cybersecurity. The main roles that organizations are advertising for are covered in the following subsections.

Penetration testers and vulnerability testers

One of the ways to secure an organization from hackers is to have its vulnerabilities identified and fixed before hackers show up. Penetration testers are essentially white hackers who compromise or try to compromise systems as requested by the owners of these systems. In security careers, penetration testing is growing in relevance in the job market. Since organizations cannot be 100% sure that the security tools they have already implemented are sufficient enough to protect them, they are always looking for people to breach them. A career in penetration testing involves the roles of using common reconnaissance or hacking tools such as Metasploit or Wireshark to test the security stature of the organization. It will also include reviewing the code that has been used to create the systems that organizations run their operations on. The only non-exciting task in this job, for many that fancy it, is writing lengthy and detailed reports of the vulnerabilities found and the fixes required.

Cybersecurity consultants

While organizations are focused on improving their security stature, they are also looking at reducing the financial burden of doing so. Hiring full-time employees just to assess the security level of an organization is being viewed as an added expense to the organization. Unlike other IT roles such as helpdesk support, some cybersecurity roles are not routine and thus can be carried out once or twice a month. In addition to this, there is a shortage of talents in cybersecurity. Therefore, employees that have these skills are changing workplaces more regularly as they are offered better remuneration packages. Therefore, organizations are increasingly having to contract third-party experts to assess their threat landscape and exposure. Cybersecurity consultancy roles are favorable to beginners as they are a way to gain real-world experience that might be required later in permanent positions. Cybersecurity consultants are often specialized in specific roles, and so anyone pursuing this role should identify a niche they are good at.

Cybersecurity managers

It is not expected that the existing system and network admins will be able to oversee the burden of cybersecurity. They might lack the expertise or be left behind by trends in cybercrime. This is why organizations are creating the position of a cybersecurity manager to oversee all cybersecurity programs on networks and systems. The roles that are played by these managers are as follows: monitor compliance with policies, ensure IT security audits are required, keep tabs on the patching or threat mitigation efforts, and manage any cybersecurity incidences. Cybersecurity managers serve as the backbone of the cybersecurity efforts of the organization, and so are expected to have a wide scope of knowledge in this field.

Cybersecurity analysts

They are the new frontlines of cybersecurity in organizations. Due to the many cybersecurity incidences that companies are facing—some of which turn out to be successful attacks as others are foiled—there has been a need to have an expert to conduct investigations. Cybersecurity analysts analyze all security incidences to obtain useful information that might be used to prevent future attacks from happening. For instance, they might trace back the path that hackers might have followed to gain access to sensitive files. It could be that the system admins are using default passwords or that one of them fell for a social engineering scam and gave out passwords. Cybersecurity analysts ensure that they provide enough information to prevent similar attacks from happening.

Cybersecurity engineers

This is an intermediate position in the cybersecurity field in which organizations are consistently looking for talents to fill. This job plays an important role in the security stature of the organization because the engineer is expected to come up with a reliable security infrastructure. This includes developing comprehensive security policies, innovative ways to prevent threats, threat mitigation or response plans, and many other security measures. The cybersecurity engineer is also expected to ensure that systems and networks cannot be breached. Therefore, all the audits, penetration tests, or security tools that are implemented rely on these inputs. Lastly, the engineer is expected to secure a buy-in from company executives for the required security tools to be acquired.

Chief Information Security Officers (CISOs)

There have been many cases where junior employees serving critical roles in cybersecurity have been unable to convince executives to authorize some purchases for security tools or enterprise-wide training of employees. The CISO role was created to give the IT department direct representation in the executive management of a company. CISOs take over the overall responsibilities of the security of the organization. They are in charge of directing operations and getting funds allocated for cybersecurity functions. They also ensure the compliance of security policies from the top down. CISO jobs are often filled by highly-learned individuals that possess both technical and management skills.

Chief Security Officers (CSOs)

This is another high ranking position in organizations that provides for the representation of all security functions to the executive. CSOs play the most important role of ensuring the security of both the physical and digital assets that organizations own. People holding this position ensure that security investments add value to the business. They do so by putting in place measures to protect the business processes so that they are never or hardly disrupted by the many cybercrime attacks that have occasioned the digital world. CSOs ensure that organizations have effective business continuity plans to prevent a scenario where a cyber attack brings all businesses to a standstill. They also ensure that enough security tools and techniques have been implemented to prevent data, monetary, and reputation losses that may arise from a cyber attack. CSO jobs are usually reserved for the few qualified individuals that have lengthy working experiences in IT and adequate training in cybersecurity.

Computer system administrators

This is not a new role in the market—it has existed for a long time. However, the demand for skills that can fill this role is going up in the market. System administrators conventionally look after the components of systems to ensure that they are working as expected. In light of cybersecurity threats, the roles in this job have increased. They include ensuring that the systems are built in a secure way, can resist common security threats, assure the security of sensitive data in case of a breach, and can continue working during attacks. System admins are mostly degree holders in IT, computer engineering, or computer science.

Cryptographers

Organizations are realizing the essence of safeguarding data in transmission and storage through encryption. This ensures that even if hackers are able to breach systems or intercept traffic, the information they steal will not be useful. The internet was originally not designed for security, and so it has become a burden for organizations to ensure end-to-end encryption of the information they exchange with customers. In addition to this, hackers are becoming more effective at infiltrating organizations and stealing data. They have been able to breach organizations that are thought to be highly secure. Once data is stolen, only encryption can make it unusable. This is why organizations are employing experts that can reliably encrypt data, emails, and internet connections. Cryptographers provide these services using the most practical encryption algorithms for each functionality. Cryptographers commonly have a degree in computer science and an added certification in cryptography.

Computer forensic experts

Computer forensic experts, just like other forensic experts, are called upon to investigate cybercrime incidences. They can identify the causes of the incidences, capture evidence that can be used in a court of law, or recover information that has been lost to hackers. Computer forensics includes lots of digital data that might be fragile to handle, especially when it is intended to be used in court. Therefore, these experts sometimes work in conjunction with professions in law. Forensic experts can reliably track where stolen data or cash has been transferred to, and so they can initiate recovery efforts. They have been known to even go through listings on several black markets and pose as buyers of stolen data as part of the efforts to recover it. Outside corporate employment, computer forensic experts can be consulted in criminal cases to examine scenes of digital crime. A typical computer forensic expert will have taken a degree course in forensics and be certified by a recognized body.

Network security engineers

Network security engineers are specialized in offering security solutions to networks. Their roles, therefore, revolve around WAN, LAN, and servers. They are responsible for implementing several network tools such as firewalls and intrusion prevention systems. They will work toward ensuring that an organization has adequate perimeter security systems to prevent attacks. They also administer critical hardware on networks such as routers and switches to ensure that they are not compromised and offer reliable services at all times. Most network security engineers will be educated in networking and certified in network security.

Information assurance technicians

Information is critical in the digital world. However, it is increasingly being targeted by cyber criminals. The focus of cybersecurity is to protect the CIA triad of information. This triad is composed of confidentiality, integrity, and availability. Information assurance technicians share the same focus. They ensure that information is always availed where needed and when needed by putting up measures for information risk management. This risk management entails all risk vectors in activities related to the use, processing, storage, and transmission of information.

Data security analysts

The data security analyst position is an entry-level one, but serves some sensitive roles in the organization. Due to the cybercrime scare, many organizations will have hired consultants to find out their vulnerabilities or audit their security systems and present their findings. There needs to be an expert to reconcile the reports from several assessments into an actionable plan to ensure that the network, systems, and data are secure. Additionally, organizations need someone who can continually monitor systems for security incidences and respond when needed. Sensitive data needs to be afforded extra protection, and its availability should also be assured. Therefore, there should be someone to secure the data so that it is secure during espionage attacks. There should also be someone to offer multiple redundancies if the availability of some data that's used for routine operations is required. Data security analysts play these roles, among many others. They will be indispensable responders to cyber attacks to ensure that the organization's data is secure.

IT security compliance analysts

Cybercrime incidences are expensive to organizations, and not just because they involve the theft of cash. Cyber breaches come bundled with the unfortunate consequences of fines for not securing personal information or not following the prescribed regulations regarding data security and disclosure of attacks to users. Companies are being fined millions. Regulatory bodies are also increasingly coming up with more stringent policies that have to be complied with. Lastly, organizations often pay much attention to the development of security policies that are aimed at reducing threat exposure and aiding in response and recovery processes. However, very little focus is paid to the adherence to these policies. IT security compliance analysts provide the needed assistance in ensuring compliance with both internal and external security policies. Internally, they ensure that employees are adhering to security policies. They might come up with measures to track and reward compliance or non-compliance.

Outside the organization, these experts ensure that the organization meets the prescribed regulatory requirements. IT security compliance analysts tend to be familiar with many frameworks that are used in the development of security policies. These frameworks include NIST and ISO 27001. These experts are also conversant with the security controls that organizations have to protect their systems and networks with. They use this knowledge to ensure that users are compliant with all applicable security policies. For instance, they might review the password strengths of the users in a system and inform those with weak passwords to change them. Lastly, they are knowledgeable of all applicable regulations that affect organizations both locally and internationally.

System security specialists

System security specialists are computer hardware and software experts that are specialized in cybersecurity. They play diverse roles in an organization to ensure security. It is noteworthy that security encompasses both physical and digital threats. Therefore, physical theft of a server is as much of a cyber threat today as is a denial of service attack. System security specialists ensure the physical security of digital assets in an organization such as servers and work stations. They also test the security measures that have been put in place to secure them, such as fire detectors, key-card access systems for servers, and other measures. These specialists are also called upon to implement security patches and test software to ensure that they are secure from initially identified threats. They also do independent assessments of the vulnerabilities faced by computers and computer systems. They can, therefore, use the common tools that are used to identify vulnerabilities in systems. System security specialists also ensure that critical systems have redundancies that can be activated during attacks to ensure business operations do not come to a standstill. They will work with other IT staff to implement continuity and disaster recovery, and mitigation plans. Due to their scope of activities, these specialists are highly knowledgeable of security across all seven layers of the ISO model.

Skills to acquire in cybersecurity

Cybersecurity is one of the most dynamic careers in the job market. While it offers quite a number of career options, the skills that you need to remain relevant in the market keep changing. This is mostly because cybersecurity is reactive to changes in the cybercrime space. Therefore, when cyber criminals change tactics, cybersecurity professionals are also expected to change. For instance, a decade ago, malware removal would be a sought-after skill in the market. However, due to automation, security tools became capable of performing this task, and so that skill lost relevance. Similarly, waves of new attacks bring emphasis to some skills and remove focus from others. For instance, the WannaCry and NotPetya attacks of 2016 brought attention to cryptography skills. For a beginner in the cybersecurity industry or an expert wishing to diversify, there are numerous skills that you may want to acquire.

HR departments are having to deal with the scarcity of cybersecurity skills in the market. While this is bad for recruiters, it is good news to people that pick up essential cybersecurity skills. There are many mitigating factors that are making cybersecurity professionals quickly accepted into the market. These include the following:

- **Preference of tech giants by many job seekers**: Since cybersecurity aligns with normal IT qualifications, experts in the industry are more focused on getting placements in big name companies. This leaves small and non-tech companies with few applicants. Therefore, applicants that strategically target jobs in smaller companies have a higher chance of being employed.
- **The widening skills gap**: There is an existing skills gap between experts and beginners in cybersecurity. HR managers are facing uphill tasks when hiring for higher security roles. Sometimes, job openings in cybersecurity could go for months without being filled. However, some approaches, such as training for the required positions in-house, are less than adequate to meet all organizational cybersecurity roles.
- **High turnover rates for cybersecurity positions**: This is a common problem for job roles that have a scarce supply of talents. Organizations are desperate to hire the right people, so they end up poaching employees from others and offering remuneration that is hard for other companies to beat.

All these challenges in the cybersecurity field should be enough for you to consider gaining skills that will make you one of the highly sought-after talents. Let's go over these skills in the following subsections.

Foundation skills

These are skills that provide the fundamentals that cybersecurity professionals need to have. They are baseline skills that everyone in the industry must ideally possess.

Risk management

Risks are the driving force behind cybersecurity. Therefore, cybersecurity professionals should be acquainted with information about risk management. As they take on some of the typical cybersecurity roles, they will be responding to some form of risk. In addition, there are some roles that will require the professionals to demonstrate the risks that are present in systems and networks to business executives in a language they understand.

Networking

One of the main attack surfaces that cyber criminals target is the network. Networks play key roles in organizations since they connect the computing infrastructure and allow most of the data exchange services to be carried out. Therefore, it is apparent that a professional in cybersecurity must have adequate knowledge of networking. There are several recognized bodies that train and certify people interested in learning networking.

Situational awareness

Attackers are evolving in regards to the attacks and tools that they are using against organizations. This means that cybersecurity professionals must be knowledgeable of the changes in cybercrime. They should know the latest attack trends and how they can be mitigated. Situational awareness allows cybersecurity professionals to understand how to best secure the organization based on the prevalent threats at a given time.

Toolkits

Contrary to what is normally depicted in movies, hacking is a slow process and is highly automated. Therefore, hackers use some toolkits to perform actions. On the cybersecurity side, professionals also use some toolkits to scan for threats or to stop attacks that are in progress. Cybersecurity professionals need to know how to use some of these toolkits or any other specialized tools provided by the organization they work for.

Security analyst skills

Many roles in cybersecurity require you to be conversant in analyzing networks and computing environments so as to detect threats and vulnerabilities. The following are some of the analytical skills that you should have.

Threat assessment

Threat assessment is vital in a cybersecurity career because the essence of security in an organization is to protect it from threats. Therefore, you are expected to know the different types of threats and their characteristics. An expert should know the vectors that these threats take and what type of effects or damage they cause. Threat assessment skills are best acquired through practical exercises that expose you to these threats. You should have this skill before entering the job market because it is vital.

Vulnerability assessment

Hand in hand with threat assessment is the skill of vulnerability assessment. Vulnerability assessment is part of the basic definition of the work of any cybersecurity personnel. The skill is used to actively seek threats that may exist in computer systems and networks. Cybersecurity experts are expected to know how to identify vulnerabilities and determine their chances of being exploited. There are several tools and techniques that can be used for detecting vulnerabilities. People seeking to start careers in this field should learn how to use these tools and how to implement some techniques. An example of a tool that can be used for vulnerability assessment is Nmap since it can scan networks to identify the connected devices and also scan the devices to identify their open ports, which can be exploited. However, Nmap uses a command-line interface, and so you have to learn how to issue the different scan commands using it. Code review is a common technique for identifying vulnerabilities where the expert can tell whether the code that's used in systems can fall to attacks. For instance, a cybersecurity professional should be able to tell whether the code for a login page can fall to SQL injection or cross-site scripting attacks. They can do this by verifying whether all inputs are validated before they are processed.

Log collection and analysis

Cybersecurity experts are expected to find historical data that can help shed more light on cybersecurity incidences, such as hacks. Furthermore, they need to be able to collect information about the operation of computers, networks, or systems when it is necessary, for example, if there are suspicious behaviors on a system and the owners want to know the cause. Log collection involves putting up automated data collection systems that timestamp activities on systems or networks. Some systems come with inbuilt logging modules, while others require third-party apps to do this. Cybersecurity professionals should know the tools that can be used for log data collection and analysis. For instance, Wireshark is a good logging tool for network connections. It can also be used to analyze the logs that are collected. You can tell which IP addresses of all the devices are communicated in the network, which ports the communication was originating from and destined for, and much more.

Active analysis

Cybersecurity professionals should be able to perform active analysis that is not based on data logs or any supportive tools. There are some attacks such as social engineering that can be hard to analyze using software tools. A cybersecurity professional is expected to know the right questions to ask or the systems to investigate. If a social engineering attack has happened, chances are that the attacker made a connection with the target via email or social media. Therefore, the victim could be asked to share suspicious emails or social media interactions. If a workstation has been hacked, the user could be asked to be honest about the websites they visited or links they clicked on. The intuitiveness of a cybersecurity expert can help gather a lot of information that tools cannot.

Incidence response

Cybersecurity professionals are expected to be ready to respond to incidences such as intrusions or suspicious network activity. When responding to an incident, they should be focused on stopping the threat, mitigating the impacts, and recovering the affected systems. Another important role they play during such scenarios is that of calming the whole organization. Let's go over some of the skills they need to do this.

Disaster recovery

Organizations should have disaster recovery plans that can be used when security disasters happen. These plans need frequent reviews and updates. In addition, they need to be implemented correctly when an actual disaster happens. Cybersecurity professionals are expected to have the skills to do all this. Disaster recovery can potentially help an organization remain stable after an attack. It is therefore given a lot of focus. Some of the common disaster recovery techniques that professionals carry out to ensure that business operations remain unaffected by disasters are activation of alternate sites and restoration of data from backups. Therefore, a cybersecurity professional should be able to at least perform these functions when called upon.

Forensics

Cyber attacks leave a lot of clues that can be used to recover what was stolen or to bring culprits to justice. While there are specialists in cyber forensics, other professionals in this line of work should have some knowledge of forensics. It is of utmost importance to learn how to preserve digital data after an attack so that some pieces of evidence are not lost. Other employees might not know the significance of this, and so cybersecurity staff members are expected to guide them after an attack has happened regarding what they can or cannot do. For instance, if employees are not informed, they could delete some programs containing evidence of break-ins or tamper with some records that could otherwise be useful for investigations.

Penetration testing skills

For those that want to still get short-term contracts before they can qualify for permanent jobs, penetration testing is a skillset that cybersecurity experts will find valuable. Since it is a niche in the greater cybersecurity industry, penetration testing is highly recognized, and so can land you into jobs with ease. Penetration testing courses teach professionals how to find weaknesses and vulnerabilities in computer systems using the same tools and techniques that malicious hackers employ. It fits the saying, *"To catch a thief, think like a thief."* Penetration testing gives you a hacker mindset that you can use to scour for any exploitable gaps in computing environments and networks. Let's go over some of the minimum pen test skills that experts in cybersecurity need to have.

Intelligence gathering

Reconnaissance is a major part of any attack. Hackers spend time just looking for information to aid or guide their attack. Cybersecurity professionals should have the same mindset to collect data that can eventually be used to attack the IT infrastructure of an organization. Some of these intelligence gathering techniques include port scanning, OS fingerprinting, data mining, checking social media posts from employees, and dumpster diving. Intelligence gathering results in intelligence that can be used to secure the systems that are used, or warn users of the dangers they expose themselves to by posting some information. For instance, a cybersecurity professional might try to seek sensitive data that users dispose of inappropriately by doing dumpster diving. He or she could discover printed copies of email communications, passwords that had been written on sticky notes, or lists of usernames on a particular system. This sensitive information ends up in dumpsters every day and so it is not disposed of in a secure way. Hackers could easily find it without breaching the organization and use it to hack.

Incidence reporting

The not-so-glossy part of a career in cybersecurity is writing lengthy reports about any findings from attack incidences or scans that have been carried out in the organization. You must learn how to correctly and clearly present findings to a non-technical audience. It is not a hard skill to learn, but people in this profession ought to have it.

Restraint

The only difference between penetration testers and malicious hackers is on which side of the law each lies. Penetration testers can become malicious hackers. For instance, a pen tester contracted by a bank might find out a vulnerability that they can exploit to initiate fund transfer without sounding alarms. The temptation to misuse this power and knowledge is massive. However, you are expected to have restraint regarding how you use your privileged access or powerful tools. Without restraint, you will chase short-term benefits of taking advantage of the access you are given to carry out cyber attacks and delete the evidence. It will only be a matter of time before you are discovered.

Security architecture skills

Cybersecurity is not just focused on threats, vulnerabilities, and attacks—it includes building strong systems that can prevent attacks from happening. The end goal of cybersecurity should be sustainable solutions that can offer services to legitimate users at all times. The security architecture in many systems is focused on strong security controls that can prevent or add an additional burden to hackers, thus reducing their effectiveness in carrying out attacks. Let's go over some of the security architecture skills that cybersecurity experts should have.

Identity and access management

Identity and access management are routine tasks that computer systems go through every day. Users have to be authenticated into their computers, network, ERPs, and apps. These systems and networks have authentication modules which, when tampered with, can give access to malicious people. In addition, there are some cases where systems could be configured incorrectly, and therefore allow users to have excessive rights. Lastly, some settings could allow guest accounts to be used to carry out sensitive functions. Part of the cybersecurity role is to ensure that identity and access management is done correctly and does not expose the organization to more threats. Cybersecurity experts need to have the know-how of several identity and access management systems. For instance, many organizations have domain controllers that manage computers connected to a certain domain. Cybersecurity experts should know how to access domain controllers and carry out some functions, such as adding or removing a user's rights.

Network configuration

Networks are indispensable in organizations and will always be in focus when security is brought up. A cybersecurity professional should be familiar with networking skills such as subnetting, network segmentation, and isolation. In addition, they should know how to set up firewalls and intrusion detection systems. Ideally, they should be able to do the basic setup and maintenance tasks in networks. They should be familiar with how the organizational network is laid out, as well and be in a position to alter it when necessary.

System hardening

Hosts, servers, and apps should not be sitting ducks for attackers to compromise. They should be hardened to resist hacking attempts so that hackers are highly inconvenienced before they can make any significant progress in breaching an organization. Hardening can be done in a number of ways, and cybersecurity professionals need to be knowledgeable of most of them. This involves applying several layers of security to prevent hackers from gaining access.

For instance, an organization could be using an ERP for routine tasks, and that keeps and protects sensitive user information. This ERP could be running on a local server. For hackers to get into the app, they might take several paths, and one of them is by compromising the server. Cybersecurity professionals could put in place intrusion prevention systems and firewalls to prevent this from happening. Hackers could use the alternative of trying to use brute-force attacks against the login interface of the app. Cybersecurity professionals could implement mechanisms to prevent multiple login attempts within a short period of time. Finally, hackers could try social engineering to try and get the employees that use the ERP system to give them passwords. Cybersecurity professionals could implement two-factor authentication and train employees about phishing attacks. Effectively, the ERP system will have been hardened and is therefore highly unlikely to be hacked. The cybersecurity career involves many such functions, and so experts in this field are expected to know about the various ways they can harden different systems.

Choosing skills to pick up based on current professional experience and skills

Cybersecurity is often occasioned by skills shortages, and so organizations are usually looking for both beginners and experts to fill up security roles. For those that are already in other careers, some of the skills and experience they have could be useful in particular niches of cybersecurity. For those that are starting their career journeys in cybersecurity, there are some skills that will thrust their career journeys forward. For beginners, a fresh start in your career should be focused on acquiring skills that can get you hired fast. Fortunately, cybersecurity is full of entry-level positions that organizations are looking to fill with beginners in the industry. The industry is also quite favorable for experienced professionals in other fields. One of the main reasons why it is hard for recruiters to find highly experienced professionals is because they almost always get hired immediately when they are in the market. Therefore, it is never too late to start your career and join this list of highly sought-after individuals. This section helps job seekers determine which skills they should pick up based on their current professional skills and experience. The following is a breakdown of some skills based on their friendliness and easy entrance into the job market for either beginners or experienced professionals.

Ethical hacking skills

Also referred to as penetration testing, ethical hacking offers learners market-ready skills that are always being sought-after by HR managers. This course is most appealing to beginners in careers. The training is hands-on and it may be easier for learners that have a strong technical background. The skills that are learned are comprehensive and can give you a major boost in the career world. Some experienced people might find it appealing, but it might not be the best choice to pursue since it puts you at an entry-level point in the cybersecurity career world. However, professionals already in the IT world, such as IT officers, will benefit from the advantages that are gained after taking this course. They will stand a chance to get promotions or better-remunerated positions in other organizations.

Application security skills

Application security entails that all processes and checks are put in place to ensure that an application is safe. Due to the massive adoption of ERPs and other customized business solutions, application security is becoming a significant concern. Training for skills in application security mostly applies to beginners and entry-level employees in IT. Beginners will be required to be conversant with app development before taking the course. The entry-level employees that are already in the job market should be actively involved in app development. Studying for application security significantly improves your chances of getting better-paid jobs in the cybersecurity industry. Experienced professionals might not find this course favorable. This is because it will lower them to entry-level jobs and might be a steep learning curve for non-technical learners.

Cloud security skills

The cloud is not an old technology, and so it has already attracted employees with the right mindset for cybersecurity. Since cloud operations are technical, most of the experienced personnel in this field will be tech-savvy. Therefore, skills in cloud security appeal most to the existing professionals in the line of cloud computing. These include cloud architects and cloud app developers. The experienced personnel will simply gain advanced skills in their line of work, thus giving them some advantage in terms of demand and remuneration. Even though beginners may still want to try venturing into cybersecurity with this course, they will face a steep learning curve and might not secure permanent jobs with a single certification in cloud security.

DevSecOps skills

DevOps is a software development phrase that refers to the integration of development and IT operations. It is aimed at ensuring that business units operate as a team in the organization, and breaking down the individualistic views of departments as independent units in organizations. It aims at allowing departments to run collaboratively, and this often involves the integration of some business operations and sharing of data. DevOps, however, introduces organizations to more risks since the risks in one department are transferred through the whole organization. DevSecOps ensures that risks such as vulnerabilities to apps are mitigated during development. Therefore, the safety controls to secure enterprise-wide apps are implemented during development. DevSecOps aligns mostly with experienced professionals in DevOps. Taking the requisite training could improve a professional's career, allowing them to get into higher-ranking positions, such as project managers.

Threat and vulnerability assessment skills

Threat and vulnerability assessment skills are used to identify the threats and weaknesses in organizations, as well as propose ways to solve them. Threat and vulnerability assessment skills appeal to both beginners and professionals in the market, but only those that are in technical fields. Taking the requisite courses will give beginners access to stable careers in the cybersecurity industry. As for professionals, these skills will drastically thrust their careers forward. Organizations are creating executive positions for people who are knowledgeable in cybersecurity, and these include Chief Information Security Officers and Chief Technology Officers. Having skills in threat and vulnerability assessment inches you closer to or allows you to be appointed to these positions.

Information security management skills

Information security management skills are focused on the top-level management of the procedures revolving around the collection, processing, and storage of information to ensure that it is well-secured. The skills you get from such courses are useful in furthering your career if you are already within the IT field. Unfortunately, beginners will not find any advantage in taking this course since it is unlikely that they will be given management positions. Experienced professionals that take the time to get the necessary training and certification in ISM will be in a better position to get executive positions in the organization relating to security. These positions include CISO and CTO.

Cybersecurity litigation support skills

To help with the legal actions that an organization may take if it is sued or when it is suing within the lines of cybersecurity, legal professions have become a necessary addition to organizations. However, normal lawyers may lack sufficient information regarding cybersecurity, and so they may need to take some training so that they have the necessary skills to litigate cybersecurity cases. The skills that are gained from this are most beneficial to existing professionals in the field of law that want to diversify the types of clients they can represent. This course is highly unfavorable to beginners as they lack the prerequisite legal knowledge in both law and cybersecurity.

Regulatory compliance and auditing skills

May acts and laws have been passed to govern cyberspaces in different regions of the world. At times, it is hard for organizations to determine whether they are compliant with all of them. For instance, there is a COPTA act in the US that bars organizations from collecting information of users under the age of 13. There are GDPR regulations being passed by the EU governing how organizations inform users about the ways they collect, process, share, and store personal data. Alongside these are many other regulations. Each comes with a set of consequences if not adhered to. The cybersecurity industry has therefore been welcoming to auditors that are more conversant with the rules of compliance to ensure that organizations are found to be fully compliant with all applicable regulations. Regulatory compliance and auditing training is normally focused on existing professionals in auditing. It may also appeal to beginners in cybersecurity, provided that they have taken a course in auditing.

Summary

This chapter has extensively looked at the issue of establishing strong careers in cybersecurity. It began by going through the general cybersecurity roles in the job market today. The listed roles, which were not exhaustive, included pen testers, cybersecurity consultants, cybersecurity manager, cybersecurity analysts, cybersecurity engineers, CISOs, CSOs, computer system administrators, cryptographers, computer forensic experts, network security engineers, information assurance technicians, data security analysis, IT security compliance analysts, and system security specialists. These, among many other cybersecurity roles, are getting a lot of demand in the job market.

We then looked at the skills that you can choose to acquire in order to be considered for any of the listed cybersecurity roles. It was noted that acquiring these skills would almost guarantee a job since the market has had a scarcity of cybersecurity professionals. The causes for this scarcity included the preference of experienced job seekers for tech giants, the widening skills gap, and the high turnover rates for such positions in many organizations. Even though these factors were causing nightmares for HR managers trying to fill the roles, they were sufficient motivators for people to pursue skills in cybersecurity. We then listed the recommended cybersecurity skills that you should acquire. These included foundation skills such as risk management, networking, situational awareness, and toolkits. The next category was made up of security analyst skills, which included threat assessment, vulnerability assessment, log collection and analysis, active analysis, incidence response, disaster recovery, and forensics. Next, we discussed penetration testing skills that you could acquire, which included intelligence gathering, incidence reporting, and restraint. Lastly, the security architecture skills that were recommended included identity and access management, network configuration, and system hardening.

The final section of this chapter looked at the most viable skills for individuals to pick based on their professional experience and skills. Since there were many skills that could have been considered, the ones that were listed reflected the market demand at the time of writing this book. Some of the recommended skills we saw included **ethical hacking,** which is ideal for beginners in cybersecurity due to the steep learning curve and the entry level jobs it offers; **application security**, which is again ideal for beginners due to its learning curve and jobs being limited to entry-level salaries; **cloud security**, which is ideal for both beginners as well as existing professionals in the IT field; **DevSecOps**, which is ideal for existing professionals in DevOps; **threat/vulnerability assessment**, which is considered ideal for both beginners and professionals in the IT field; **information security management** and **cybersecurity litigation support**, which are considered ideal for existing professionals in the IT and law fields, respectively; and **regulatory compliance and auditing,** which is considered most appealing to existing professionals in the auditing field.

This chapter has therefore provided you with sufficient guidelines so that you can choose a role in the cybersecurity industry that appeals to you. In the next chapter, we analyze the different types of hackers, and their mindsets and social skills.

Further reading

The following resources can be used so that you can gain more knowledge regarding what was covered in this chapter:

- *Cyber Security Jobs, Roles, and Requirements*: https://www.charteroak.edu/cybersecurity/cybersecurity-jobs-roles-requirements.php
- https://insights.dice.com/cybersecurity-skills/
- *10 critical security skills every IT team needs*: https://www.cio.com/article/3228965/10-critical-security-skills-every-it-team-needs.html
- *Top 5 Must-Learn Cybersecurity Courses and Certifications*: https://www.cbronline.com/opinion/top-5-cybersecurity-courses
- *THE 8 MOST IN-DEMAND CYBERSECURITY SKILLS FOR 2019*: http://techgenix.com/in-demand-cybersecurity-skills/
- *These Are the Most In-Demand Cyber Security Skills for 2017*: https://techspective.net/2017/02/28/demand-cyber-security-skills-2017/
- *The 20 Hottest Security Skills and Competencies*: https://www.bankinfosecurity.com/20-hottest-security-skills-competencies-a-2024

5
Attacker Mindset

There has been an accelerated growth of cybercrime over the last decade. Costs related to cybersecurity and cyber attacks have also burgeoned, with organizations having to pay more to keep their infrastructure secure. McAfee, a leading cybersecurity company, reported that the cost of cybercrime in 2017 was $600 billion. Individual attacks were estimated to have cost $5 million in the same year with $2.75 million having been lost to downtime and productivity loss. The cost of securing organizations was estimated to be $81 billion in 2016. Since the cost of cybersecurity solutions has also increased, the total cost of securing organizations has also been going up. Therefore, the world economy is losing a lot of money to cybercrime. This money could have been put to more productive use, but it is either ending up in the hands of cybercriminals or being spent on cybersecurity solutions.

Therefore, it is imperative to view hackers from a psychological perspective in order to understand what drives them, thereby contemplating what can be done to stop them. This chapter will explore the category and traits of hackers, as well as their way of thinking. We will eventually find out what drives a hacker and, to that end, the following topics will be covered in the chapter:

- The category of hackers
- The traits of hackers
- How hackers think
- What can be learned

The category of hackers

To best understand why there are so many cases of cybercrime, and why they will possibly keep on rising, it is important to understand the psychology of the perpetrators. Cybercriminals have the technical know-how to penetrate systems and networks to steal data, money, or compromise the integrity of the systems. The following are the main categories of hackers:

- **Black hats**: These are malicious hackers that purposefully penetrate systems and networks for financial or self-gain
- **White hats**: They are vigilante hackers that try and find vulnerabilities that can be used by black hats to attack systems so that mitigation measures can be taken
- **Grey hats**: They are black hats that have reformed and become security consultants
- **Hacktivists**: These are groups of hackers that join hands in hacking exercises, often to make a political statement aimed at pushing for social change, such as freedom of speech
- **Cyber terrorists**: These are hackers that use their skills for hacks targeted at the loss of life, damage to critical infrastructure, significant bodily harm, and spreading intimidation to groups of people

It can be assumed that grey and white hats will not use their skills to carry out cyber attacks, and, if they do, the attacks will be designed to help the victim learn more about vulnerabilities and how they can be mitigated. Black hats will target individuals and organizations if they believe that there are financial gains that they can make from the attack. Hacktivists can target government agencies or corporate that have huge societal influence, and will do so to pass a message. Cyber terrorists will attack critical infrastructure such as nuclear energy facilities.

The traits of hackers

To understand the psychology that drives hackers to carry out crimes that are almost impossible to pull off, it is important to understand their traits. The traits observed with the majority of them appear similar; however, this should not be a cause of complacency. Organizations must be invested in exploring new use cases and finding out if there are more. The common traits observed in most cybercriminals are listed in the following sections.

They are patient

Hacking is a process, not just a one-off act. Hackers have been known to take their time to first study their targets. They do observations of how the system they are targeting operates, how secure it is, the humans that use it, and the times that it is active. Once they have done reconnaissance, they scan the system and identify its technical specifications, as well as the vulnerabilities it may be having. Only when sure of the vulnerabilities, will the hackers try to breach the system to steal data and money, or to compromise it. These stages can be replicated on other targets, such as networks or users. It is evident that each stage takes time, and this is why hackers have to be patient. If they attack without knowing the security systems in place, the attack could flop and the organization could be triggered to secure the system even more. In addition to this, hackers are also patient when learning how to hack. Veteran hackers have studied programming languages in order to be able to read code or reverse engineer programs to find out where vulnerabilities exist. To become such an expert that you can analyze code written in different languages, one definitely has to spend a lot of time learning how to code. Hackers invest their time in this to prepare for their cybercrime activities.

They are determined

At the moment, cybercrime is a catch-up game, whereby cybercriminals seem to always have an upper hand. Many old hacking techniques and tools will not work today due to the sophistication of cybersecurity tools. Systems that could have been exploited a few years ago through vulnerabilities such as SQL injection, have also been patched and are fully secure. However, hacking is still on the rise, which means that hackers are constantly coming up with new techniques and tools that cybersecurity companies are not aware of. They are also actively searching for new vulnerabilities to exploit. This just shows how determined hackers are. Hackers have also been targeting large corporations that are expected to have state-of-the-art security. However, this is not enough to stop the hackers, as previous incidences have shown. For instance, Facebook, with a user base of 2 billion people, was hacked in 2018 and data belonging to 50 million users stolen. To many people, it could be assumed that Facebook has so many security features that it would just be time wastage to try and hack it. However, hackers have proven just how determined they are to bring down any target they aim at.

They are insensitive

Hackers engage in crime and do not care about the victims. For instance, the 2016 WannaCry attack led to many deaths in hospitals after computers supporting crucial processes and services were encrypted. To the hackers, this was not a concern and, despite WannaCry having a kill-switch, they decided to let the ransomware keep on encrypting more computers even if they were used for life-support purposes. Another set of hackers have been targeting the elderly through vishing, where they call them and:

- Claim to be grandchildren in urgent need of money
- Claim to be law enforcement officers and inform the elderly that they are wanted for a crime, then threaten to arrest them if they do not pay some money as a fine
- Claim to be from their banks requesting credentials such as ATM PIN numbers
- Claim to be from the IRS and demand some payments

In all these incidents, the elderly are forced to comply and send money to the hackers. The way in which a hacker can call just to steal from vulnerable and elderly people, just shows how insensitive they are. Hackers often do not show mercy to their targets until they get what they want.

They are risk-takers

The fight against cybercrime has intensified and hackers risk many years behind bars if caught. However, hacking is still going on. Some of the cybercriminals are known by their pseudo names and will often leave their signatures wherever they have hacked. A good example is a hacker known as Higinio Ochoa who was caught in 2012 by the FBI after leaving a clumsy message after his hack. As was the norm after every attack, Ochoa left a signature via a message taped on his girlfriend's stomach and uploaded it on Twitter. However, Ochoa had forgotten to remove meta information from the image that the FBI used to track and arrest him. Ochoa had stolen data from the FBI, yet had the guts to try and taunt the agency, which is known for tracking down all types of criminals with a high success rate. This incidence shows how risk-taking hackers are. They are not afraid of breaking laws and informing law enforcement officers that they are the ones responsible.

A growing trend in cybercrime is social engineering, where users have been tricked into handing sensitive details, or even transferring money to hackers. With the increasing cybersecurity budgets for organizations to buy more effective tools and security services, the channels for attacking systems and networks directly are reducing. However, hackers are exploiting other avenues to hack into highly secured organizations, and they are doing this through social engineering. There have been multiple hacks where it has been reported that the hackers simply coerced users into sending them money or giving them passwords. An increasingly common technique is business email compromise, where hackers are spoofing emails of executive employees and instructing junior employees to send money or passwords to certain accounts or emails. The use of coercion is working so effectively because hackers are exploiting flaws in the communication channels used by organizations. It has become normal for executives to order around junior employees and even to break protocol. Therefore, if the junior employees are asked by a spoofed email to send money to an overseas account, they will yield, simply because that is what the real executive does. Hackers have perfected their coercion skills as well, to a point that it is hard for the targets to say no. Hackers will refine the stories they will tell the users they target before sending them. If it is a call they are making, they will know what to say, depending on how the targets respond. Some social engineers even make physical appearances before targets to gain their trust. Therefore, coercion is simply one of the many essential tricks that hackers possess. They are coercive.

They are careful

The traces of a cybercriminal are hardly ever recovered. They are also hardly ever arrested or convicted. Cybercrime networks are hardly ever broken. All this is because cybercriminals employ a lot of caution in their malicious activities. From the planning phase of an attack, cybercriminals will start exercising caution, and use communication tools and techniques that make it hard for the messages to be traceable. Encryption, self-destructing emails, spoofed emails, and dark web communication tools are commonly used. During an attack, hackers will also cover their trails. They will use IP addresses from VPNs or proxies routed through other VPNs and proxies. The flow of data will be such that it is hard to trace where hackers came from and where stolen data was routed to. Additionally, hackers will operate systematically, where each of them knows what to do and when. Funds stolen directly from targets are not directly cashed into the hacker's banks since this would make it easy for them to be tracked. Instead, ghost accounts opened in overseas banks that do not have as many restrictions are used. Alternatively, money obtained from cybercrime passes through money laundering schemes till it cannot be traced back to the cybercrime incident. With the advent of cryptocurrencies that come with privacy controls aimed at anonymizing transacting parties, it is even easier for hackers to cleanse their money by converting it to cryptocurrencies and then withdrawing it or buying assets using the cryptocurrencies and liquidating them later on.

The FBI has been successful in apprehending some cybercriminals, but it is just a small number of them that get caught in unfortunate circumstances. For instance, the FBI has been said to list its own fake malware on such sites only to arrest those that buy the malware. In response to this, both buyers and sellers in the market become extra-cautious when transacting. Even when a hacker is arrested, it is hard for the enforcement agencies to arrest another because they do not operate using real names, and will quickly cut off communication if they are suspicious. At the moment, cybercrime is operating as an underground economy that is thriving, and the appropriate steps have been taken by players in the economy to protect its existence. Therefore, cybercriminals will keep on acting with a great deal of caution to protect themselves and others. Hacking networks are hard to break, due to the high levels of secrecy employed by hackers. For instance, it is known that there are dark web sites where one can purchase highly effective malware. However, not just anyone can buy. Most of these markets use invitation-only systems and, even then, none of the hackers in the market dare to divulge any information that could be used to bust any of the hackers.

They are deviant

Cybercriminals participate in anti-social behaviors which break the law and cause suffering to other people. For example, stealing all the retirement savings that an elderly person has made, by simply getting access to the credentials of their bank accounts and withdrawing all the money found. No society expects its own to do such things. Cybercriminals also defy laws. They will engage in fraud, theft, destruction of resources, and identity theft, among other crimes. In any case, cybercriminals are not typical people. They are hardened to steal without mercy and break rules without fearing any consequences. Therefore, hackers will tend to be divergent from the norm, and will be ready to engage in malicious acts despite knowing that it is wrong to do so.

Social characteristics of hackers

Having looked at the psychological make-up of hackers, it is good to look at their characteristics. These characteristics help explain what influences their criminal minds to act in the ways they do. The social characteristics are as follows:

Lack of social skills

Hackers tend to be withdrawn and introverted. They will not have much of a social life outside hacking, and this explains why they are inconsequential and ready to take risks. If hackers had a stable family and several dependents, they would be less drawn towards engaging in cybercrime as they would fear being arrested and leaving the dependents without a breadwinner. The lack of social skills also presents another problem, where the hackers will be soulless and thus merciless in their attacks. They do not view the other side of the target, such as the people that depend on the organization they are trying to attack. They will do these things without any emotions attached.

They have an inferiority complex

In many types of crimes, some of the perpetrators are people with an inferiority complex, and thus compensate for this by hurting others or damaging assets. An inferiority complex is where an individual lacks self-esteem, doubts their own capabilities, and feels that they do not measure up to some standards. Such a person will feel weak and, thus, to compensate for this, they will try and do something to prove that they are strong. Some hackers have these social characteristics, and this makes them very dangerous. If the hacker feels that the world sees him or her as a weakling, he will be ready to prove that he is not by hacking. Sometimes this feeling gets to employees in organizations and they eventually become insider threats. For instance, an employee kept under constant pressure and highly criticized by their boss for never delivering, or not being good enough, could be pushed to the edge and decide to strike back to prove that they are strong. Hackers that suffer from inferiority complexes are prone to carrying out cyber attacks that can cause heavy damage, as they will be trying to show others just how powerful they are. Such hackers are also not worried about the consequences of their actions, as their main objective is to send a message to those that had shown them disrespect or looked down on their abilities.

They are radical

This mostly applies to cyber terrorists and hacktivists. Hacktivists are radical and will do anything to overhaul what they do not like. For instance, hacktivists could stand up against the arrest of an influential journalist due to the existence of laws that limit the freedom of expression. They could be ready to force such laws to be done away with by unleashing waves of attacks against government agencies and top government officials. Cyber terrorists borrow from the ideals of the terrorist groups they are affiliated with, and mostly these ideals are from radical views. For instance, cyber terrorists from a group such as Al Qaeda could be against the interference of Westerners in local wars and could end up destroying infrastructure in the Western countries to promote the message that they are not wanted and must leave. Other cybercriminals will have their own radical views that they will base their actions on. Radicalism helps the cybercriminals escape the guilt of the negative impacts of what they do. For instance, if cyber terrorism leads to the destruction of a nuclear energy plant, and, consequently, to the deaths of the workers in such a plant, the perpetrators will be shielded from the guilt of killing innocent people by their radical beliefs.

They are rebellious

Crime is itself an act of rebellion against laws and societal ethics. Cybercrime is, therefore, an extension of this rebellion, except that the crime is conducted via a computer network or computing device. Cybercriminals take bold stands against the law and tend to gang up when they do so. They can form organized hacking groups or cyber-crime support structures. These groups, or structures, bring like-minded people together, and they can be highly effective, since all the members already disregard laws, morality, and ethics. They also possess tools, techniques, and skills that they can use against the people, bodies, or agencies they are rebelling against. Rebellion has many causes, but the main cause in the case of skilled people turning to hacktivism and cybercrime is economic need. To some extent, there exists an imbalance in the society, where wealth lies with a small percentage of people. Some people rebel, with the hope that their rebellion will lead to the redistribution of the wealth held by only a few. In other cases, people turn to cybercrime as a rebellion as a result of deprivation and oppression. There are countries where citizens live under oppressive governments, and the only way to fight such governments is to rebel. People might decide to join others that have rebelled, and contribute in fights against oppression, by hacking people in the oppressive governments and destroying some crucial infrastructure that benefits such governments. For instance, hackers may engage in hacking activities that will lead to the economic sabotage of the country, thus forcing the oppressive government to step down. Therefore, sometimes hackers are created by extreme circumstances that require them to rebel, with the hopes of making a difference. However, the means of achieving the change they hope to see ends up blurring the lines between the good they want to achieve and the bad they have to do to achieve it.

They lack social support

It was stated that cybercriminals lack social skills. As a consequence, they fail to associate with people who can give them social support. Hackers will tend to be withdrawn and act on their own. When they are passing through difficult moments, they have no one to turn to. They, instead, decide to lash out in their anger or depression at other people by hacking them. At such low points, hackers will lack any remorse for their targets. If they rob the elderly of all the money saved, they will not feel a thing. If the hackers destroy infrastructure worth billions of dollars, they will still not feel a thing. Therefore, the lack of social support is, at times, the cause of extreme cases of cybercrime where many people are attacked, lives are lost, or the most vulnerable are attacked.

It is noteworthy that the discussed social characteristics might differ in hackers. For instance, one might have a social life but, due to oppression, they may decide to join a hacktivist group to support a rebellion against the oppressors. Having looked at the social predispositions of hackers that influence their decisions and shape their minds, we can now look at how they think.

How hackers think (motivators)

Now that we have acquired an understanding of the traits and social skills of a hacker, let's address the elephant in the room—the psychology of hackers, or more appropriately, how hackers think. The following are some of the thoughts that hackers have and that encourage normal people to turn to the life of cybercrime:

Getting money (monetary gain)

As organizations are becoming increasingly concerned about the cost of a single cybercrime attack, cybercriminals are at the point in their careers where they are making more money than ever. Hacking is evidently profitable, and hacking incidences have shown this. Business Insider claimed in 2015 that hackers, relatively, make $80,000 a month. Hacking is like a business, and there are suppliers and customers interacting with the seller, who, in this case, is a hacker. Hackers do not have to directly engage in hacking to make money as there are many other ways of making a sustainable income in such a business. To begin with, they can make and sell exploits to other hackers. Some exploit kits are rented, where other hackers can use them for a given period as agreed during renting. Some hackers own botnets. Botnets are networks made up of many computers that have been infected with malware that can be used to force them to participate in attacks. Botnets are used in DDoS attacks, where they send more traffic than a target can handle, causing it to cease handling all legitimate requests. Since the advent of the IoT, many of these small devices that are connected to the internet were found to be lacking basic security features. They have thus been continually infected with malware which makes them botnets, and some of them have been used in attacks against renowned targets. A hacker who owns such malware gets many requests from other hackers to rent them the tool for a given duration, and the tool is paid for.

Lastly, hackers also make money from cyber attacks. There are very many types of cyber attacks and each yields money to the hackers in a different way. Ransomware attacks generate money for the hackers after the victims pay for the decryption of their computers. Phishing attacks, to gain credentials from users, only generate money when the hacker steals data or money from the systems they have gained access to. Personal data is being specifically targeted as it is fetching a lot more money in the underground cybercrime markets. There have been some public postings for stolen personal data. One hacker posted the following:

- $100,000 for 48,000 records from a healthcare organization in Missouri
- $200,000 for 210,000 records from a healthcare organization in the Midwestern US
- $400,000 for 397,000 records from a hospital in Georgia

Media houses followed up with the hacker, who did not disclose the names of the healthcare organizations, but claimed that they had been offered an opportunity to cover the stolen data, instead of letting it be leaked out, yet they refused to take the chance. The hacker said that already one of the records had been bought. The records were said to contain names, social security numbers, birth dates, physical addresses and insurance information of the patients that had visited the hospital.

Therefore, the sale of stolen data is another way of generating revenue. Based on the hacker's sentiments, it also seems that extorting the hacked companies to buy back the stolen records is still another way of generating income.

Another way that hackers make money is by offering obfuscation services to other hackers. Malware writers can write highly-effective malware, but it could be detectable by antivirus scanners. There are expert malware-writers that know their way around antivirus programs, thus they are contracted to obfuscate malware from being detected by such programs. The experts are paid a certain amount by each malware-writer that seeks their services. Lastly, hackers offer their hacking services to other hackers and get a commission of the proceeds from the hacks.

Greed

Cybercrime offers fast rewards since hackers can make millions from a single attack. The lure of making millions in a few days is drawing more people, including highly-intelligent professionals, into cybercrime. This is coupled with the fact that hackers today do not even need to know how to code, because they can rent the hacking tools. As was covered before, there are expert hackers who rent out exploit kits. There are others who rent out botnets to be used to carry out DDoS attacks. Therefore, newcomers to hacking think that they will find it quite easy to start off today due to the readily available tools. The existing hackers are already making money and will not be willing to stop doing so because of their greed. Due to this greed, hackers will keep on coming up with new hacking tools to sustain their sources of income. Greed also motivates them to keep looking for vulnerabilities to exploit in systems. A hacker knows that a new vulnerability, unknown to others, could easily translate to millions, and so they are ready to undertake scanning across several systems used by different organizations just to find one that has vulnerabilities. Greed is also a motivator in phishing, where a hacker goes to make clones of authoritative companies, write phishing emails laid out exactly like those of authoritative companies, or use spoof email addresses of executives in organizations to be used for hacking. The hacker is greedy for money and will do all it takes to create the perfect tool or technique to carry out a successful cyber-attack.

Political power

There are cybercrimes that are based on political beliefs which some hackers want to oppose or promote. There have been claims of state-sponsored hacking groups in several countries. The countries facilitate the hacking groups with all the resources they require in order to carry out the attacks. The attacks carried out are aimed at passing a message of the cyberspace superiority of one country over another. For instance, there have been very many hacking incidences against the US which have been attributed to state-sponsored hacking groups in some Asian countries. Many companies in the US have fallen victim to these attackers. It is said that a certain nation has been specifically targeting its hacks to steal secrets from these companies. Therefore, the products that the companies make will be easily replicated and, if they are used for communication purposes, the hackers will know how to compromise such products. Hackers that carry out cyber attacks with political motivation can be a big menace to targets because the hackers get resources from high-ranking politicians. In the case of state-sponsored hacking groups, the attackers are conditioned to behave like an army and will take orders to attack from those high in command. Hackers that have this type of thinking are not mainly motivated by greed or money. They are motivated by an illusion of patriotism to their own countries.

Apart from state-sponsored hacking groups, there are hacktivists which comprise of hackers that want to push for a certain societal or political change. Hacktivists will generally attack governments or specific organizations. When hacktivists are against the government, their operations are indeed political and the hackers will work towards having their voices heard.

Religious extremism

It has, however, been alleged that it was not ISIS behind these texts, rather, another country. This does not, however, discount the fact that an external entity already had the contact details of the family members of US military officers and proceeded to send threatening messages to them. Religious extremism is a motivator to hacking, and terrorist groups have been radicalizing those that join the groups to attack certain people or countries using any means they can. Religious extremist groups have been making news due to their technological advancements and presence in the cyberspace. Groups such as ISIS have promoted their ideals and recruited new members through the internet. Secret communications have been held by leaders of these terrorist groups on the dark web. Finally, terrorist groups have been moving towards hacking. While foot soldiers in terrorist groups make physical attacks to promote their radical interpretations of their own religion, terrorists now have other teams to carry out cyber attacks. This could stem from the fact that some groups, such as ISIS, opened their gates for everyone to join saying that there was an opportunity for anyone to support the group's ideals. In 2017, pro-ISIS hackers hacked 800 school websites. When visitors tried loading these pages, they would be redirected to videos containing ISIS propaganda. Investigations revealed that these school websites were developed by a company called SchoolDesk, which had probably been attacked, and updates pushed to the codes of the school website to redirect users to the ISIS propaganda video. In May 2018, alleged ISIS hackers started sending text messages to wives of US military personnel which contained threats to their lives and those of their children.

Curiosity

There are intelligent people who occasionally want to try and see what some codes do. They end up inadvertently hacking into organizations, even though that was not their motive. For instance, computer science students might be taught about SQL injection. A curious student might want to try out what they learned. While many of the current websites have been built with security considerations in place to prevent such attacks, old websites that are not maintained, might not be so protected. Therefore, the student could try to hack an old website and end up compromising it using an SQL injection statement. Such hackers could be innocent, but they can still cause damage. Even more dangerous is the possibility of curiosity leading to one becoming a cybercriminal after finding out that it is possible to break into poorly secured web-based systems.

What can be learned from the psychology of hackers?

From the discussions above, hacking can be better understood by looking at it from a psychological perspective. The traits of hackers, as presented, show that maintaining healthy social lives can help reduce cybercrime. People that lack social lives or like to lead isolated lives could be checked up on to make sure that they do not fall into cybercrime. It has been said that hackers are both patient and determined. These two traits have far-reaching implications for cybersecurity approaches in organizations. Since hackers will not relent easily, and will also take their time to find a vulnerability in the organization, it is prudent for organizations to adopt cyber resilience rather than cyber defense. Unlike cyber defense, cyber resilience ensures that an organization is protected from attackers, and, in the event that an attack happens, business processes will not be adversely affected. It has also been discussed that hackers are coercive. This, therefore, means that employees can easily fall prey. Organizations must, consequently, invest in programs to train their employees on how to protect themselves from hackers. Alongside this, organizations must set up clear procedures on how credentials can be shared, and also how a transfer of funds can be authorized. Hackers have been said to be careful in their attacks and this affects how organizations should monitor their systems and networks. Minor observations of abnormal activities on networks should not be ignored as hackers might be making a move. Additionally, organizations should invest in intrusion prevention systems to prevent some activities, such as network scanning, that might be used by attackers. Based on how attackers think, it can be learned that the main motivator for them is money, thus all resources that they can steal and make money from should be highly secured. Organizations that store personal data should employ extra security measures, such as encrypting their databases. Additionally, since some hacking events are politically motivated, governments in other countries have to take the initiative to follow up with the attackers and seek diplomatic resolutions.

Summary

The chapter has focused on what drives hackers and has discussed their psychological make-up and thought patterns. In the psychological make-up section, we have looked at the traits which define most hackers. These traits include patience, determination, insensitivity, risk-taking, coercion, carefulness, defiance, lack of social skills, radicalism, and rebellion, among others. Most of these traits help profile attackers and can be used to prepare an organization for hacking incidences. The patience and determination show just how far a hacker is willing to go. Insensitivity rules out appeals for mercy as a countermeasure to hacking events. The risk-taking trait shows that the hackers are not afraid of the law catching up with them, as it hardly ever does. Coercion and carefulness show how meticulous hackers are in their attacks and can get the best of targets, even before they can suspect they are being attacked. These traits also show that it may be hard to try and recover what has been stolen after an attack and thus more attention should be paid to protecting an organization from the attack in the first place. Radicalism and rebellion also add to the understanding of hackers as people who are not so remorseful and have an internal motivation to carry out their attacks. The chapter then looked at how hackers think and showed that their motivators are financial gain, greed, politics, religious extremism, and curiosity. Lastly, the chapter has looked at what can be learned from the psychology of the hackers covered.

Moving ahead, we will discuss the three pillars of security in the next chapter. This will give you an insight into ramping up the security infrastructure in an organization and thereby averting a data breach.

Further reading

The following are resources that can be used to gain more knowledge on this chapter:

- http://blog.wallix.com/the-psychology-of-the-cyber-criminal
- https://www.ripublication.com/irph/ijict_spl/ijictv4n3spl_06.pdf
- https://blog.avast.com/psychology-of-cybercrime
- https://pdfs.semanticscholar.org/3302/e173939ae434ad30f91d4c60d69f5e4a05e3.pdf
- https://www.donau-uni.ac.at/de/department/gpa/informatik/DanubeUniversityHackersStudy.pdf
- https://www.sans.org/reading-room/whitepapers/incident/paper/36077

6
Understanding Reactive, Proactive, and Operational Security

Cybersecurity is gaining importance due to the increased number of cyberattacks and the huge losses that victims are reporting. In many organizations, however, the implementation of cybersecurity comes as a consequence of a threat or an attack. Organizations can decide to mount reactive, proactive, and operational cyber defenses, or a combination of the three depending on financial capabilities and levels of exposure to threats. This chapter will go through the three types of approaches to implementing cybersecurity and help you to choose the optimal one for your company.

In this chapter, we will cover the following topics:

- Proactive cyber defense
- Reactive cybersecurity
- Operational security
- The significance of the three pillars of security

Proactive cyber defense

Proactive cyber defense is focused on anticipating attacks and offensively protecting the targets (computers, systems, and networks) whenever an attack is launched. The intention is to aggressively disrupt the attack or the preparation for an attack by the threat vector. This renders the attack vector less effective, or capable of being repulsed with ease. Proactive cyber defense is arguably the best implementation of cybersecurity even though many organizations do not give it much thought. This approach foresees oncoming attacks and readies an arsenal of defense systems and strategies to disrupt these attacks or make them ineffective. Company assets are therefore seldom put at risk since the threat does not come into contact with them. Despite these advantages, many organizations opt to remain reactive or use operation cybersecurity due to a number of reasons, which we will outline next.

Small and medium-sized enterprises

Small and medium-sized businesses (SMEs) tend to be thinly stretched in terms of finances and thus will not easily adopt proactive security as it is expensive to maintain. Understandably, they do not want to allocate resources that could mean other operations will suffer.

SMEs are also put off the implementation of some cybersecurity measures in favor of their business operations. Since proactive cybersecurity is quite involved and often needs immediate action to avert possible attacks, it can be seen as bothersome and inconvenient by SMEs. They want a cybersecurity strategy that bends to their schedule and not the other way round.

SMEs are also known to be quite slow in seeking professional help for their cybersecurity concerns. They will give priority to off-the-shelf security systems if they have decent reviews. However, in the changing cybersecurity scene, where tech giants such as Facebook are becoming victims, it is no longer safe to just deploy security systems without understanding the threat landscape and what needs to be covered.

Lastly, SMEs have long been reactive to cyberattacks and thus will shun proactive security strategies. They will only intensify their security after they fall prey to an attack.

Large organizations

Large corporations often feel they are too big to be effectively managed by a proactive security strategy. Since proactive security takes control of the whole organization, there are many areas that it cannot cover. For instance, all employees might not be trained about a certain attack before it happens.

In addition, large companies are usually concerned about their reputation. Proactive security adds extra eyes and ears that might eventually expose threats that face the organization. Moreover, some measures, such as an urgent request for all employees to undertake a certain training, might go out in a negative light to show that the company is under attack.

Worrying attack trends

Symantec, a leading cybersecurity products company, released a report on the advanced cyberattack techniques that had maximum effectiveness on targets. They are as listed as follows:

- **Deploying legitimate software on attacked computers**: To prevent discovery by antivirus programs and still keep tabs on attacked computers, cyberattackers will install seemingly legitimate software. After the removal of the malware that caused an attack, the antivirus tools would not remove the legitimate software, thus leaving the computer under the eye of attackers.
- **Using company resources to move stolen assets**: To stick around after an attack, cybercriminals will use company resources to move around any stolen intellectual property without arousing suspicion. Therefore, instead of directly uploading information assets to their servers, they create fake communication through which the data is sent to a compromised email that they control.
- **Building more attack tools within the victim's network or servers**: Instead of using prepackaged attacks, some cyber attackers assemble their attack tools within the victim. This was especially effective for organizations that had firewalls that could thwart the entry of malware tools into the organization's network.
- **Spear-phishing employees using corporate accounts**: Another tactic that was discovered was the use of hacked corporate emails to target other employees. These would have higher rates of success than spoofed emails.

These tactics were a few among many that cannot be easily stopped by reactive or operational security. The attacks were built specifically to beat these two conventional security strategies. Proactive security identifies these and many other preeminent attacks and works to make them ineffective or less effective to the organization. The following are the key areas that proactive security puts a focus on:

- **Asset management**: In this security approach, all the devices in the organization have to be known. Therefore, there should be an updated register of all the devices connected to the network and sufficient details to determine their users or functions.
- **Software inventory**: To prevent the installation of malicious or unwanted programs, proactive security includes taking an inventory of the software that users are allowed to run on their computers and mobile devices, as well as the software in servers.
- **Hardware and software configuration**: The configurations in devices and software should be validated and updated as needed, to ensure that they do not expose the company to threats.
- **Vulnerability assessment**: The threats that an organization is exposed to should be known. In addition, their risk and impacts must also be determined.
- **Malware security**: There should be tools that can offer antivirus protection to the organization.
- **Employee training**: Since attackers have been targeting employees through phishing scams and social engineering, proactive defense includes training employees on common phishing or social engineering attacks and how they can guard against cyberattacks.

Implementing proactive security

As you can see, despite being an effective method, proactive security might not be the first choice for many organizations. However, with the changing dynamics of cyberattacks, proactive security will perhaps become the go-to methodology in the coming years. In this section, we'll look into the various aspects of implementing proactive security. The following are some elements that need to be taken into account when formulating a proactive security strategy.

Vulnerability assessment

This involves scanning organizational networks, devices, and systems to discover their vulnerabilities. The scans are ideally done both outside and within the organization's network to give a well-rounded report. The identified threats must then be mediated to prevent possible exploitation.

Penetration testing

This involves authorizing penetration tests against a company's internal and external IT infrastructure to further identify any flaws that hackers might use to attack a company. Penetration tests take the form of actual attacks and can thus be viewed as replicas of how a hacker would try to breach an organization and thus how they can be denied the chance to do so. Penetration tests normally include the following:

- **Network reconnaissance**: All the computers within a specified scope are detected, the OS and services of these computers are then determined. In addition, DNS records are obtained to further identify the systems running on the network.
- **Enumeration**: The next step is to determine the versions of the OS and services in each computer. The services can also be probed to help determine their configurations.
- **Exploitation**: Any flaws and vulnerabilities in the services running on the network are identified. Exploitation tools and techniques are then used to attack the services. For instance, the firewall could be running a service that cannot handle traffic past a certain limit. A botnet can thus be used to flood the firewall with traffic past its limits.
- **Validation**: After successful exploitation, the vulnerability is validated and prioritized for mitigation.

Social-engineering assessment

This is aimed at ensuring that employees are ready to face social-engineering attacks without yielding to the tricks and gimmicks used by cyber criminals.

Web-application security assessment

This assessment focuses on the vulnerabilities in apps that are commonly exploited by hackers. Organizations must test both the threats and the impacts of a successful breach to a web app. Upon discovery of the threats, the app should be patched or put offline to prevent hackers from using them as attack surfaces. In addition, the impact of successful intrusions should be determined to help the organization further increase its security layers. For instance, the impacts of a successful breach past the login interface can be mitigated by having only the less valuable data exposed to hackers. Sensitive data could be moved to a layer with a higher level of security using techniques such as encryption.

In summary, proactive security includes all the techniques that can prevent an attack from happening in the first place. This approach is taken by companies that anticipate potentially negative situations and cannot risk their reputation.

Reactive cybersecurity

It may not always be possible to foresee oncoming attacks. In addition, it might be expensive for some companies to keep so many threat-monitoring tools running if the organization seldom gets attacked. Reactive security is an approach that, instead of anticipating cybersecurity incidences, responds to the past or present threats after they have happened. Therefore, only when an organization is targeted by hackers and breached does reactive security kick in. Using this approach, the victim organization assesses the threat and the impacts the cyberattack had. Using this information, security measures are installed to prevent similar attacks in the future.

The reactive security strategy makes financial and business sense to many business executives, and that is why many organizations are stuck in it. The executives are mostly focused on reducing expenses and maximizing profits. In addition, business requirements, threats, and many other factors continually change. Therefore, it becomes quite expensive to deploy proactive security measures that are mostly based on assumptions of the threats that could happen in the future. The reality is that the threats will change and so will the business. For instance, a business that relies on a locally hosted website to make sales might choose to to adopt a cloud app. Security in the cloud is offered by the vendor and thus the company will hardly need to focus on it. If they had a proactive security strategy, they might be at a loss since the expensive tools or services acquired to predict and protect the website will no longer be required. With a reactive security strategy, the business will not feel a pinch since the strategy welcomes these changes.

To achieve minimal wastage of resources, many organizations consider this security strategy. It is also more conventional since it deals with cybersecurity incidents once they happen. The business is put in a position where it dictates the security infrastructure. Since it is normally problematic for IT leaders to calculate the return on cybersecurity investments, this strategy gives management a better picture of the amount to spend. The amount is determined based on the attacks that the organization is targeted with. The strategy is also simple for management to understand. There is a cause-effect relationship. The occurrence of a cybersecurity incidence necessitates spending on IT security. This is easier for business executives to understand as compared to the proactive strategy where the security investments are done to invisible attacks that might never happen.

Implementing a reactive security strategy

Since the strategy is based on the occurrence of an attack for a response to be initiated, there has to be a highly efficient monitoring system. In addition, since the occurrence of an attack might lead to a loss of services, the strategy must also have a highly functional backup and disaster-recovery element. To prevent future similar attacks, organizations need to understand what caused the previous attacks. This strategy, therefore, must include forensics investigations. The following is how all these components are implemented in the organization.

Monitoring

Instead of having active defenses to prevent the occurrence of an attack, organizations use highly effective monitoring tools to be on the lookout for suspicious activities on computers, systems, and networks. When suspicious behaviors or attacks are detected, alerts are sent out so that the appropriate response can be taken. For instance, an organization might install an intrusion-detection system on its network to be on the lookout for reconnaissance scans, illegitimate traffic, malware, and other types of threats. When it detects the threats, it might notify the IT department or an integrated security tool to counter these threats.

Response

The type of response depends on the threat and the extent of the attack. If the attack is ongoing, the response will focus on stopping the attack. For instance, if there is a lot of illegitimate traffic directed toward a certain server, the IT department might opt to take the server offline or reconfigure its IP address so that the attacks no longer reach it. If the attack is a breach to a system, the IT team might change the access credentials and kill all sessions, thus forcing the attackers out of the system. An attack that has already happened will elicit a different type of response. The IT team has to prevent repeat attacks or the spread of malware from the victim. Therefore, if a server was targeted, it might be disconnected from the network and isolated physically. If a system faced a brute-force attack and the login system was compromised, the login module could be temporarily taken out to prevent further attacks. The steps taken to respond to the attack can affect the impacts. However, the organization still needs to ensure that its clients are not adversely affected, hence the following measure is taken.

Disaster-recovery

The reactive security strategy is heavily reliant on the organization's ability to bounce back after an attack. Disaster-recovery plans are therefore the key components of the strategy. The priorities in disaster-recovery might differ depending on the organization and the type of attack that occurred. There are five main components that are given attention during disaster-recovery: computers, hardware, network, software, and data. They are elaborated upon here:

- Computers refer to the workstations and servers in a network. After an attack has happened, they need to be checked upon to determine whether they were affected. Enterprise antivirus systems can be used to initiate simultaneous scans to help with this. The hardware refers to any computing hardware in the organization, such as network routers, desktops, firewalls, and computer peripherals. Cybersecurity incidences still include physical theft or destruction of these hardware. Therefore, if a physical attack has happened, it is necessary to determine that all hardware is still in place and to replace any sensitive hardware that has been compromised or stolen. For instance, if a router has been stolen or destroyed, a replacement should be installed. Similarly, servers running sensitive systems should be replaced if they have been destroyed or stolen.

- The network includes all forms of connectivity in the network. If, for instance, the wireless network has been breached, it is prudent for its SSID or password to be changed, hence forcing out the hackers. If the connection to the service provider has been compromised, a backup service provider should be engaged. This will ensure that the organization does not remain offline.
- Software includes both the operating systems and the applications that normally run in an organization. Some attackers will have tools that can attack a specific version of software. Therefore, when an attack occurs, the organization should consider updating to the latest OS versions. These versions will come with patches that will prevent similar attacks from recurring. In addition, some hackers might misconfigure some software. For instance, they might reconfigure the router to sabotage communication. Therefore, in such cases, the software needs to be configured to the correct settings. In the cases where the attacked software is infected with malware, the IT team can uninstall it and provide alternatives to keep the organization going.
- The data is arguably the most important digital asset, thus it should be prioritized in disaster-recovery. If mission-critical data has been modified or stolen, the IT team should reinstate the most recent backup to roll back the changes made or to make the data available to users that need it. Due to the vulnerability of data, the IT team must also ensure that, before restoration, the relevant systems are free from malware or a backdoor that can be used by attackers to gain unauthorized access to the data.

Forensic investigations

The reactive security strategy is aimed at ensuring that attacks are not repeated. Therefore, their causes must be fully known and any factors that mediated the success of the attack should be identified. For instance, a system breach might occur simply because of the use of default passwords by system admins. The forensic investigations will uncover that the attack was a breach past the login controls and it was mediated by the use of the default credentials. The organization will thus have a full picture and implement better security controls to prevent the same attack from reoccurring. For instance, in this case, the organization might opt to implement two-factor authentication and create a security policy that bars system admins from using default passwords. By the end of the forensic investigations, the organization should know all the mitigation measures it must take to secure itself.

In some cases, forensic investigations are coupled with retrieval efforts. For instance, if money has been stolen, the forensics might include tracing back the money trails to find out where it has been sent. There have been some real-life cases where money was stolen by cybercriminals and recovered by forensic investigators. Ubiquity networks is one of these organizations where $40,000,000 was stolen through social engineering and forensic investigations were able to trace and recover $8,000,000. Besides money, forensic investigations can recover data. Most of the stolen data ends up on dark-web markets. Forensic investigators can scour the dark-web markets for new listings of certain types of data. They can then pose as buyers and retrieve the data from the hackers before it is sold to other people.

In conclusion, it is not always economically feasible for an organization to adopt proactive security. Most organizations use the reactive cybersecurity strategy due to its simplicity and appeal to business executives. The reactive approach is designed to only act when a substantial threat is detected or an attack has happened. The approach seeks to stop the attacks and prevent excessive damage to the company's assets. The strategy covers computers, hardware, software, network, and data. It has four key steps: monitoring, response, disaster-recovery, and forensic investigations. These steps work hand in hand to ensure that the organization survives the cyberattacks with minimal impacts on its business operations and that the causes of the security attacks are identified and mitigated to prevent future attacks.

Overview of operational security

Operational security is often regarded as the convergence point of operational risks and cybersecurity. It is the middle ground between proactive and reactive security. This approach to cybersecurity addresses the conflicting business and security needs that organizations usually face. Business executives will want to manage cybersecurity from the top down so that it aligns with other business processes. However, they lack the technical knowledge to connect cybersecurity and business processes. For instance, they could know the basics of firewalls and antivirus programs, but they cannot tell how these tools connect with their business processes and employees. To the executives, it is just a matter of having cybersecurity tools.

However, the reality is much different. Cybersecurity is not about having two or three security tools, it is about safeguarding the confidentiality, integrity, and availability of data. Business executives will understandably lack the knowledge of all the security tools or measures required to safeguard the CIA triad of information. They will just know the few tools they are familiar with and assume that cybersecurity spending only revolves around those tools.

Cybersecurity is complex and highly technical since it must involve the entirety of the organization. It involves the people, processes, devices, and services within the given organization; all business operations are part of cybersecurity.

The operational security approach stitches together the organization's processes with cybersecurity. This, therefore, deters operational risks that might threaten the business. There are many operational cybersecurity risks that organizations are exposed to daily. For instance, there are conventional IT risks, such as unauthorized access to data, denial-of-service attacks, and social engineering. In addition, legal risks emanate from the regulations surrounding IT operations, such as the collection, storage, and sharing of data. Thirdly, there are third-party risks that come from vendors and suppliers. These are just a few of the many operational risks that face an organization and must be handled to prevent the risk of data loss, lawsuits, and reputation. The operational security strategy covers all these risks using a clever implementation plan, which we'll discuss next.

Implementing operation security

Operational security is divided into three lines of defense: risk management, cybersecurity management, and audits:

- **The first line of defense is risk management.** Here, the different risks that affect a business' operations are handled. In this line, the key focus is risk analysis and management. The different risks across the scope of the business have to be identified. The key risk indicators for each of these risks have to be established. The probability of the occurrence of each of these risks then has to be determined. This has to be followed by the assessment of the severity of the occurrence of each risk. Using this information, the operational risks can be ranked or tabulated in a matrix to determine the priority of solving them.

- **The second line of defense is cybersecurity management.** This includes all the processes involved in securing the organization from the operational risks identified by the first line. The second line of defense starts with security policies. These help mitigate the introduction of risks into the business. This is followed by the definition of key risk indicators. These definitions help to alert the IT team when a risk event has occurred. The definition of key risk indicators is followed by cybersecurity standards. The standards outline the execution of different cybersecurity strategies to mitigate or prevent the defined risks from happening. The second line of defense ends with cybersecurity-management tools, which are used to view the cybersecurity stature of the organization.

- **The last line of defense in operation security is auditing.** There are two types of auditing: internal and external. This line of defense ensures that all the other lines of defense have been correctly implemented. It also helps identify areas of weakness in the security strategy.

The significance of the three security pillars

Organizations have varying needs, risk exposures, and access to resources. Cybersecurity, however, is a cross-cutting concern and any organization can be a target or a victim. This chapter has gone through the three security strategies that organizations can deploy in their organizations. While they can function independently, the strategies work best when intertwined. They are complementary in nature and can offer organizations protection from multiple fronts.

The proactive security approach ensures that very few attacks manage to hit the organization. It is focused on predicting and neutralizing threats, and hardening attack surfaces so that it is difficult for an attacker to penetrate the organizational network or systems. The reactive security approach is the contrast of proactive security. The reactive security approach works by responding to threats only when they happen. Therefore, a lot more time and resources are spent on core business objectives instead of cybersecurity. The reactive security approach ensures that, whenever an attack happens, the organization is able to recover and can identify the causal factors and seal them to prevent future attacks. In addition, reactive security involves possible tracking and recovery of stolen assets from the organization. The operational security approach works with people and processes. It identifies the risks that can be met during business operations and then creates security solutions to prevent any adverse effects of these risks. In addition, it ensures that the organization is regularly audited to detect any weaknesses in the security strategy.

The three security strategies, when combined, act as pillars to form a formidable defense from attacks. They also offer multiple layers of security, with proactive security preventing most attacks from occurring, operational security guarding business operations against the attacks, and reactive security ensuring that the business is resilient enough to survive the attack and form future defenses against similar attacks. Of importance during the consideration of the security strategies are the business, needs, exposure to cybersecurity threats, and available resources. Each of the strategies can fit different organizations to varying degrees depending on these three factors.

Security operations and continuous monitoring

Security monitoring is an integral process in cybersecurity. Security monitoring provides any organization with the ability to detect and analyze events from the enterprise network, applications, endpoints, and user activities. Typically, **security operations and continuous monitoring (SOC)** has three elements: **people**, **process**, and **technology**.

Technology helps drive the monitoring of assets, such as networks, applications, endpoints, servers, web applications, and generates alerts by automatic correlation and analysis:

A photo from a Microsoft SOC

The **people** component in SOC focuses on validating these alerts manually and categorizing them.

The **process** component is all about analyzing the alerts/logs and either identifies a threat and provides detailed information to the remediation team or marks it as false positive:

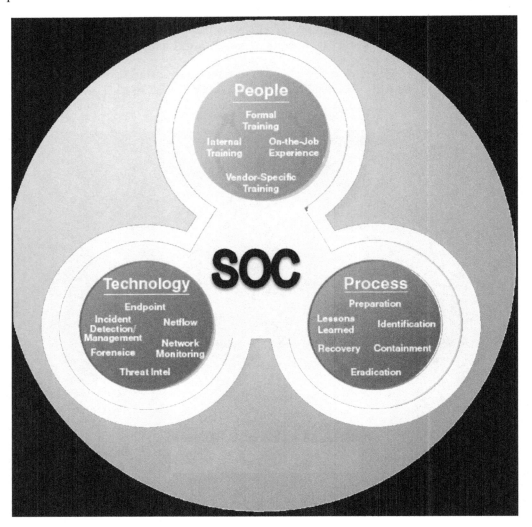

SOC also has to align its purpose with the business goals and vision of the organization. SOC needs to build its monitoring strategy to fulfill the business needs. SOC in general is a 24/7 operation, and this is by design so that SOC analysts, proper processes, and the detection technologies can help to reduce the gap between time to detection versus when the attack happened by processing data from internal corporate sources and correlating them with the known threat information from a wide range of external sources. With enriched and actionable threat intelligence, advanced analytics capabilities, data contextualization, and the right skills in place, an SOC can also act proactively to deter and stop attacks. An SOC always relies on intelligence, such as malware data, indicators of compromise and attack information, and threat and vulnerability reports by security vendors and application vendors. Modern SOCs need to embrace security automation and machine learning to reach the highest level of maturity. Other than the core technology of SIEM, threat-intelligence feeds, and various data feeds, SOC can leverage technologies such as intrusion-detection tools, antivirus integrations, DLP feeds, workflows, and reporting tools. SOC can be achieved in three different ways: captive SOC or self-managed SOC, co-managed SOC, and fully managed SOC by a third party.

Captive SOC (self-managed SOC)

Captive SOC is security monitoring that is managed in-house, with their own talents or trained resources. Captive SOC is run from a premise or facility that is fully controlled by the organization itself. In this scenario, the organization fully owns the responsibility of choosing their own SIEM tool, managing the tool, and running the operations, they also are responsible for training their analysts to staying up to date.

Co-managed SOC

When you are not in a position to have a self-managed SOC, the second option is to have a co-managed SOC. In a co-managed SOC model scenario, you are partnering with another service provider to share your workload, technology, or the operational overload. In this model, you can optimize your operations by offloading some of the responsibilities to the SOC service vendor, for example you may choose to monitor the daytime shift, and let the vendor manage the night shifts, you can have the SIEM owned by the vendor and have your resources manage the operations, or you can own the SIEM and offload the operations to a vendor. In a co-managed way of running SOC, you have the opportunity to be more agile and maintain a high level of operational excellence by applying service-level agreements on the vendor and bring up the SOC in less time than is required in a fully owned SOC; you almost tap into a matured operating SOC. One of the other factors that will work in your favor is that you will be able to almost immediately tap into the resource skill pool of your vendor, should you lose your own, or in the case of vendor-managed analysts, you never have to worry about losing a talent, as they will maintain the pool. If you choose a service provider that has a well-trained and experienced analyst pool, this automatically benefits your security operations. On the other hand, if you choose to co-manage the SIEM, you can share the cost of the license, maintenance, and operations. This eases your business to some extent, but not completely, as you might still be responsible for the incident response and analysis with shared resources between you and the vendor, manage the governance from your end, and also own the risk management of your business, monitor the SLAs with the vendor, and monitor the quality of service from the vendor so that the quality of detection and operation is not degraded. The following diagram shows the layers in a co-managed SOC:

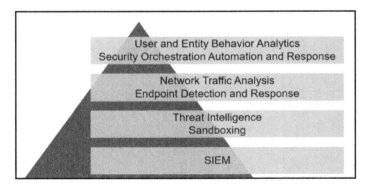

Fully managed SOC

Fully managed SOC has been the talk of the industry for a few years now. This model of operations provides you with the ability to outsource or offload the entire SOC process to a third-party vendor, with full access to its trained resources, SIEM and detection technologies, and proven processes. Your SOC gets a boost from 0 to 100 in no time. Organizations will usually send all the telemetry, visibility data, and logs to the vendor-managed SOC data centers, from where the **managed security service provider (MSSP)** will analyze the data for security incidents/events. The benefit of an MSSP is higher than the other two models, because you as an organization will almost immediately get access to a matured SOC. An outcome-based result can be expected from MSSP, providing highly accurate detection and response, with advanced level-detection and response technologies. MSSPs have a very experienced and skilled pool of staff to monitor, analyze, and investigate. Scalability and crisis management is another benefit of a fully managed SOC, where you don't have to worry about whether you need to monitor more devices or applications for any reason, or if there is a major incident and you might need additional resources to help through that situation. MSSPs normally have affiliations and access to agencies and vendors who provide highly enriched and actionable threat data that is relevant to your business, which is crucial for advanced detection capabilities. One other benefit of having a fully managed SOC is the industry-level visibility and threat data sharing; if another attack is noticed with another customer of a similar type, that attack information and threat intelligence is almost immediately available to you as an advisory and within the detection infrastructure. In general, MSSP vendors will have access to large data centers for storage and retention for you to take advantage of it. The only part that you may still have to own is the governance of your SOC and remediation of threat in case of an attack. The current MSSP model is the most popular SOC model.

To learn how Microsoft operates SOC, check out https://www.microsoft.com/security/blog/2019/02/21/lessons-learned-from-the-microsoft-soc-part-1-organization/. To learn how Google operates SOC, visit https://medium.com/google-cloud/google-cloud-platform-security-operations-center-soc-data-lake-4b31e011f622. To learn how FireEye helps how to build SOC, https://www.fireeye.com/services/mandiant-cyber-defense-center-development.html.

Proactive versus reactive security

The range of cyberattacks and their sophistication is on the rise today. All the attacks in recent days were successful in bypassing the existing security solutions, traditional or advanced. These attacks were successful because they were able to hide within the legitimate realm of our network and infrastructure. Our current security solutions are designed to detect based on scanning for known issues, filtering or dropping bad things, or even trying to monitor the identity and user habits, but these are not able to deter the attacks. The primary reason is that these are still focused on reacting to the security event, responding to the security findings of the security events that happened, and planning for how to recover from them. In other words: a reactive security response. A reactive response is good, but it is not holding the ground to a level where it can compete with the advanced attacks of these days. We need to have the focus redirected toward a proactive security response. The industry is already moving from a reactive to a proactive security response. This is a paradigm shift in security framework and methodologies on how we predict, analyze and respond to threats. Unlike reactive forms of security response, proactive methodologies provide greater and more in-depth visibility into the attack infrastructure. In simple words, the proactive method looks at the attacker's view of the attack surface and tries to predict the attacks and apply proper measures to prevent them.

As the logic goes, the reactive model of security response is the mindset of, *"If and when there is an attack, the systems and security analysts will respond to it."* It's about laying a trap with known attack parameters and methods, and waiting for the monitoring and detection systems to react to it. In the reactive form, the attention is always given to forming a strong perimeter defense to thwart the attacks that will attempt to penetrate the network. This form of security is localized toward the particular business unit and its activities; it does not take advantage of the attacks of a similar nature against another business or industry verticals. Reactive security does not provide a 360-degree view of the threat landscape but a reactive way of achieving security operations is always simpler, faster to bring up and with less operational cost. The reactive way of security monitoring can be further enhanced with data feeds from antivirus detection systems, vulnerability scanners, and DLP systems. The flip side of such a model is that it will always react to the security detection after the breach or compromise has happened.

The proactive way of security monitoring and response wins here. It is an intelligence-driven model, where the system is enriched with actionable intelligence data, from multiple internal and external sources, working in line with the existing real-time monitoring systems. This proactive method will have visibility to the entire threat landscape and all phases of the cyber-kill chain, and not just focusing on one or partial phases of the kill chain. One of the key aspects of proactive security is threat hunting, which allows analysts to get more insight into the network and systems, by trying to uncover anomalies or any abnormal patterns in the network behavior, any known bad files in the systems, or registry entries that can be found from previously known attacks. As an analyst, you can also look for known **indicators of compromise (IOCs)** in the network to find any signs of compromise. Threat hunting is a continuous process and always tries to look for new sets of information as received from threat-intelligence sources. Threat hunting can also be done automatically by looking into network behavior, system anomalies, timeline analysis of certain events, and baseline data of the network and system for a period of time.

The threat intelligence system and its importance

Every organization is extremely worried about the data they hold and how to secure it. The sensitivity toward data is at an all-time peak. In our effort to keep data safe and be proactive in detecting any threat toward it, we must have proper and effective threat intelligence in place. Threat intelligence can be achieved by acquiring specific threat information (intelligence) about various systems, processes, network, applications, perimeter defense mechanisms, and other IT assets. This data is then collected, analyzed, and enriched to provide proactive and actionable threat intelligence. One of the reasons threat intelligence is so important is because the threats of the current generation are highly sophisticated, and difficult to detect. We must acquire very specific information and perform a search for the signs of compromise with actionable content from any threat-intel source. To stay ahead of advanced threats, it is essential that we feed our analytic and correlation systems with proper threat data.

Any effective and matured threat-intelligence system must be able to collect and categorize threat information in real time to produce actionable threat intelligence for the SIEM and incident-response systems to analyze and correlate the collected threat information with the security alerts and events they are monitoring. These threat alerts from the threat-intel system will also empower the SOC professionals to create custom signatures for further detection. Threat intelligence systems gather various information related to incidents, events and logs, security vulnerabilities, and recent and past attack data. This includes detection data from security and network devices of the organization along with information from external threat feeds. You can also set up a honeypot system to collect attack information and use it as threat data. Data collection needs to be focused and meaningful for the organization that intends to use it, because every business is different, with distinct needs and types of infrastructure. Threat intelligence collection and feed need to suit each business. Non-relevant intelligence data will lead to wrong assumptions, so the potential to miss the attack or compromise is greater. For the threat intelligence to be effective, the collection of intelligence data must be done in a centralized manner, as the systems collects threat and vulnerability information from a wide range of locations and devices to correlate data. You must collect data from both internal and external sources, as combined they will provide more detailed information on threats and attack vectors specific to your industry or organization. Also focus on collecting information about any ongoing global attack and its attack vectors, related mitigation instructions and detection parameters from agencies such as government CERT, NIST, and ENISA, along with industry sources, such as Cisco, Symantec, McAfee, Microsoft, and RSA. You may also focus on open source threat intel, such as OSINT, SANS Internet Storm Center, and Open Threat Exchange. All this collected threat information needs to be properly categorized and segregated based on threat types, and its importance to the business entity and function. It can, for example, be based on the geolocation of the business unit, business applications you are using, and IT infrastructures. Geolocation is important for identifying where the threat originated from so that you can focus on those business locations of yours as priority as they may have been affected; this could also help establish whether it is a targeted attack toward your organization or not or maybe towards a country. This scenario can help you pinpoint the most affected business function, application, or unit, and gives you room for remediation in advance or at least on time, before it's too late. It will also help you to define proper mitigation and detection strategies, allowing you to focus on effectively using your resources, as they are always limited regardless of the size of the organization.

A successful and matured threat-intelligence system must be able to generate and distribute reports about all of their findings and related investigations to help others involved in the security protection, investigation, and monitoring process to carry out their necessary work at various levels of operations, engineering, and strategic decision-making by governance bodies. Reporting can be via real-time methods or by publishing online advisories. The Security Threat Intelligence Advisory might also be shared among industry peers via threat-exchange mechanisms such as STIX or Traffic Light Protocol, for everyone to take advantage of and stay ahead of any attacks.

Digital forensics and real-time incident response with SIEM

As we have witnessed the rise in cyberattacks in the past few years, we are convinced that prevention and monitoring are just the initial steps toward being prepared against any cybersecurity attacks. What we should do is develop more capabilities toward threat hunting, internal threat intelligence, and strong incident response empowered with digital forensics investigation.

Most of the organizations in the industry today are already using SIEM as their primary and central monitoring platform. Traditionally, we have been using SIEM as a platform that receives information from the rest of the network, as mentioned earlier in this chapter, to correlate and identify threats and security incidents. In essence, SIEM has always acted like a device that listened and didn't say a word. In today's cybersecurity scenario, it is prudent for SIEM to take a much larger role in the whole process to say things and collaborate in taking actions. One prominent activity that SIEM can be tasked with is to integrate with Digital Forensic platforms to receive richer and more tactical information in real-time. The digital evidence is extremely volatile, and this drives the response time for any security incident. The fragile and crucial nature of digital evidence in cybersecurity incidents forces us to approach the problem in a fully automated way. The need for a human factor in responding to incidents and traditional methods of evidence acquisition, such as cloning disks, is no longer serving efficiently in the race with time it takes to complete any cyber-attack; the attacks are successful before you even notice.

This calls for an automated way of collecting digital evidence from a suspected device and we should do it before it's too late. We need to integrate this telemetry with SIEM to trigger a collection of evidence on endpoints, just like a security camera starts recording with the help of motion sensor. This provides us with detailed information about what took place and with more accurate evidence, which is collected at the right time: the time when the incident took place and not later. Capturing the state of a compromised machine right after it provides shell access to cyber criminals—providing initial analysis of the collected evidence and making everything ready for a deep dive investigation—will help us turn the tables on the bad guys. Actually, this is only the beginning, we should also develop systems/platforms that will automatically analyze collected evidence and enrich this with threat intelligence to become faster and more accurate.

Getting started with security automation and orchestration

Let's start with why we need **Security Automation and Orchestration (SA&O)**. With the rapid growth of single-point security solutions, most IT teams find themselves in troubled waters as this has lead to ineffective monitoring of security environments along with subpar incident response management. Grappling with a plethora of solutions that weren't designed to work in tandem not only wastes time and resources but also weighs heavy on an organization's budget. This is where SA&O comes to the rescue as it saves an organization's precious time by enabling the point solutions to work together, thereby paving way for a centralized orchestration of incident-response actions. To be honest, there is a huge skill shortage in this area and as a result that section is in the book. Before we move ahead of what you need to learn, it's also good to understand what those terms mean.

Security orchestration is a method of connecting and integrating different security systems and processes. Orchestration serves as the connecting layer for your security operations. This saves time otherwise spent jumping from tool to tool in an effort to piece together information, enabling faster, more efficient, and accurate responses.

Security automation is the automatic handling of a task in an information or cybersecurity system. You can automate multiple tasks within a single product or system, but security orchestration is required in order to automate many tasks or security processes between other products, tools, or systems.

Security automation automatically handles the most tedious, and time-intensive tasks so that once you orchestrate your tools together, you can leverage streamlined playbooks or workflows to automate entire processes. This means that the moment a security issue arises, your workflows immediately kick into action, correlating data between tools, conducting deeper investigations, escalating alerts, and aiding in the response, as shown in the following diagram:

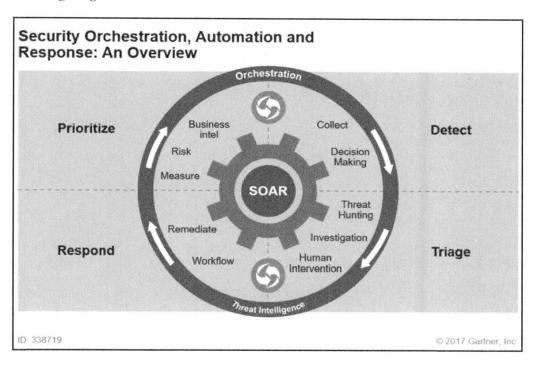

Automation and orchestration can enable security teams to prioritize and manage efficiency, and time-consuming response of alerts coming in from detection, and SIEM tools. It's important to learn how to use the automation orchestration, especially when it comes to investigating and remediating incidents. We saw CISO to a level 1 security analyst who believed that everything can be automated, which can be true but they also believed that it could be done at once! Without proper documentation there would be less benefit of automation and orchestration. Even for the most ambitious expert, automating every incident and every step in your incident-response workflow is as realistic as trying to boil the ocean. It's much more effective to walk before you run, especially when you become part of an enterprise security team, where typically multiple cross-functional teams are involved across a variety of different technologies.

For the last few years, security automation and orchestration has become a hot topic in the cybersecurity industry. So in this section, we will share some tips to help you take your first steps toward leveraging automation and orchestration.

Automation is not as easy as it sounds, you need to know when it can be used, and how to follow a workflow, to be successful.

Once you identify the security use case of security automation and orchestration, you can deliver a measurable impact. Here are three tips to help you identify great use cases for security automation and orchestration.

Step 1 – start small

Having a smaller task or playbook will help you learn SA&O. Having a small playbook/demo lab with a limited set of automation tasks can often provide a great learning path. One example is checking an IP across multiple reputation services and computing a weighted reputation score. Another might be to create or update a ticketing system. The key concept here is to automate key parts of a larger workflow so that you're able to work more efficiently and avoid context switching, as well as the need to copy and paste across multiple interfaces.

To help you get started, you can ask yourself the following questions, where your answers will form a map that essentially says *"Start here"*:

- What are your top business drivers and priorities?
- What's driving your strategies right now? The need for risk management, overall growth, stronger ROI, adherence to regulatory concerns such as GDPR?
- What are the metrics that matter? Could it be an increase in the number of incidents investigated, for instance? Improved response time and MTTR? Cost management?

Step 2 – learn to analyze (incidents)

Once you get familiar with SA&O, you can move to the next step. Examining the operations plans for workflows will help you master more complex scenarios.

Here is an example. As phishing attacks are still the number-one entry point for many cyberattacks, learning to examine a suspected phishing email can be useful. Instead of repeating the same steps again and again, you can automate the repetitive actions, such as enriching an event with reputation data from a threat intelligence service, and then insert your staff into the workflow so they can make a close or escalation decision.

Over time, the more you start smaller and go step by step to more complex automation, you will be learning to fully automate the process. The benefit of this approach is that it allows you to devote your analysts, who are always in high demand, to more complex issues.

As a beginner, it's always good to learn the common incidents. Try to master the top-five incidents, get familiar with the vendors, and analyze them. Find out whether they require information to be gathered and actions to be taken on threat-intelligence feeds, firewalls, email server, and network devices' centralized credential stores. The more complex use cases will touch more systems as well as more teams, which brings us to the next step.

Step 3 – learn to monitor wisely

The more you invest time in learning to analyze, the faster you can get to this final step, where you will need to find out how those analyzed steps can be automated. Then it's also important to define a set of metrics that can be used to measure the steps, which run back text help to build a report within the SOC. One common metric is **Mean Time to Resolution (MTTR)**, which is a service-level metric for desktop support that measures the average elapsed time from when an incident is reported until the incident is resolved. This metric should decrease as a result of the efficiencies gained through security automation and orchestration.

Of course, the continuous improvement will add value to your skillset. If automation means investigating incidents in minutes instead of hours or days, you can quickly calculate those costs and even assess the benefits of the extra time of the analysts to focus on other, more critical work which may need automation or cannot be automated. Soon, you'll be able to leverage your new best practices and processes across the organization for the ultimate orchestration and automation benefits.

Three common security orchestration, automation, and response use cases

Mastering use cases will help you gain lots of experience, so here are the top-three cases for you to focus on.

Phishing emails

Phishing emails have become one of the most critical issues faced by organizations over the past several years. Some of the most recent high-profile data breaches have resulted from carefully crafted phishing emails. Security orchestration, automation, and response is perfectly positioned to enable the automatic triage and examination of suspected phishing emails by extracting artifacts from the email, then performing additional enrichment on these artifacts and, if necessary, containing the malicious email and any malicious payloads.

Malicious network traffic

Alerts regarding malicious traffic could be received directly, or forwarded by a SIEM. Regardless, if you lean how to automate and orchestrate actions surrounding these types of events, you can save lots of time.

Once a log has been received, analysts use the data-enrichment tools, such as threat intelligence, reputation services, and IT asset inventories, and tools such as `nslookup` and `whois`. Analysts then determine whether the indicators appear to be malicious, at which point containment and further investigation would begin. If you use automation and orchestration, this process will be done automatically. Using the same automatization, searching for additional instances of the same indicator across the organization, and then alerting analysts to any additionally detected occurrences would be easier. Automated or semi-automated containment is also possible; for example, blocking an IP address or URL via the firewall or proxy, or isolating a host pending further investigation, depicted as follows:

WHOIS search results

Domain Name: ERDALOZKAYA.COM
Registry Domain ID: 1545081292_DOMAIN_COM-VRSN
Registrar WHOIS Server: whois.crazydomains.com
Registrar URL: http://www.crazydomains.com
Updated Date: 2019-02-24T14:28:17Z
Creation Date: 2009-03-03T03:44:43Z
Registry Expiry Date: 2022-03-03T03:44:43Z
Registrar: Crazy Domains FZ-LLC
Registrar IANA ID: 1291
Registrar Abuse Contact Email: abuse@crazydomains.com
Registrar Abuse Contact Phone: +61 894 220 890
Domain Status: ok https://icann.org/epp#ok
Name Server: ANGELA.NS.CLOUDFLARE.COM
Name Server: JERRY.NS.CLOUDFLARE.COM
DNSSEC: unsigned
URL of the ICANN Whois Inaccuracy Complaint Form: https://www.icann.org/wicf/
>>> Last update of whois database: 2019-03-12T11:58:15Z <<<

Figure 1: A sample search result from a whois search

Next, we will look at vulnerability management and how it can enhance monitoring efforts.

Vulnerability management

Security orchestration automation is not intended to be a vulnerability-management platform and will never replace today's robust vulnerability-management systems, however there are some aspects that can help us. They can be used to ensure that the security team is made aware of any new vulnerabilities. Automation can be used to query a database of vulnerabilities to gather additional information on the vulnerability, query Active Directory or CMDB for asset information, or query a SIEM or EDR for events. Based on vulnerability, host, or event information, the case could be automatically upgraded or reassigned, or the host could even be temporarily isolated until appropriate mitigation tasks could be performed.

Summary

This chapter was all about why you need to learn operational security. We covered what proactive, reactive, and operational security mean, the significance of those pillars, as well as what a Security Operations Center is and why you need to understand it.

While this chapter focused on the operational and technical aspects of cybersecurity, the next chapter will throw some light on the importance of human elements, such as if you want to choose any career, how to pick a mentor in your field. We will look at the importance of interpersonal networking, because security is never achieved alone, and you will need information and contacts to get important information, guidance, or even land a job.

Further reading

Check out the following resources for more information on the topics covered in this chapter:

- https://www.symantec.com/connect/blogs/top-5-priorities-proactive-cybersecurity
- https://www.fortynorthsecurity.com/
- https://www.stickman.com.au/reactive-cyber-security-approach-put-business/
- https://www.netfortris.com/blog/proactive-vs.-reactive-whats-your-network-security-strategy
- https://www.openaccessgovernment.org/reactive-mentality-on-cybersecurity/60036/
- https://www.ready.gov/business/implementation/IT
- https://www.disasterrecovery.org/
- https://www.accenture.com/t20170803T055319Z__w__/us-en/_acnmedia/PDF-7/Accenture-Cyber-Risk-Convergence-Of-Operational-Risk-And-Cyber-Security.pdf

7
Networking, Mentoring, and Shadowing

To ensure that you have a smooth start to, and progress through, your career, there are three essential processes that you can follow. These are **mentoring**, **shadowing**, and **networking**. Mentoring involves a one-to-one relationship between you and a professional who can give you timely advice, motivation, and direction. Shadowing involves going to the workplace with a professional attitude and observing what they do. This allows you to discover more about the career you intend to pursue by watching what actually takes place in a normal workday. Lastly, networking involves building professional links with other people within, and outside, your line of work. Networking helps you get information, guidance, and support from others when it comes to developing your career, or switching from one career to another. This chapter will discuss the importance of these three essentials in your career in the following topics:

- Mentoring
- Networking
- Shadowing

Mentoring

Mentorship is important both in your education and career. There is always the excitement of getting things done all by yourself so that you can attribute all the success to yourself. Getting a job all by yourself is a significant achievement. Planning your career development all by yourself is also a significant achievement, or so it seems. However, the reality is quite different from expectations. You might have the best of ideas, but not actually know how to execute them. Your plan for growing in your career might not exactly fall into place in real life. Your expectations of getting a job by merely spending hours on job boards, applying for positions that you are qualified for, might not go as you expected. This is why you need a mentor to give you guidance and, also, to monitor the steps that you take. Mentoring is a one-to-one relationship where you seek the continued support and advice of a more experienced professional to guide you through any stage of career development. The following is a detailed list of the reasons why mentors are necessary to one's career life:

They provide knowledge and wisdom

The best mentors, as we shall see later in the chapter, are professionals that have lengthy experience in their fields. They tend to have lots of knowledge that someone starting his or her career would benefit from. For instance, a mentor will be best placed to tell you the right programming languages and frameworks to learn. From a beginner's perspective, the best languages and frameworks are those fetching most money in the market. Programmers who have been working in the field for a long time know how hyped up languages and frameworks end up. Therefore, they might tell you to focus on other languages and frameworks. The same goes for many other professions. Besides this, you can tap into their wealth of knowledge. You can approach a mentor when you are faced with dilemmas or hard choices to make and they will help you make the best decisions.

They give insights on where you should improve

Mentors are good at identifying faults that you may have overlooked. These faults might be in your projects, your decisions, your execution, or your plans. You may have downplayed these faults assuming that they would not have any significant impact on your personal or career development. Mentors will be brutally honest and tell you that you need to correct areas where you have had faults. This is how you get to improve. Constructive criticism from mentors often helps people attain most of their goals as they will have eliminated the faults that were preventing them from being successful. Without a mentor, you rely on self-criticism which is, at times, deceptive, as it leads you to think that you are better or worse than you actually are. Mentors will give you a true reflection of yourself and tell you what you can do to improve.

They give encouragement

Your career path might not be as smooth as you had imagined or planned. Sometimes you will face challenges and you will be on the brink of quitting. Without any motivation, you will decide to quit, take a break, or forfeit your success. Mentors come with encouragement that can keep you going. Oprah Winfrey, an inspirational entrepreneur, defined a mentor as *"someone that allows you to see the hope inside yourself."* A mentor's principal concern in your engagement is to ensure that you achieve your goals and, when you are almost caving in, they are there to get you back up. Therefore, mentors will hardly let you stop, and, when you are facing the most challenging of obstacles, they will encourage you to keep going, and give guidance on how you should do that.

Mentors create boundaries and ensure discipline

Taking charge of your life or career is a huge responsibility and you must be committed to it. However, you will naturally try to give yourself a break or follow the least cumbersome path to success. You will also run into many distractions. These distractions, taking unnecessary breaks, or looking for shortcuts, might delay your success. This is why mentors have a strict sense of discipline and create boundaries in respect of what you can or cannot do. These are what help create a solid work ethic, unshaken focus, and help you set your priorities in the right way.

Mentors give unfiltered opinions

You will have very many ideas which will convincingly sound achievable to you and others. However, mentors view such ideas from different perspectives. Based on their observations from the different perspectives, mentors can give their honest opinions regarding the viability of your ideas. Mentors can help you identify ideas that have potential in the long term so that you can act on them. For instance, if you want to learn a new framework at an inflated cost just because there are openings paying attractive salaries, a mentor could advise you on whether you should commit to learning the language. It could simply be a wave passing, and, after a year of learning the framework, a new one could be released rendering you jobless. These insights might be lacking in your decision making, and that is why you should consult your mentor before committing.

They are trustworthy advisers

When working on sensitive projects, especially those that involve proprietary information, it becomes hard to trust anyone but yourself. Sharing such information, or even ideas, with the wrong people can lead to duplication of the product that you plan on making. Therefore, there is a challenge when you have to ask another party to give you fresh ideas or new insights into what you are working on. Mentors act as third parties without any stake in your ideas and will be happy to share with you their advice on sensitive projects. However, you should still exercise caution in what you divulge to others. Mentors will hardly sell out your ideas or steal proprietary information that you share with them confidentially.

They can be good connectors

As will be discussed later in the chapter, there is a lot of value in professional connections. Mentors will often be willing to give you access to professionals in the industry who can provide some support for what you are doing, or aiming to achieve. Mentors can take you to events, introduce you to opportunities, or link you with recognized professionals that you would otherwise never meet.

They have lengthy experience that you can learn from

Mentors often have a lot of experience that you can learn from. They have been in your shoes, they have made informed decisions, they have made mistakes, and they have learned from the school of experience. With a mentor, you do not have to go through the same challenges they went through, or make the same mistakes they did. They will share with you their stories and their mistakes so that you do not have to repeat them. They will also share with you the wise decisions or sacrifices they made to achieve something big.

Mentors are satisfied by your success

Mentors, unlike many other professionals, are not in your life just to enrich themselves. Mentors are free; thus, they are not motivated by financial gains from you. Mentors derive satisfaction from watching you succeed. They will, therefore, be willing to support you and connect you with professionals in your industry. Some people who end up being successful after several tries want to help others become successful, through mentoring.

The list of benefits that come from having a mentor is long. You can have the best ideas or plans, but, during execution, you might need someone who has done something similar before to give you insights about the mistakes to avoid and the decisions to make at each stage. You could be hitting a snag with each idea or project you have, just because you do not have someone else to guide you. Having looked at the importance of having a mentor, you ought to understand how to choose one and the following section gives tips on how to do it.

How to choose a mentor

Mentors are the reasons behind the success of many people. However, not every mentor will take you to success, and that is why, before approaching them, you should consider a few things. The following are what you should look for:

Compatibility

You should look for a mentor that you can work with comfortably without strain. Your first few interactions with potential mentors should be used as an opportunity to gauge whether you are compatible with them. If there is a sense of discomfort or a conflict of ideals, it is best not to take the mentorship relationship any further. If the mentor is assigned by a company, you can request for them to be changed.

To gauge your compatibility with a mentor, you should look at their worldviews, ideals, and philosophies. Their views or ideals might not be the same as yours, but they should be reasonable. You should avoid people that demonstrate signs of extremism in their views, as they might end up enslaving your personality to follow one strict path. You should also avoid mentors who have stark differences with you that might get in the way of the two of you working together. You should not try and force the mentorship relationship: follow your instincts. When you feel that you might end up getting into a long-term conflict with the mentor, it is best to cut off links with them.

The mentor's strengths and weaknesses

You will be looking for someone to emulate, and this is why you should look at their strengths and weaknesses. Mentors that have too many weaknesses could have a negative effect on you. It is never good to have to spend too much energy trying to accommodate the weaknesses of a mentor. However, you should also consider that no one is perfect and a few flaws are acceptable. Some important qualities you should pay attention to when assessing a mentor are their empathy, honesty, timekeeping, dedication, and their listening skills. Listening skills, particularly, are of great importance, as much of the time that you will be interacting with the mentor will involve you presenting your challenges to them. If the mentor never lends listening ears, it is probably best to highlight this to them or cut off the mentorship ties with them.

Contrast

Previously, we mentioned that you should look for a mentor you are compatible with. However, you ought to know that you need a mentor who is outside your comfort zone. Your mentor should not be based on your best friend's traits. You need someone that contrasts with you so as to encourage you to step out of your comfort zone. For instance, if you are poor at timekeeping, you need a mentor who is strict on time because this will push you to start trying to keep time. Therefore, you should be open to having a mentor who thinks or acts differently, provided that their traits will help you move out of your comfort zone. You should also be open to being mentored by someone outside your industry. If you are a web developer, a football coach could still be your mentor. Such a person has a different outlook on life than someone within your professional circles and will look at your challenges from a different perspective as would another programmer.

Expertise

In mentorship, titles or years of experience do not matter, but expertise does. The best choice for a mentor is someone who has gone through different challenges, or has had several experiences that you can learn from. You cannot be assured that, simply because someone holds a high office in a particular organization, they will make a great mentor. They could have gotten to such positions without facing major obstacles, or by being pulled up by someone influential. You would be better off having an armed forces veteran as your mentor or someone that has overcome many life challenges to get to where they are today. Their experience will be helpful to you and you will learn from it.

Trust

We had mentioned that mentors are trustworthy with confidential information, but you have to do your part in finding a mentor that is trustworthy. Mostly, you will end up sharing with your mentor some information in confidence. Therefore, it is best if you can trust them. Trust has to be two-way and you should trust your mentor just as much as they trust you. To avoid getting in unwanted scenarios where you share sensitive information with the wrong person, it is best to take your relationship with the mentor slowly. You should take time building up some ground rules on how you will interact with your mentor, and, after several sessions, you will learn whether the mentor is trustworthy. The mentor will also find you sufficiently trustworthy to share with you their own personal information.

These factors to consider while seeking out a mentor will help you to find someone trustworthy, reliable and best-placed to help you grow. Once you are in a good relationship with your mentor, you must make the most out of it and grow your career, or move closer to achieving your life goals. After you have found a good mentor, you should be curious, and ready to leave your comfort zone; you should be honest, appreciate feedback or constructive criticism, and ensure that there is mutual respect between the two of you. The next section looks at yet another important part of your professional life: networking.

Networking

Networking is the building of relationships that help you get information, guidance, and support in your career. Networking has proven benefits of helping one advance more quickly in your career, get better compensation for your skills, develop career mobility, and get more satisfaction from your work life. Networking can be said to be social capital. The more people that you have in your network, the more social capital you have. This capital can be used to get information, opportunities, exposure, more networks, and long-term support in your career. With social capital, you can also advance and develop your career more quickly. An effective network must be built with certain considerations to ensure that you derive maximum social capital from it. The two most important considerations are network size and composition. Network size involves the number of contacts that you have. These contacts determine the opportunities that you have access to from your network. However, network size alone is not sufficient to give you enough social capital to grow your career as you could have many low-level contacts. This is why network composition is the most important factor in your network. Network composition is simply the type of people that make up your network. It is important to ensure that your network has contacts from different social environments, demographics and organizational statuses. Social environments or contexts include colleagues at your workplace, family members, and communities, among others. It is good to build a network with a mix of different social environments. This improves your chances of getting opportunities passed to, or shared, with them. Having contacts from different demographics plays a big role in opening you up for careers in distant places. Your current location might be saturated with people who have the same skills as you, but overseas there might be an acute lack of people with such skill sets. A diverse demographic network helps you get such opportunities, and this could accelerate your career development. Lastly, contacts with different organizational statuses are important in your network. If you only have contacts holding executive statuses, you can get promotions or well-paying jobs. If you have contacts with lower organizational statuses, you get many opportunities passed to you that you could apply for. There are benefits of having contacts that hold junior, middle, and senior level jobs.

Networking is vital to your career growth and ensures that you build reputable relations over a period of time. The following are some of the benefits of networking:

Job opportunities

The contacts in a network help in starting or building your career. The contacts could be HR personnel, individuals working in organizations with job vacancies, or executives in organizations. Such contacts could help you to get jobs easily, with minimal struggle. There is a statistic that 80% of jobs are not advertised on job boards. Therefore, relying on applying for jobs from sites such as **indeed** is not as nearly effective as having contacts who can inform you when there are job vacancies. While other job seekers are competing for the 20% of the jobs posted on job boards, you stand a better chance of landing jobs passed to you by contacts that work in the organization with the vacancy. A network can also be helpful in getting jobs that are outside your locale. As discussed before, there could be places that have a shortage of a skillset; as a result, they will be willing to not only hire, but compensate more, someone from overseas. For instance, there might be a non-profit organization working in a remote place in Africa which cannot find a reliable local developer skilled in a certain framework. If you have a contact within the country, they could offer you the job with several perks. Lastly, contacts within your network can serve as good referrals if you get job interviews within organizations that they work for. This significantly increases your chances of getting hired.

Career advice and support

Your network contacts who have lengthy stays in particular industries are a source of valuable career advice and support. They can give you advice at every stage of your career and support you as they grow. Without this advice, you could follow a potentially dangerous career path that will not lead you to better opportunities. For instance, you could make the mistake of staying in one company that continually abuses and unfairly compensates you, due to a lack of advice from experienced people, that there is a point at which you have to switch employers. You can also stay in a career with limited growth prospects, and a contact that has been in the same shoes could give advice on whether you should try a career change. It is very easy to get stuck in an unpromising career while there are other opportunities. Your professional network can help prevent such a scenario, through sound career advice and support.

Building confidence

Growing your network involves meeting new people and engaging them in conversation, so that you can build a professional relationship with them. Each time you approach a new person to build a new link, you step outside your comfort zone. This allows you to gain confidence and develop essential social skills that will benefit you in your life. The more you go to events, or other places, to meet professionals so that you can build your network, the more confidence you gain. Ultimately, it becomes effortless for you to approach anyone and build a professional relationship with them.

Developing personal relationships

Some of the strongest and long-lasting relationships are built from your professional contacts. The main goal of building your network is to get professionals that can help you grow your career. However, there are times when these professional relationships develop into something more. This is because it is inevitable that you will stumble upon a contact who shares the same goals and has almost the same mindset. This causes the professional relationship to become a personal relationship. Such a relationship is likely to stay strong for a long period of time.

Access to resources

Your network can be utilized as a source of many resources for career needs. Each contact, if well-utilized, could have something to offer. Some contacts have inside information about organizations that you are applying to for jobs. Other connections can help you polish your CV. There are others that are HRs or executives who can offer you opportunities in their companies. Lastly, there are contacts that will continually send you lists of vacancies that you are qualified for,and possibly link you up with professionals who can help you get the job. In short, there are so many resources that you can harvest from a network. These resources can be used to help with career growth and success.

Discovery

You can limit your potential by not exploring some paths. However, many people fail to reach their full potential in life because they do not discover things that they can flourish at. With a professional network, you are presented with different types of people that can broaden your mindset. This helps you discover career options that you may not have thought of initially. For instance, a web developer working a 9-5 job in one organization could discover sites that they can work as freelancers and get additional income, or easily get two jobs, and quit the 9-5. Therefore, a professional network serves as a free outlet for new ideas that you can discover and explore. Without the network, you would probably never get to know about the ideas.

Tips for establishing a professional network

Having taken a look at the benefits of a professional network, it is important to go over the tips for establishing a professional network that can yield one these benefits. Not every professional network will have these advantages, especially if it is not established in a thoughtful way. It is noteworthy that networking where you can meet new professionals, can happen in different ways. Some of these ways include meeting people in person, attending industry events, connecting over social media networks such as LinkedIn, or meeting in public places. These are just a few of the many places where you can engage with others as a professional and add them to your network. The following are some of the tips that you should follow when networking.

Build genuine relationships

Strong professional networks are established on genuine relationships. Networking is not as simple as approaching a stranger, having a short conversation, and telling them that you want to add them to your professional network. This will likely lead to a superficial network and it will not bear any fruit. When in a scenario where you wish to grow your network, you must first create a genuine relationship with the people you are targeting. You should listen to what they say, add to their talk, reciprocate what they share, and find out their interests and goals. It is best to assume that you are creating a lifelong friendship rather than just aiming to using strangers to gain social capital. You could invite the person you are interacting with to another event, or offer to show them one of your products that matches their interests. If they connect with you in a way that is not superficial, they will most likely be more open to you and give you advice, support, resources, and links, in your professional relationship.

Offer to help

You should build relationships in which you are not considered a pest who only wants to gain without offering anything in return. It is good to show support and generosity to other people that you want to connect with. You could ask strangers about the project that they are working on, and, if you have skills that can help them, you should offer to help. You could even recommend someone who can help out if you lack the skills to do so. Therefore, be as ready to offer assistance to others as you are ready to ask others for help. In the process of asking for help, or offering it to others, you can build a meaningful professional relationship.

Diversify your events

Events offer some of the best places for linking up with new people who share your interests. For instance, going to a developers' event will help you link with other developers. You can also try going to events that have professionals from other fields. Additionally, you can try improving your chances of meeting even more people by seeking to be a speaker rather than an attendee. For instance, if you have information that some developers could benefit from, you could offer to give a small talk either at the beginning or end of a developers' meeting. Appearing as a speaker at an event improves your credibility in front of others and gets you recognized by many people. This could ease the process of starting conversations with others after the event, and they could become contacts in your network. You might also be sought by other attendees to be in their networks if they enjoyed your presentation. In summary, try attending events that you did not consider previously, and also seek opportunities to appear as one of the speakers during an event.

Keep in touch

Communication is key in any relationship. Therefore, you should remember to keep in touch with the contacts in your network every once in a while. This is critical in strengthening your relationships, and possibly expanding your network. You could periodically say hello to each and offer to catch up with them in upcoming events if they are willing to attend. Social media is also another way to remain in touch with your network. You should try to have your contacts added as connects on LinkedIn. On LinkedIn, you could periodically send them messages, like their posts, or endorse their skills. This enables you to remain relevant to them and they will also keep you in mind just in case they have opportunities that may benefit you.

Shadowing

When starting your career straight from campus, you can opt not to wait till you are on-boarded in an organization, and, instead, follow shadowing. Shadowing is, however, not limited to those joining the workforce. Those that have established careers can do it, probably to learn more about an organization or to get insights about a career they want to switch to. Job shadowing allows those who are already in their careers to test whether another career choice would be ideal for them before they make a bold move to switch careers. Shadowing is a career development process where one accompanies a professional to the workplace and observes what their job entails.

For job seekers that are new in the market and have not joined the workforce, shadowing allows them to learn more about prospective companies to join. There is a lot that can be learned about companies just through job shadowing. For instance, one can learn about the culture of an organization you want to join when you are within the organization's premises. You can see how employees are treated, how focused each employee is, what employee relationships are like, as well as the overall working atmosphere in the organization. By observing the cultural differences in an organization, you are more informed about the types of workplaces you want to end up in. For instance, through job shadowing, you are able to observe how employees that dress casually differ from those in organizations which are strict and where all employees have to wear suits and ties. The following is a breakdown of the different types of job shadowing:

Regular briefings

This is a type of shadowing that aims to help you learn more about a specific task carried out by employees. Therefore, it involves you shadowing an employee only when carrying out specific activities. For instance, a prospective engineering employee who has just completed campus could go to a site, only when an important task is being carried out. Regular briefings allow you to get a better understanding of roles that are important to these industries. Unlike other types of shadowing, regular briefings require a lot of planning and timing to ensure that the host gets you at the right place and time to observe the specific task being carried out.

Observation

This is where you go only to observe what the host or other employees do in a normal workday. This type of job shadowing is passive and you are not normally allowed to try carrying out what you have observed. Observation can happen through attendance at meetings or simply by watching the host and other employees work. Observation is simple and allows you to learn a lot about the organizational culture, work ethics, and work atmosphere in an organization.

Hands-on

This is where you are given some tasks to carry out in an actual workplace. It involves observation followed by a hands-on exercise. For instance, you can observe how computers in an organization are dusted off and, after that, you can take a blower and repeat the dusting off process. Hands-on job shadowing is quite risky as inexperienced people can make mistakes when carrying out tasks and these mistakes could financially impact the organization. This is why there are only a few organizations that can offer this. Most organizations will have strict guidelines so that, when you are allowed to carry out some tasks, the financial implications are not significant if an accident occurs.

Preparing for job shadowing

Job shadowing offers a learning experience that you should take advantage of. The following sections are some of the ways you should prepare for a job shadowing exercise.

Preparing questions beforehand

Job shadowing allows you to interact with people working in careers that you may wish to take up in the future. Therefore, it is important to prepare some questions in good time that will help paint a better picture of what the host or other employees do, and to help you discover some tips on the skills that you should develop before joining the workplace.

Taking notes

There is a lot that can be learned from a job shadowing exercise and it is hard to keep it all in mind. It is therefore handy to have a notebook to take notes of important things said or done in the workplace.

Picking an appropriate time

As was discussed above, one type of job shadowing involves regular briefings where a specific task is observed at a certain time and place. It is therefore essential to pick the right time for such a job shadowing exercise. There are other organizations that are seasonal; therefore, you should also ensure that you go during the most convenient times, either when there is a reduced workload and employees can interact more freely, or when there is a full workload when you can see employees working at their peak performance.

Gratitude

After attending a job shadowing exercise, it is important to show gratitude to the organization and the host. Therefore, it is advisable to write a thank you note that you will give at the end of the tour, acknowledging that you appreciated the opportunity to learn more about a particular line of work in the organization. The note could also mention the prospects of joining the organization in future through opportunities such as internships.

Summary

This chapter has looked at three important processes in career growth and development. Mentoring has been exhaustively discussed as a relationship between one person and a professional who has lengthy experience in an industry and who can give career growth and development guidance. The chapter has looked at the reasons why a mentor is important in one's life. Some of the listed reasons include mentors being sources of knowledge, giving insights on how to improve, giving encouragement, instilling discipline in your life, giving opinions, and giving advice. The chapter has also looked at the best ways of choosing a mentor and has highlighted that you should look at compatibility, strengths and weaknesses, contrast, expertise, and trust.

Networking has also been covered as a method of building relationships that help you to get information, guidance, and support. It has been described as a way of gaining social capital that can be used to build your career. The benefits of networking have been listed as getting access to job opportunities, getting a source of career advice and support, building your confidence, developing personal relationships, getting access to resources, and discovering new paths. The chapter has given a few tips that should be followed when networking and they include building genuine relationships, offering to help, varying the events you attend, and keeping in touch with your network.

Lastly, the chapter has looked at shadowing, which is a method of developing your career by accompanying a professional to a workplace and observing what their job entails. The types of job shadowing that have been highlighted include regular briefings, observation, and hands-on experience. Some of the ways that you can make the most out of a job shadowing exercise include preparing questions to ask, taking notes, picking the most appropriate times, and showing gratitude.

Venturing ahead, we will discuss how to set up a lab environment and carry out penetration testing in the next chapter. This will give you hands-on experience of cyber security lab set-up and to do self-assessment by getting acquainted with various technologies pertaining to this domain.

Further reading

The following are resources that can be used to gain more knowledge on this chapter:

1. https://career.oregonstate.edu/students/networking
2. https://www.elmhurst.edu/academics/career-education/mentoring-and-shadowing/
3. https://www.inc.com/john-rampton/10-reasons-why-a-mentor-is-a-must.html
4. https://www.td.org/insights/understanding-the-value-of-networking-for-job-and-career-development
5. https://www.topresume.com/career-advice/importance-of-networking-for-career-success
6. https://www.summitsearchgroup.com/why-having-a-mentor-is-so-important-for-your-career/
7. https://www.unl.edu/mentoring/why-mentoring-important
8. https://www.thebalancecareers.com/what-is-job-shadowing-2062024
9. https://www.livecareer.com/career/advice/jobs/job-shadowing
10. https://www.businessinsider.com/7-career-benefits-of-a-strong-network-2013-2?IR=T
11. https://www.thebalancecareers.com/job-shadowing-is-effective-on-the-job-training-1919285

8

Cybersecurity Labs

Traditional teaching methods have been observed to be ineffective for cybersecurity training. Theoretical approaches just give details on some aspects of cybersecurity, but they rarely impart skills to the learner. This is why hands-on experience is required, so that a learner can apply the principles they have learned to a real-world environment. Hands-on training allows for skills to be learned more efficiently and learners can appreciate the importance of all the tiny details. For instance, a flaw in the configuration of a firewall could lead to a network breach.

The IT world is agile and requires people to rapidly acquire new knowledge. It is likely that you will keep acquiring new skills for the better part of your cybersecurity career as you adjust to new market trends. It is, therefore, of great importance to know the avenues that you can use to acquire new skills or grow your existing ones. The advantage of cybersecurity training is that you don't need to enroll in a college in order to learn. There are several platforms available on the internet where you can learn either free of charge, or for a small fee.

However, there are several concerns that you have to bear in mind when it comes to online training. One of them is that the choice you make will greatly affect your outcome. Therefore, choosing the wrong learning platform will serve to your disadvantage. In addition to this, your commitment to learning will always affect how well or quickly you learn new skills. If you are keen and focused, you will quickly acquire new knowledge and skills. Therefore, if you have challenges with concentrating for long periods of time, it is best to choose training that is led by an instructor. This chapter will give you an overview of three popular training options that you may choose from, depending on your preferences and abilities:

- Instructor-led training (ILT)
- Virtual instructor-led training (VILT)
- Self-study

ILT

ILT is often referred to as a traditional learning method. This method involves the physical presence of an instructor who interacts with students, with the goal of imparting to them new skills or developing the skills that the instructor already possesses. Technology has made ILT quite easy. It is suitable for training where there are complex topics that require expert, hands-on experience.

In ILT, the training is offered in training circles. Students get to work together in the same physical space and they can assist each other with challenges. The collaboration between students often plays a key role in the success of this method of training. Students can interact with each other by sharing challenges, experiences, tips, and tricks that can make the training easier or more fun. The end effect is that complex topics become more accessible due to the synergy between the students.

The cons of this type of training include limited accessibility, as students usually have to travel to get to the training venue. Additionally, they have to proceed at the same pace. This method is also expensive, and most of the expenses cannot be evaded. The reach of this type of training is also limited because the trainer and students have to meet physically. However, institutions are also offering boot camp sessions, which are shorter training events that can be rotated regularly in different locations. This improves the reach and accessibility of the training program.

VILT

This is an extension of ILT that is powered by the internet. In VILT, there are virtual instructor-led classes on the internet. Both students and instructors do not have to travel to attend a class since they can participate from anywhere provided that they have a stable internet connection. The institutions offering this training have the advantage of not having to rent rooms for students to study in. There is more flexibility with this learning model since students can take up other tasks before and after the classes. The classes are also more time-efficient and will start and end at predefined times. The quality of training can also be high, since the institution is able to hire qualified personnel from anywhere, as long as they have a reliable internet connection.

However, VILT comes with its own set of challenges. To begin with, it is virtual and, therefore, comes with self-discipline requirements for the learners. Students have to avoid distractions such as phones while the training is going on. It is tempting for students, without physical supervision, to wander away from the training and be distracted by other things in their environment. Some estimates show that the attention-span for a VILT is 25%. This means that many students do wander off during the training session. The scope for interacting with instructors is also limited. This type of training tends to have many students per session, reducing the chance for each student to voice their concerns or ask questions to the instructor. The instructor is also unable to connect with the students. This is because one of the ways instructors know whether students understand what is being taught is by looking at their body language. VILT does not offer the best medium for instructors to observe non-verbal communication from their students. Finally, there is a limitation to the practicality of this type of training. Students are sent resources through PDFs, video clips, or manuals. However, these resources are not always optimized for different screen sizes and it can be uncomfortable for some students to actually follow the training.

Self-study

This is where learners follow text-based or video training modules and learn at their own pace. It requires self-discipline from the learner, in terms of time management and willingness to complete challenges in the lessons.

The benefits of this type of learning are numerous and range from flexibility to cost-effectiveness. In this type of training, the student does not have to go at the pace of other students or that of the trainer. Fast learners will complete it quickly, while slow learners will have the chance to stretch their learning timelines over a longer duration so that they can grasp what is being taught. This method of learning is also cost-effective. Institutions that offer self-study modules often price them cheaply or for free. For instance, you can learn many skills by watching and using YouTube tutorials, which are free of charge. A course that might cost thousands of dollars to take in college could be priced at under $1,000.

Self-study and assessment modules have been gaining traction due to the large number of people that want to learn at their own pace and convenience. Cybersecurity is seeing an increase in the number of experts due to these learning platforms. The industry is quickly responding to the shortage in the number of trained specialists. Projections suggest that in 2020, there will be a shortage of 1.5 million cybersecurity personnel, but this might just be averted.

One of the best methods for doing self-study and assessment in cybersecurity is through online cybersecurity labs. These expose you to real-world threats that you will have to respond to. There is a wide selection of labs that you can perform on the internet. However, some of them are costly.

This chapter focuses on the cheaper alternatives where you can set up and utilize security labs free of charge. It explores labs that are meant to improve your mastery of different types of threats and their resolutions.

Self-study cybersecurity labs

We will now discuss a number of online platforms that a cybersecurity professional can use for learning purposes. Some of the tools that will be covered are live and require authorization from the target to use. Therefore, exercise caution and do not run tests on highly sensitive or highly guarded websites. The end goal is to learn more about cybersecurity, so do focus on the results or reports given at the end of each exercise.

The cross-site scripting (XSS) lab

To begin with, a simple security lab that you can carry out is an XSS attack, which can be found at `https://pentest-tools.com/website-vulnerability-scanning/xss-scanner-online`:

Figure 1: The landing page for XSS Scanner

The XSS online scanner is a free online tool that is used for detecting XSS attacks and vulnerabilities on websites. In XSS attacks, hackers inject malicious JavaScript in trusted websites. The script can then be used to harm the affected websites and their visitors in a number of ways, such as by reading sensitive page content, injecting malicious scripts, cookie stealing, and website defacement.

The security lab is quite simple to carry out, since you are only expected to have a URL of a website to be scanned. The scanner will go through the provided website by trying to identify all the pages that have exploitable avenues for XSS attacks, such as contact forms and search boxes. The tool will then attempt XSS attacks on each of the potentially vulnerable pages. The scanner will then give a report of its findings concerning the XSS vulnerabilities that were found on the entire website.

The XSS scanner supports light and full scans. A light scan is less comprehensive as the maximum number of URLs that can be scanned is set at 20 and the maximum active scan duration is two minutes. The full scan is more comprehensive and can support a maximum of 500 URLs and a scan duration of 30 minutes.

To perform a scan, a user is required to provide three parameters:

- The URL of the web application to be scanned
- The type of scan
- Confirmation that they have the authorization to scan the target application

It is important to note that the scanner generates HTTP requests that can be flagged as attacks on the server side, although they are not harmful. This is why you should mostly use the XSS Scanner on authorized targets to avoid prosecution for security violations. The tool provides a detailed report of identified XSS vulnerabilities or attacks. The report can then be used to fix the vulnerabilities before attackers can exploit them.

The Secure Socket Layer (SSL) configuration lab

This is a cybersecurity lab that is offered by Wormly. You can refer to it at `https://www.wormly.com/test_ssl`. It allows you to conduct a deep analysis of the SSL configuration of a web server. This is an important test since misconfigured SSL can introduce security vulnerabilities that can be exploited by cybercriminals to steal data that is stored, sent, or received by the server or can be exploited to carry out **Denial of Service (DoS)** attacks. Additionally, a misconfigured SSL web server can slow down websites, thereby degrading a user's experience.

In this lab, a cybersecurity expert can identify the security configuration weaknesses or errors in web servers. It is important to note that SSL certificates are vital for securing communication between web clients and web servers. The SSL certificate ensures that all data that is exchanged between a web server and a browser is kept private and secure through encryption:

Figure 2: The Wormly SSL server test tool user interface

Wormly offers a simplified interface where you can enter either the URL or public IP address of the web application whose SSL server is to be scanned. You can then click on the **Start SSL test** button to begin the test.

The tool provides important information about the SSL certificate that is in use, such as validity duration and trust level. The report also includes security information such as whether the encryption ciphers in use are strong, the public key size, the security protocols in use, and their version and performance information, such as SSL handshake size, TLS stateless resume, and SSL session cache. This information allows you to identify any weaknesses in SSL configuration so that appropriate measures can be taken to correct the weaknesses before criminals can exploit them. A cybersecurity expert will easily interpret and fix the errors that this tool highlights.

Acunetix Vulnerability Scanner

This is a security auditing tool that can be found at `https://www.acunetix.com/vulnerability-scanner`. It is used by cybersecurity professionals to identify vulnerabilities in web applications that are hosted on the cloud. The use of web applications has increased over the last decade. At the same time, criminals are exploiting the vulnerabilities that are in internet protocols to cause havoc and to benefit financially by stealing confidential information that is sold on the black market. This tool, therefore, provides webmasters or cybersecurity professionals with a free cloud-based system that they can use to detect two of the most common vulnerabilities in web applications. The free version of the tool has limited functionalities compared to the paid version, but it can still provide valuable information that can be used to harden a given web application.

The tool offers an interface with a control panel where a user can select the type of scan, the vulnerabilities to be scanned, reports, settings, and the target system. After a user provides the required information, the scan is conducted and a detailed report outlining the detected vulnerabilities is generated. The security tool also suggests suitable actions that a user can take to remedy the loopholes.

Acunetix is a useful security tool that can detect more than 4,500 web application vulnerabilities. Moreover, it can scan open source and custom-built applications to detect security loopholes that can be used to compromise the security of web applications. Acunetix online scanner can also scan perimeter servers for weaknesses and give suggestions on the appropriate cause of action to rectify these weaknesses. The security tool is, therefore, an effective security tool for detecting and rectifying security weaknesses in web applications.

Sucuri

Sucuri is another free online malware that can be viewed at `https://sitecheck.sucuri.net/`. It is a security scanner that cybersecurity professionals can use to find out the vulnerabilities in a website. The system provides an interface where users enter the URL of the websites to be scanned. The security tool will then scan the websites for known malware, blacklisting status, errors, and out-of-date software.

The Sucuri system can also be used to ensure that a given web application is clean, fast, and protected. In case malware is detected, the concerned security profession will be able to delete it so that the performance and security of the application are not compromised. The security tool can also detect out-of-date software, such as content management systems, which are common sources of security vulnerability. It will, therefore, be possible to update the software to secure versions in order to minimize exposure to security risks.

Valhalla

Valhalla is a comprehensive online cybersecurity lab. You can visit its website at `https://halls-of-valhalla.org/beta/challenges`. It allows users to undertake various security-related challenges for points. The challenges offered by the website include SQL injection, debugging, encryption, XSS, and reconnaissance. In reconnaissance, users are required to gather intelligence about a given target. Reconnaissance plays a big role in penetration testing, which forms the bulk of a cybersecurity career.

The goal of penetration testing is to discover the security loopholes in a given system, so that they can be rectified to reduce exposure to security risks. For this process to succeed, you must have adequate intelligence about the target. Intelligence gathering is, therefore, an important step in penetration testing and the Valhalla security lab will offer various services that will give you a hands-on experience on intelligence gathering. The reconnaissance challenge has three tasks for you to complete and to then check whether your answers are correct. The other cybersecurity labs feature the same layout of three labs. In all the challenges, the site offers hints and support that a user can utilize to complete the given tasks. A user is also allowed to access successfully completed solutions so that they can learn from them. The following screenshot shows the Valhalla user interface:

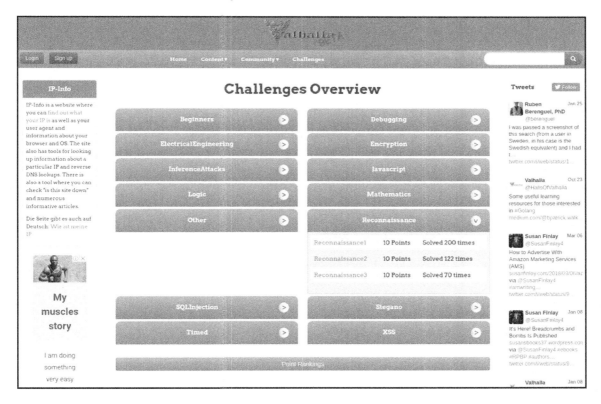

Figure 3: The Valhalla user interface

The user is required to go to the Valhalla website and select the category of challenges that they want to attempt. The user will then select the level and begin working on the challenge. For example, a user may be required to gather appropriate intelligence that can enable them to find out the login credentials of one of the accounts in the system. Using this information, the user will gain access to the system and proceed to gather more intelligence that will allow them access to confidential information.

F-Secure Router Checker

This is a networking security lab that helps you to check whether a router has been hijacked by cybercriminals. It can be found at `https://www.f-secure.com/en/web/home_global/router-checker`. A common threat today is DNS hijacking; one of the ways in which it is carried out is through unauthorized modifications of a router's configurations so that a third party can monitor, control, or redirect the traffic that is passing through the router. This security lab teaches you how to easily check whether a router has fallen victim to DNS hijacking. This knowledge can help victims stop attacks early enough before any significant damage is done. For example, in a situation where a router's DNS has been hijacked, a quick test using this tool will detect the attack and recommend an appropriate cause of action. This will prevent a user from being redirected to fake versions of genuine sites, such as in online banking, where their records or login credentials can be stolen and used to access their bank accounts. The tool is also important because it detects vulnerabilities or misconfigured settings in routers that can be exploited by criminals to harm users.

F-Secure Router Checker provides the interface shown in the following screenshot to allow users to analyze the settings of their routers for vulnerabilities. A user, therefore, needs to access the F-Secure website, and then select **Online Tools** and they will be directed to the router checker tool. Provided that they are connected to the internet, they just need to click on the **Check your router** button to start the analysis. After a few minutes, a report with the relevant information regarding the health of the router will be displayed with appropriate suggestions on how the issues can be rectified. The tool offers more tests for other devices, but these are offered at a subscription fee and so they might not be ideal for learning purposes:

Figure 4: The F-Secure Router Checker tool

Now, let's explore Hacking-Lab in the next section to further strengthen our knowledge base.

Hacking-Lab

Hacking-Lab can be visited at `https://www.hacking-lab.com/Remote_Sec_Lab/`. Hacking-Lab is a free online ethical hacking lab that offers a virtual platform where you can conduct penetration tests. The tool also incorporates several computer network and security challenges that you can attempt in order to build hands-on experience on various networking and security aspects. Hacking-Lab's goal is to promote awareness of ethics in information security. This is achieved using cybersecurity competitions that test important aspects of cybersecurity such as forensics, cryptography, reverse engineering, and cyber defense. The tool is provided for free to foster an environment that creates cyber protection by equipping cybersecurity professionals with relevant knowledge and skills. The tool is also licensed to a number of universities worldwide for educational purposes with the goal of building young cyber talent that can meet the needs of the current business environment and encourage learners to pursue careers in cybersecurity.

The following screenshot shows the Hacking-Labs dashboard; there is also a section on **Security Events**, which lists events that you can join, such as free hacking challenges. Most of these events are delivered online and, therefore, you don't need any special software to undertake the cybersecurity challenges. To use the lab, you just need to register your Hacking-Lab account and then register for a free hacking challenge event that is running. A lot can be learned from the challenges, as they simulate how criminals take advantage of the vulnerabilities in applications in order to compromise their security. You can, therefore, gain hands-on experience of how to identify security loopholes in applications, and learn about the measures, such as system hardening, that can be taken to minimize exposure to various security risks:

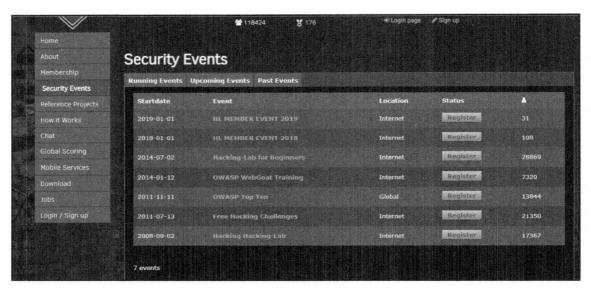

Figure 5: The Hacking-Lab control panel

Now that you've gained an insight into Hacking-Lab, let's move our focus to the Root Me password generator.

The Root Me password generator

The Root Me password generator can be visited at `https://www.root-me.org/spip.php?page=outilsamp;inc=passwordamp;lang=en`. To date, weak passwords are still a major threat to the security of organizational data and systems. The Root Me password generator is a security tool used to generate user passwords that users can then use to gain access to their account. The following screenshot shows the user interface for the password generator. There are a number of fields that a user is required to enter, such as password length and additional characters, before clicking on the **Generate password** button. The tool will then use brute force to try and guess the correct password for a given user account. This tool is important because when conducting a penetration test, it is common for a user to try and access accounts with weak passwords. The tool will, therefore, be used to identify weak passwords and develop an effective password policy that will ensure that users select passwords that cannot be hacked using common password hacking tools:

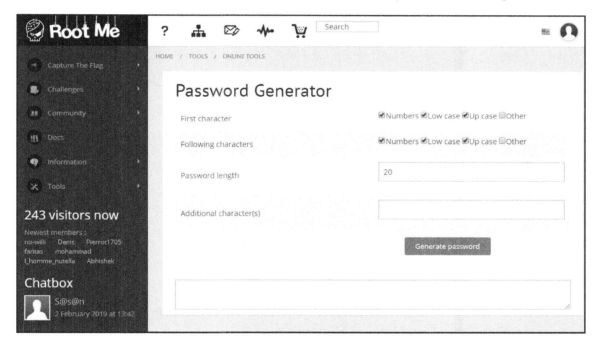

Figure 6: The Root Me password generator user interface

In the next section, we will explore the essentials of CTF365.

CTF365

CTF365 can be visited at `https://ctf365.com/`. CTF365 is a cybersecurity training gamification tool that offers numerous real-life games where players build the defenses for their systems, such as virtual private servers, in order to defend them from attacks. At the same time, the players try to attack systems developed by others in the network. This tool is useful because it simulates what happens in real life, as far as cybersecurity is concerned. Security professionals are expected to build and protect computer systems that are constantly under attack by criminals trying to destroy, modify, or steal data from systems. CTF365 uses a fun, entertaining, challenging, and community-driven approach to equip security professionals with the skills they need to be effective in the current information-security field.

According to the developers of the security training tool, the best way to learn is through applications. Gamification excels in this aspect by increasing the learner's engagement and improving their retention rate and the speed of their learning curve. The tool is free for not-for-profit information security conferences. You can also enjoy a 30-day trial period for individual use and training. To participate, all that is required is the installation of OpenVPN to use the security tool. Moreover, you need two important files: your VPN username and password file and your config file. The two files should be copied to the following location: `C:\Program files\OpenVPN\config\`. Then, search in Windows for `OpenVPN GUI`, right-click on it, and select **Run as an administrator**. After the tool starts, you should right-click on the OpenVPN GUI icon and select **Connect**. This will allow you to connect to CTF365 and build the necessary systems and their defenses for practice and, at the same time, try to attack the systems developed by others in the community.

Mozilla Observatory

You can access Mozilla Observatory at `https://observatory.mozilla.org/`. Mozilla Observatory is a free and open source website security scanner that works on top of a Python code base. Mozilla claims that the tool has helped over 125,000 security professionals to configure their sites in a secure manner. It is, therefore, a great avenue for cybersecurity enthusiasts to learn. To use the tool, you just need to copy and paste the URL or domain name of a website into the Observatory, and then click on the **Scan Me** button. A scan will be conducted and a security report about the website will then be presented. The report includes important security elements such as OWASP header security and TSL best practices. The Observatory is also capable of performing third-party tests from SSL Labs, High-Tech Bridge, and HSTS preload. The security tool also provides links to quality resources that can be used to rectify the identified security issues.

The report is useful for web developers and security admins because it allows them to identify the vulnerabilities on their websites, thus making them safer. A big advantage of this tool is that a user can also schedule automatic security scans after a certain duration. This helps in the monitoring of the website, as the user is notified if their website has any newly developed security issues.

Free online training providers

It is pretty understandable that cybersecurity is a niche area and the resources available are limited. Therefore, it is extremely difficult to find training courses that cater to the needs of new talent interested in the subject. However, there are few training providers that offer free-of-cost cybersecurity training for young enthusiastic minds. We go through these training providers in the following sections.

IT master's degrees and Charles Sturt University

Consider free university short courses: if you are considering enrolling in a master's degree, why not *"try before you enroll"*? Enrolling in these webinar-based free short courses, such as the one available at Charles Sturt University (CSU), offers an insight into how IT master's degrees can create a collaborative learning environment that is also an opportunity to engage with other students and build networks. Passing course exams will earn you a certificate of achievement, and may even qualify you for a master's degree credit.

Dr. Erdal Ozkaya is also a lecturer at CSU and has delivered many free short courses. There are always new ones available, so check out the website yourself. You can visit the CSU website at `https://www.itmasters.edu.au/about-it-masters/free-short-courses/`:

Figure 7: The landing page for the Charles Sturt University website

This free short course is usually four weeks long and is based online, where you have weekly assessments. At the end of this, you will have one final online exam and, if you pass the exam, you will get a certificate:

Certificate of Achievement
Short Course: Network Security Administrator Certification

This is to certify that

has successfully completed the Short Course

Network Security Administrator Certification

Grade: Credit (73/100)

Lecturer: Erdal Ozkaya

Completed: July 2, 2018

Martin Hale
CEO, IT Masters
Adjunct Senior Lecturer, CSU

IT Masters
itmasters.edu.au

Charles Sturt University

Figure 8: A sample Certificate of Achievement awarded to a student of Charles Sturt University

Microsoft Learn

The skills that are required to advance your career and earn your spot at the top do not come easily. Now there's a more rewarding approach to hands-on learning that helps you achieve your goals faster. You can earn points, levels, and achieve more! You can find out more at `https://docs.microsoft.com/en-us/learn/`:

Figure 9: A screenshot from a lecture on Windows Security and Forensics on Microsoft Learn

edX

At edX, you can find online courses in the humanities field, including the study of classical cultures, languages, and literature. Courses are offered from major universities around the world and are available for free; you simply select the course that you want to enroll in. You can find edX at `www.edx.org`:

Figure 10: The landing page for edX

Khan Academy

Khan Academy offers practice exercises, instructional videos, and a personalized learning dashboard that empower learners to study at their own pace in and outside of the classroom. They offer math, science, computer programming, history, art history, economics, and more. You can find Khan Academy at `https://www.khanacademy.org/`:

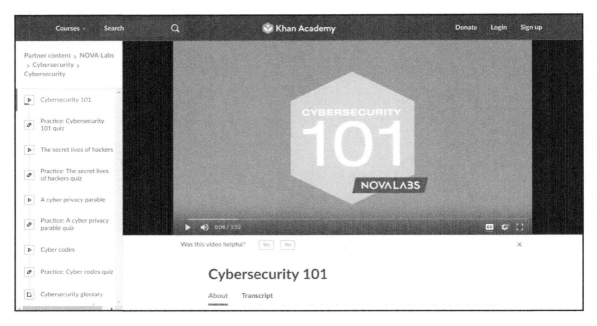

Figure 11: A screenshot of a Cybersecurity 101 course on Khan Academy

Cybersecurity: Attack and Defense Strategies

Here is a book sample from Packt Publishing that can help you to go to the next level of cybersecurity:

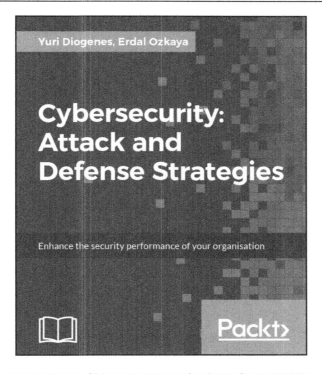

Figure 12: Cover page of Cybersecurity: Attack and Defense Strategies from Packt Publishing

This book uses a practical approach of the cybersecurity kill chain to explain the different phases of the attack, which includes the rationale behind each phase, followed by scenarios and examples that brings the theory into practice.

Building your own test lab

Everything begins with having the right hardware, which, at the very least, supports virtualization. If you have Windows 8 or 10 Pro, then you can just use the built-in Hyper-V. For this, you will need to learn how to install a **virtual machine** (**VM**) and a hypervisor, which is typically done in Microsoft Hyper-V, Oracle VirtualBox, or VMware (Fusion and Workstation are not free):

- How to install Hyper-V in Windows 10: `https://blogs.technet.microsoft.com/canitpro/2015/09/08/step-by-step-enabling-hyper-v-for-use-on-windows-10/`
- How to install Oracle VirtualBox: `https://docs.oracle.com/cd/E26217_01/E26796/html/qs-create-vm.html`

Once you have done this, you will need to start setting up a network. The following links will help you to get started.

The preceding URLs can help you set the network up as well. For the attacking machine, you can set up a Kali box or download a pre-built image from OffensiveSecurity at `https:/ /www.offensive-security.com/kali-linux-vmware-virtualbox-image-download/`.

To learn more about firewalls, go to the pfSense website, which can be found at `https:// pfsense.org/download/`. Additionally, you can refer to the guides that you find on the internet, or to books that will help you to install other machines that will expand your lab environment (Packt Publishing has a number of great books on this topic).

For instance, you could install an Ubuntu VM and set it up as a DNS server. Afterward, you could install a CentOS VM and use it as your web server with the appropriate Apache (or Nginx), MySQL, and PHP/Perl/Python (LAMP stack) software. Optionally, you could use the pre-built images from the websites listed, or install some of the applications on the newly-deployed VMs. The following links will give you ready-to-use VM images that you can deploy in your lab:

- **Metasploitable3**: A Windows-based vulnerable environment with CTF-style flags; it can be found at `https://github.com/rapid7/metasploitable3`.
- **Metasploitable2**: A Linux-based vulnerable environment; it can be found at `https://community.rapid7.com/docs/DOC-1875`.
- **PentesterLab exercises**: PentesterLab provides preconfigured VM images and courses that teach you how to perform exploitation. There are both free and paid exercises; it can be found at `https://pentesterlab.com/exercises/`
- **Kioptrix VMs**: These are vulnerable, ready-to-go VMs; they can be found at `http://www.kioptrix.com/blog/test-page/`.
- **Vulnhub**: These are vulnerable, ready-to-go VMs; they can be found at `https://www.vulnhub.com/`.
- **OWASP Multillidae**: A vulnerable web application; it can be found at `https://www.owasp.org/index.php/OWASP_Mutillidae_2_Project`.
- **OWASP WebGoat**: A vulnerable web application; it can be found at `https://www.owasp.org/index.php/Category:OWASP_WebGoat_Project`.
- **OWASP SecurityShepherd**: A training environment to practice web and mobile application security; it can be found at `https://github.com/OWASP/SecurityShepherd`.

- **OWASP GoatDroid**: This offers training for secure Android development; it can be found at `https://github.com/jackMannino/OWASP-GoatDroid-Project`.
- **SuperSecureBank**: A vulnerable web application representing a fictional bank; it can be found at `https://github.com/SecurityInnovation/SuperSecureBank`.

Summary

In this chapter, we looked at an avenue for training through cybersecurity labs. It began with a cross-examination of the types of online learning methods and discussed ILT, VILT, and self-study. We then explored the benefits of self-study and why it is gaining wide acceptance in the cybersecurity industry. This method of learning is also helping to address the shortage of sufficiently trained skillsets in the cybersecurity field. Additionally, a number of online cybersecurity labs are available, both free and paid, but this chapter focused on the free labs that anyone can perform without spending a dime. The first lab is an XSS exercise that can be used to figure out whether a website has components that are vulnerable to XSS. The next lab is an SSL test to check whether a website is running on a server with misconfigured SSL. The third test is a cloud-based vulnerability scan that can be used to detect more than 4,500 vulnerabilities in web applications.

The fourth lab is a malware scanning tool that could be used to detect whether a website has any known malware, outdated software, or other security errors. The fifth tool is more comprehensive, as it features a platform offering a number of cybersecurity challenges that a user can try solving. The sixth lab is a network security tool that cybersecurity professionals can use to check whether a router is a victim of DNS hijacking. The seventh is another comprehensive lab where users can participate in a number of challenges from an attacker's perspective and exploit vulnerabilities in dummy targets. The eighth lab focuses on password security and gives learners a chance to try and generate passwords that users are likely to create and use in systems. Here, you can check a number of parameters and provide certain characters that are likely to be in a password, and the tool will generate highly-probable passwords.

The ninth lab is a gamification cybersecurity training platform in which the user can create systems and defend them from attacks. Alongside this, they can also attack systems created by other users on the platform. The last lab was a tool from Mozilla, called Mozilla Observatory. The tool is a website security scanner that generates in-depth reports on the vulnerabilities that are on a website. These labs are a sure way for a cybersecurity enthusiast to continue learning and assess their skills. Some of the labs might not be too engaging, as they feature automated tests. However, the reports generated are important. You should try and find out how the details contained in the lab reports affect the website.

Finally, there are many other cybersecurity training platforms that you can use to advance your knowledge. Some of the best platforms charge a premium to allow you to carry out simulations, but it could be worthwhile trying out these premium platforms. However, you should at least consider doing a number of the free labs to get a preview of what to expect from the premium tools. Cybersecurity is quite involving, and a career in this field will always be filled with new learning opportunities. You should, therefore, be proactive in trying out any other security lab that you come across.

In the next chapter, we will take a close look at the various knowledge checks and certifications that are quintessential to kickstarting your career in cybersecurity.

Further reading

The following list of resources can be used to gain more knowledge on the topics in this chapter:

- https://security.stackexchange.com/questions/147337/are-there-free-online-penetration-testing-labs-that-i-can-safely-hack-with-my-co.
- https://www.fraunhofer.de/en/research/fields-of-research/communication-knowledge/it-security/cybersecurity-training-labs.html.
- https://www.tripwire.com/state-of-security/security-data-protection/cyber-security/cybersecurity-skills-training-medium-best-instructor-led-training-king/.
- https://www.cybintsolutions.com/hands-on-skills-in-cyber-security-education/.
- https://www.researchgate.net/publication/254034726_Online_assessment_for_hands-on_cyber_security_training_in_a_virtual_lab.
- Wargames to learn security concepts: http://overthewire.org/wargames.
- Hack.me mini-challenges built by community contributors: https://hack.me/explore/.
- Running your own CTF: https://github.com/facebook/fbctf/blob/master/README.md.
- Hack This Site, offering training for web applications: https://www.hackthissite.org.

Knowledge Check and Certifications

9

With eLearning becoming more popular than the traditional classroom approach, many people are acquiring important skills without stepping into a classroom. Some organizations have opted to offer free training programs, particularly in the field of cybersecurity, to increase the number of professionals that can reliably counter cybercriminals. In addition, there are many threats that specifically target users in organizations. Organizations are responding to these crimes by enrolling employees in online classes instead of the traditional seminar to teach basic concepts. Learning cybersecurity skills online is highly convenient, especially for those aspiring to start careers in it. The eLearning space is full of incredible knowledge sources. There are fears that some do not offer quality training. Other learning platforms do not cover all the requirements of a given course. However, there are some learning platforms that are licensed to offer training and can give learners certifications to prove that they went through a recognized platform and met all assessment expectations, and were awarded a certificate. This chapter will look at the need to be certified and how to choose the right places and certifications to study for. It will discuss the following:

- The need to get a certification
- Choosing certifications and vendors
- Certifications, to show what you know

The need to get a certification

In the current market, certifications could impact your career, whether you are employed or working as a freelancer. The following are some of the reasons why you should strive to get certifications.

They show employers that you take initiative

In the job market, having a college degree is just the norm. Most degrees tend not to specialize fully in a certain field. However, taking a certification course in cybersecurity makes you stand out from the crowd. While completing a degree course is still valuable, you get an added advantage by having a certification in a certain niche. Certifications often offer skills that are highly relevant to specific jobs. For instance, if you take a penetration testing course, you get skills that are highly relevant for all security analyst jobs. Having a certification is, therefore, highly valuable. It shows employers that you took the initiative to hone your skills in a specific niche, thus you are better qualified for the job you are applying to.

They reflect your abilities in a specific niche

There are fears in the job market of onboarding highly qualified candidates on paper that have poor practical skills. Degrees tend to be misleading since a student could have passed in the easy and less relevant courses to a job but failed in the most important courses. In addition, the assessments in degree programs tend not to be thorough. They do not expose learners to challenging situations where their abilities are tested to the fullest. The degree certificate will not reflect the strong or weak points of a candidate. On the contrary, certifications tend to be thorough and learners have to prove their skills in several assessments to be considered successful in the course. Some certifications also provide details about the performance of a learner in specific modules. They assure employers that the skills taught were assessed to the full extent and you showed competence in all of them. Therefore, employers will have fewer worries about onboarding you.

They equip you with knowledge for a specific job

The cybersecurity field is highly reactive to change. New threats will trigger new skill requirements, and companies will start looking for experts that have these skills. Degree programs tend to be slow to change, thus it is hard for universities to alter their courses just because of a new threat. Fortunately, certifications are robust and many vendors will assess the need for skills in the market and tailor their training accordingly. Taking some certifications early enough gives you the advantage of getting in-demand jobs with a good salary. Degree programs are not designed to give learners such rapid training to capitalize on gaps that arise in the market.

They can kickstart a career in cybersecurity

The advantage of certification courses is that they are not fixated on your undergraduate degree. While having a relevant IT degree is good, it is not always important and neither is it used as a delimiter to the people that can take certifications. Therefore, if you want to start a new career altogether, taking certifications will be beneficial. They will save the cost and time of going back to university to take a four-year degree.

They give your clients confidence

This applies to professionals that work outside formal companies, those who provide consultancy or auditing services as sole contractors. Clients will be understandably hesitant to trust such people with sensitive data and systems. Being a certified expert in your field gives your clients confidence in your abilities. They are assured that you are a professional and thus can be trusted with all the necessary data and systems.

They market you

Certifications show that you have more skills than the average degree holder in a certain field. In the workplace, certifications can lead HR to consider you for promotions to higher ranks or to increase your remuneration to match market rates. For those that operate outside formal employers, certifications work to your advantage as they show clients that you are more skilled than other freelancers or temps. The names of the reputable institutions where you got a certification may also work to your advantage. Employers will overlook other applicants if they find that you have certifications in various areas.

Choosing certifications and vendors

There are some factors that you should consider before committing to taking a certification and with a given vendor, let's look at them now.

The reputation of the vendor

Vendors that have been in the eLearning space for some time are recognized by many organizations. Start-ups, on the other hand, are viewed with suspicion. It is therefore wiser to take certifications with vendors that are known or have been offering training for several years.

The length of the course

Certifications are given after the successful completion of a course. Most courses run for a few months, mostly three or four. However, some vendors extend the duration of courses and often have learners go up to six months for a course, while others offering it in four months. Assessing the duration of the course is important to ensure that you are not taken advantage of through longer courses with higher fees.

Feedback from former learners

Some vendors have well-established feedback mechanisms where former students leave feedback about their instructors and the overall quality of the course. Some instructors are simply not good while some courses are not in-depth. Taking the time to review feedback from students on websites, Google Reviews, and social media pages might save you some frustration later on.

Support for learners

Some online learning platforms are poorly structured where learners are only given materials and automated tests after certain periods of time. It is therefore important for you to do research on the level of support that learners are given while taking the course.

The credibility of the certification

Certifications should be provided by learning institutions that are licensed to do so. However, some websites offer their own certifications, which are not recognized anywhere. Therefore, before enrolling in a course, it is important to check whether the company offering it is licensed to do so.

Job market demands

The job market dictates the skills that you should have. Ideally, learners should look for courses that lead to in-demand careers. For instance, the rise of cyberattacks has caused the market to develop an increased demand for penetration testers. Getting a pen test certification puts you ahead in the job market.

Effective cybersecurity requires participation from all

Ask a random person on the street what cybersecurity means, and you might get a response that refers to the most recent big data breach. It's hard to ignore being constantly told by major news outlets that the *private* in private information is a bad joke, and that not a single person who has ever entered so much as their favorite color into an online form is safe from black-market traders, unscrupulous governments, internet hacktivists, and whatever other threats you can possibly imagine. Push the question a little further, and your random person on the street might tell you all the things they do to stay safe online—and all the things they don't do. At the very least, you would probably conclude that awareness of cybersecurity issues has dramatically increased in the public sphere. Awareness is, to be sure, a crucial step in bolstering security, whether in a corporate context or a more personal one. But awareness is not enough.

As members of a digital, networked society, we shouldn't simply be aware of our problems. Rather, we should be fixing them. We often fail to do that, though, choosing instead to just accept bad outcomes rather than address their root causes.

This is completely understandable when you think about the fact that security problems often seem insurmountable. What can we as individuals do, even if it's just to protect our own personal information? There are too many points of failure, too many factors that are out of one person's hands.

So rather than struggle independently with rudimentary tools and limited help from others, the most logical choice is to shift our focus and embrace a new standard: a culture of cybersecurity. To put it another way, we need a collective effort to share valuable security knowledge, strategies, best practices, and more with our fellow digital citizens. If we want effective cybersecurity, we all have to play a part.

What's in it for me?

There's some truth in saying that laziness is a key element of human nature, but that excuse is too simplistic and dismissive. It's not that we can't be bothered to exercise due diligence, it's that we haven't been properly motivated. *"What's in it for me?"* is a fundamental unspoken question of cybersecurity—one that demands our attention.

When we cast blame on average users for failing to regularly change their many passwords across many different sites and systems, we seem averse to understanding why they've failed to do so. Only when it is too late, when users' own identities are stolen, do they acknowledge the importance of such a security practice.

What impetus did they have to incorporate this practice sooner, though? Too often, they've simply been told what to do without truly understanding why they need to do it. Maybe they read a brief, *Top 10 User Security Guidelines* article, on the web or maybe a colleague hurriedly mentioned a few personal security tips on a lunch break. Maybe their employer sent out a security-minded email that the user didn't really take seriously. While these actions provide a decent start, they aren't sufficient. Superficial commentary alone won't foster an adequate or comprehensive cybersecurity culture.

The key to fostering this culture, then, is substance. One of the most substantive ways to inspire others to be proactive is to get them to relate to the situation. People often fall into the trap of thinking about their computer use too abstractly, as if what they do online is far removed from actual real-world consequences. To get them to understand the gravity of their digital actions, we need to get them to shed this outdated mode of thinking.

When the average computer user leaves their house to go to work, they lock the front door. What about when they leave their desk to go to lunch? Do they leave their workstation unlocked for any passerby to use? Just like physical doors, we open cyber doors all the time—and when such doors open to something personal or sensitive in nature, we must lock them behind us to keep that information secure.

Not everything in the cyberworld has an analogue in the real world, and that can present a unique challenge in fostering a security-conscious climate. To go back to the passwords example, the average homeowner probably doesn't visit a locksmith every month to have the lock to their front door changed.

If you can communicate to users, however, that time is a critical component of any hacker's attempt at brute-force password cracking, the importance of regularly changing passwords becomes more obvious. In this case, the answer to *"What's in it for me?"* is simple: you stay one step ahead of attackers who are always refining their methods, and your critical information stays safe.

A culture of continuous monitoring

An effective cybersecurity culture has many dimensions, but one of the most important is continuous monitoring. For all of us as users, being able to monitor our online presence for misuse is crucial. Unfortunately, it's easy to feel that your online presence is stretched thin, and that much of it is beyond your control. That's why it's helpful to keep an inventory of your website accounts, passwords, and email addresses.

Password managers such as **KeePass** and **LastPass** make this much easier, while also using encryption to keep the inventory confidential. You can also use email as a hub for all of your other account activity. Many websites and services have options to send email alerts when key account configurations change. The quicker you're informed about these changes, the quicker you can confirm—or deny—their validity and take appropriate action.

This can mean the difference between finding out immediately that a hacker has changed your online bank account password, and finding out when you next sign in—after a massive withdrawal.

It's not just end users who need to contribute to a strong cybersecurity culture—businesses have a lot of catching up to do as well. Just like with users, continuous monitoring is essential. Minding your data, whether in transit or at rest, is a proactive approach to security that is often sorely lacking in the enterprise world.

Many of the breaches that we've all heard about weren't noticed until months, or even years, after the breach actually happened. Attackers exfiltrated data off servers so long ago that it's hard to know exactly what was stolen. This is the last position you want your business to be in, and it's vital to have solutions, such as **Security Information and Event Management (SIEM)**, always keeping your cybersecurity personnel up to date on any suspicious activity right when it happens. After all, it's the people in your organization who spread and maintain your culture, not the automated machines and software. There's no better way to assure the growth and development of a strong culture of security than through training and certification. Taking a master class and earning a certification, such as the *CyberSec First Responder: Threat Detection and Response* credential offered by CertNexsus (Logical Operations), will prepare your team to face any threat.

Don't wait another week, or month, to start changing the culture around you. Take action today, whether it's pursuing a cert, upgrading security software and tools, or even just changing those long-dormant passwords. The more effort that each of us puts into creating a culture of cybersecurity, the brighter our shared digital future will be.

The usual perception of cybersecurity among the masses revolves around data breaches. However, most people fail to understand why such breaches occur in the first place. While all the netizens were furious during the Facebook data breach that affected almost 50,000,000 users, no one was willing to get to the root cause of such attacks. This knowledge gap acts as fodder on which cybercriminals breed. Therefore, it is imperative to bridge this gap in a holistic manner to thwart cybersecurity challenges.

In the next section, we will talk about the various certifications needed for cybersecurity professionals to hone their skills and stay ahead of bad actors.

CompTIA Security+

This certification is actually a good starting point for security professionals, which is offered by CompTIA. It gives the individual an opportunity to gain knowledge about security infrastructure, identity management, risk evaluation and mitigation, and also a fair amount of cryptographic knowledge. This could be a good start for individuals working as system administrators and in IT infrastructure services. It might give you that overlap in transitioning from an existing role toward more a security-centric role. One of the best parts of this certification is that its vendor-neutral, which means it covers skills in general security concepts and is not focused toward any particular product. It is considered an entry-level certification by many, but it can also be useful if you have at least a few years of IT experience. The CompTIA Security+ certification is also approved by the US DoD Directive 8140/8570.01-M requirements. There are many options available to complete this certification, but you can also choose to do it in the self-paced manner, all by yourself, and then attempt the exam.

CompTIA PenTest+

This certification from CompTIA offers hands-on, performance-based, and multiple-choice questions, to ensure each candidate possesses the skills, knowledge, and ability to perform tasks on systems. The PenTest+ exam also includes management skills used to plan, scope, and manage weaknesses, not just to exploit them. You will gain penetration-testing, vulnerability-assessment, and management skills; this exam meets the ISO17024 standards and is ANSI-certified.

CompTIA Cybersecurity Analyst (CySA+)

This is another certification offered by CompTIA, to allow individuals to gain skills for behavioral analytics for networks and devices, so that they can prevent and detect cybersecurity threats. CySA+ is considered an intermediate-level cybersecurity analyst certification. This certification focuses on teaching you about intrusion-detection and response skills, along with some coverage of advanced persistent threats. You will be able to gain skills about how to perform data analysis on the threat data collected from various sources and interpret the results of your analysis to identify threats, risks, and vulnerabilities for your business and organization. You will also gain skills relating to how to use various threat-detection tools once you complete this training. This certification also meets the US DoD Directive 8570.01-M requirements.

CompTIA Advanced Security Practitioner (CASP+)

CASP+ is the ideal certification for technical professionals who wish to remain immersed in technology as opposed to strictly managing. CASP+ validates advanced-level competency in risk management, enterprise security operations and architecture, research and collaboration, and integration of enterprise security.

For more details, visit: `https://certification.comptia.org/certifications/comptia-advanced-security-practitioner`.

Here is the CompTIA cybersecurity career pathway:

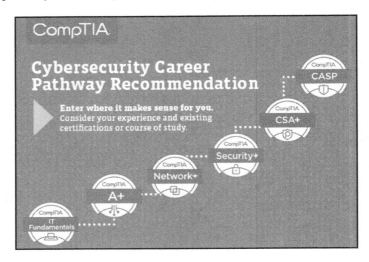

EC-Council, Certified Ethical Hacker (CEH)

This is one of the few very popular certifications in the cybersecurity community from the past decade or so. I never see any decline in enthusiasm from professionals who want to start in cybersecurity or just want to understand the attacker's perspective behind any security breaches and attacks. This certification is offered by EC-Council, they also offer a range of other certifications for security professionals. This certification focuses on the *"White Hat Hacker"*—a concept that defines how you can use the same techniques as the bad guys to proactively find and prevent attacks. It teaches you how to think like an attacker, and learn how actual attacks are carried out and using what means. This certification also exposes you to the knowledge of hacking practices, such as foot-printing, reconnaissance, scanning the network for vulnerabilities, enumeration, and knowing the internal working mechanisms of Trojans, worms, and viruses. It also teaches you about how to use sniffers, how DoS and DDoS attacks work, and how you can use social engineering when you are doing a threat assessment. Apart from focusing on network-based and social engineering attacks, CEH brings in the concepts of web hacking, how webservers are attacked and what you can expect when you are preventing such an attack, and SQL injection attacks and how to perform them on your corporate applications to find vulnerabilities proactively. Last but not least, this also covers evading IDS, firewalls, and honeypots. This certification can be best achieved by attending any five-day training course, and it is highly recommended to take this as classroom-based so that you can gain more as a team and get the opportunity to use the lab set up by the trainers to give you first-hand experience.

EC-Council, Computer Hacking Forensic Investigator (CHFI)

EC-Council also offers another certification for individuals who wish to take up a career in the digital forensics space: **Computer Hacking Forensic Investigator**, commonly known as **CHFI**. As the demand for forensic investigators is at its peak with the rise in cyberattacks, this certification gives you the jump start to be one of those digital forensic investigators who helps the industry to find out evidence in a post-breach scenario. As mentioned in our earlier chapters, a digital forensic investigation is the process of identifying the evidence and analyzing it to create reports so that the findings can support the legal process to prosecute criminals, and so you can use the information to prevent future attacks. The CHFI certification will expose you to the concepts and processes of computer investigation and analysis techniques to determine pertinent legal evidence. This evidence may be required for a wide range of computer crime or any other forms of digital misuse, which may include theft of trade secrets, theft of or destruction of intellectual property, and fraud. During the CHFI certification and training process, you will learn about using various methods to discover data from a computer system involved in digital crime, or in certain cases recovering deleted, encrypted, or damaged files.

EC-Council cybersecurity career pathway

The following shows pathways as recommended by the EC-Council:

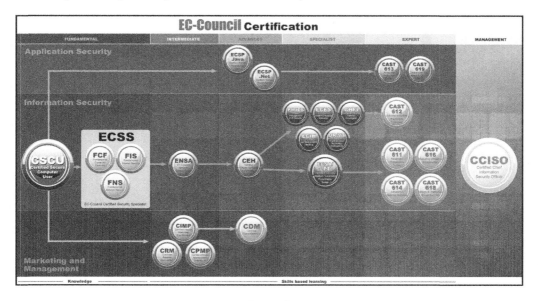

For more information about the full list of EC-Council certifications, check out their website: https://www.eccouncil.org/.

Certified Information Systems Security Professional (CISSP)

Certified Information Systems Security Professional, or **CISSP** as it is known in the industry, is a certification granted by the **International Information System Security Certification Consortium**, known as **(ISC)²**. This is one of the must-have certifications for professionals and is very highly regarded in the security community. CISSP focuses on a variety of topics related to information security. As part of this certification process, you will have to learn about eight domains of security:

- Security and risk management
- Asset security
- Security architecture and engineering
- Communication and network security
- **Identity and Access Management (IAM)**
- Security assessment and testing
- Security operations
- Software development security

Unlike other certifications where you may plan to target them without prior experience in security, CISSP mandates you have at least full-time experience of five years in two or more of its eight domains. But they also offer waiver of one year, for candidates who have a four-year college degree or a master's degree. Does this mean that candidates who do not have the required experience cannot achieve this certification? No, even they can appear for this certification, but they will then be receiving Associate of (ISC)² designation once they pass the required CISSP examination, and that will be valid for a maximum of six years. Within this period of six years, you will need to obtain the required experience and submit it to (ISC)² for certification as a CISSP. Upon acceptance of the professional experience requirements by (ISC)², the certification will be converted to CISSP status. You can train with any nearby institutes, online providers, or independent study by reading and learning from the various books available in the market.

Certified Cloud Security Professional (CCSP)

If you are already working in cloud technology, and are looking to advance your career from a cloud security perspective, this is the certification that you should start with. It is jointly designed by (ISC)² and the **Cloud Security Alliance (CSA)** to provide skill enhancement for cloud security professionals by providing the required knowledge and skills, by covering topics such as cloud security design, implementation, architecture, operations, controls, and compliance with regulatory frameworks. This professional certification will allow candidates to learn the following six domains, focusing on cloud security:

- Architectural concepts and design requirements
- Cloud data security
- Cloud platform and infrastructure security
- Cloud application security
- Operations
- Legal and compliance

There is certain basic experience that you are required to have: a minimum of five years' work experience in information technology, out of which three years must be in information security and one year in one or more of the six domains of the CCSP. A candidate that doesn't have the required experience to become a CCSP may become an Associate of (ISC)² by successfully passing the CCSP examination.

The Associate of (ISC)^2 will then have six years to earn the five years of required experience. Alternatively, you can appear for this certification without any prior experience, but you will then receive an Associate of (ISC)^2 designation once you pass the required CCSP examination, and that will be valid for a maximum of six years. After five years of gaining experience, you can claim the CCSP certification:

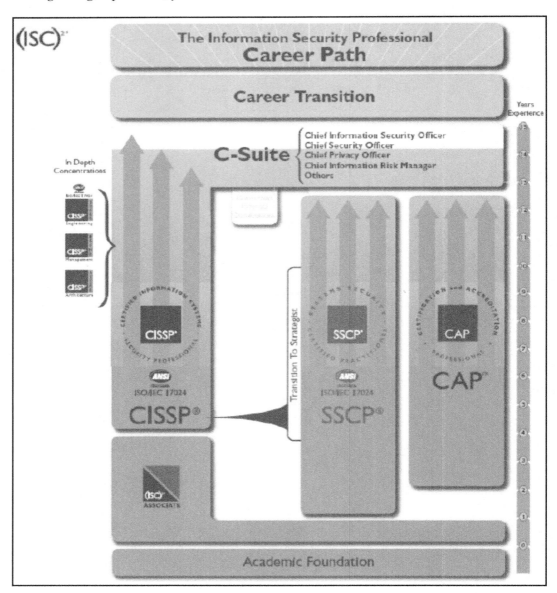

Certified Information Systems Auditor (CISA)

Certified Information Systems Auditor is an IT Certification offered by **Information Systems Audit and Control Association (ISACA)**, a well-known body. If you want to make IT Auditing into a career, CISA is the certification that you should work toward. CISA teaches you skills in the fields of audit, security, and control of information and systems. This is highly accepted globally and has become a de-facto standard when it comes to security-audit certifications. If you already conduct Information System audits, are a security professional with existing experience, or work as an IT consultant, Privacy Officer, or Information Security Officer, this might be a valuable certification to have for your experience and skills. A minimum of five years of information security work experience, with a minimum of three years of information security management work experience is necessary for this certification. This certificate will help you learn about five domains and acquire comprehensive and in-depth knowledge:

- **Domain 1**: The Process of Auditing Information Systems
- **Domain 2**: Governance and Management of IT
- **Domain 3**: Information Systems Acquisition, Development and Implementation
- **Domain 4**: Information Systems Operations, Maintenance and Service Management
- **Domain 5**: Protection of Information Assets

Certified Information Security Manager (CISM)

Certified Information Security Manager is also offered by ISACA. This is mainly focused toward IT Professionals who are responsible for managing and governing information security systems for their organizations. This certification will help you learn the skills needed to manage security risk, security program development and how to manage security governance, incident management, and response-related activities. Like CISA, CISM also requires a minimum of five years of security work experience; out of five years, three years must be in information-security management. You can also appear for the exam, and provide evidence in the five years after passing the exam. CISM focuses on the following five domains:

- **Domain 1**: Information Security Governance
- **Domain 2**: Information Risk Management

- **Domain 3**: Information Security Program Development
- **Domain 4**: Information Security Program Management
- **Domain 5**: Incident Management and Response

Which (ISC)^2 Certification is right for you?

You can always visit the (ISC)^2 website for more up-to-date information: `https://www.isc2.org/certifications/ultimate-guides`:

Global Information Assurance Certification (GIAC) Certifications

GIAC is one of the largest certification entities with many highly-regarded and deeply technical certifications for cybersecurity. GIAC is primarily formed by SANS Institute to provide high-quality security training for professionals worldwide. There are many flagship certifications under the umbrella of GIAC. Some of them are mentioned here (you can research the rest of the certifications at www.giac.org/certifications/categories):

Get Certified: Roadmap

GIAC offers over 30 cyber security certifications in security administration, management, legal, audit, forensics and software security. A Certification Roadmap has been created to help you determine what certifications are right for specific job needs or career goals. Each GIAC certification is designed to stand on its own, and represents a certified individual's mastery of a particular set of knowledge and skills. There is no particular "order" in which GIAC certifications must be earned; though we recommend that candidates master lower level concepts before moving on to more advanced topics.

GIAC certifications align with individual job based disciplines and typically correspond to topics presented in SANS full 5-6 day courses. GIAC certification attempts have a 4 month time frame.

GIAC Information Security Fundamentals (GISF)

GISF will provide you with the opportunity to learn and demonstrate the key information security concepts to understand the threats and risks to information and information assets. This certification will also help you learn how to identify best practices that can be used to protect information and information assets. This may be treated as an entry-level certification from GIAC. You need to study the following topics for the certification:

- AAA and access controls
- Application security
- Computer math

- Cryptographic algorithms and attacks
- Fundamentals of cryptography
- History of cryptography
- Network addressing and protocols
- Network attacks
- Network communication fundamentals
- Network security technology
- Risk management principles and security policy
- Systems security

GIAC Security Essentials Certification (GSEC)

GSEC is an entry-level certification. This will provide you with the ability to develop skills beyond the simple concepts and terminology of cybersecurity. You will have to study the following topics for the GSEC certification:

- Access control and password management
- Active defense
- Contingency plans
- Critical controls
- Cryptography
- Cryptography algorithms and deployment
- Cryptography application
- Defense in depth
- Defensible network architecture
- Endpoint security
- Enforcing Windows security policy
- Incident handling and response
- IT risk management
- **Linux security**: Structure, permissions, and access
- **Linux services**: Hardening and securing
- **Linux**: Monitoring and attack detection
- **Linux**: Security utilities
- Log management and SIEM
- Malicious code and exploit mitigation

- Network device security
- Network security devices
- Networking and protocols
- Securing Windows network services
- Security policy
- Threat hunting
- Virtualization and cloud security
- Vulnerability scanning and penetration testing
- Web communication security
- Windows access controls
- Windows as a service
- Windows automation, auditing, and forensics
- Windows security infrastructure
- Wireless network security

GIAC Certified Perimeter Protection Analyst (GPPA)

GPPA provides you an opportunity to learn the skills needed to secure the modern-day perimeter, which goes beyond the corporate firewalls and perimeter devices, as there are assets in the cloud, and the use of mobile devices poses a challenge. This certification addresses those challenges while still giving you the ability to learn about traditional protection, and you will gain the ability to design, configure, and monitor routers, firewalls, and other perimeter-defense systems. The topics that this certification will cover are as follows:

- Advanced perimeter protection
- Cloud security
- Creating and auditing a rulebase
- Host-based detection and DLP
- IPv6 and ICMPv6
- Log collection and analysis
- **Network based Intrusion Detection and Prevention (NIPS/NIDS)**
- Packet fragmentation
- Perimeter concepts and IP fundamentals

- Routers security and network access control
- Securing hosts and services
- Static and stateful packet filtering
- TCP/IP protocols
- VPN basics and implementation
- Vulnerability assessment and auditing
- Wireless design and security

GIAC Certified Intrusion Analyst (GCIA)

GCIA is one of the most prestigious and well-regarded certifications for security professionals who wish to continue their journey in Security Incident Handling. This certification is also equally valuable for seasoned cybersecurity professionals. Attempting GCIA certification will require you to understand security incidents and how to deal with an incident, post- or during a cyberattack. To attempt the certification exam, you will need to gain knowledge on the following topics:

- Advanced analysis and network forensics
- Advanced IDS concepts
- Application protocols
- Concepts of TCP/IP and the link layer
- Concepts of DNS, IP headers and fragmentation, IPv6, TCP, UDP, and ICMP
- IDS fundamentals and network architecture
- IDS rules
- Network traffic analysis
- Packet engineering
- SiLK and other traffic analysis tools
- Wireshark fundamentals

SANS certifications

SANS is one of the largest sources of information-security training in the world. It offers training through several delivery methods: live and virtual, classroom-style, online at your own pace or webcast with live instruction, guided study with a local mentor, or privately at your workplace where even your most remote colleagues can join in via Simulcast.

As SANS has a lot of training options, I recommend you visit their website to find a course that will work with your needs: `https://www.sans.org/courses/`:

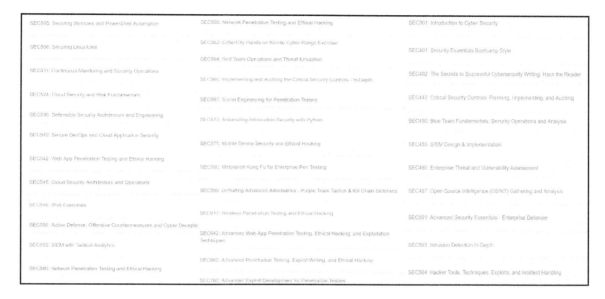

To make your job easier, SANS has created a roadmap, which can be found at `https://www.sans.org/cyber-security-skills-roadmap`:

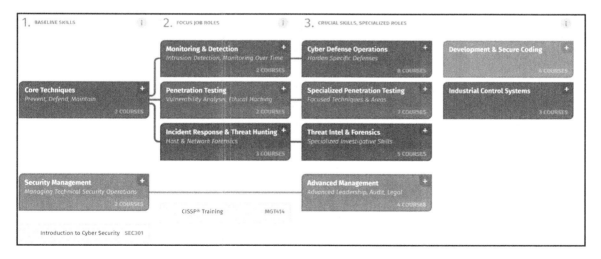

Cisco certifications

Cisco offers top-of-the-line industry certifications, and it is also a great way to kickstart your security career, if you want to focus on the network security side of the cyber world. Cisco certifications are mainly split into four major categories, the first is the entry-level certification, **CCENT**, the second is associate certifications, which is the **CCNA** and **CCDA** range of certifications, the third is the professional certifications which cover the **CCNP** and **CCDP** range, and the last one is the expert level, which covers the **CCIE** and **CCDE** range. For more serious professionals who want to get deeper into network design, architecture, and security, Cisco certifications also cover architect certifications under the acronym **CCAr**. The best part of the Cisco certifications is that they have split each level into nine different categories to make it easy for you to choose the path you want to take for your career and specific technical field: Routing & Switching, Design, Industrial Network, Network Security, Service Provider, Service Provider Operations, Storage Networking, Voice, Datacenter, and Wireless. The split also makes sense because the network subject is huge and you cannot learn everything in one certification. Well, you may choose to have the certifications in all the nine categories, if you have enough time and resources (I am aware of very few people in the real world who have a series of these certifications), it's just that you have to take them one by one, and gain expertise in them. Let's look at some of these certifications (the rest of them can be found at
`www.cisco.com/c/en/us/training-events/training-certifications/certifications.ht`
`ml`).

Cisco Certified Entry Networking Technician (CCENT)

This is an entry-level, basic certification. As a result of this certification attempt, you will learn the basic concepts of networking, how to perform jobs such as network support, and how to implement, operate, and troubleshoot a small enterprise or branch network. You will also learn basics of network security. This certification certainly opens up careers in networking if you are looking for one. This is also the foundation for other certifications from Cisco, such as CCNA. Because this is a very basic type of certification, in my opinion, anyone who is in the field of IT can try this:

- Basic understanding of **Quality of Service (QoS)**.
- A module on virtualization and cloud services.

- Exposure to network programmability related to WAN, access and core segments.
- Learn foundational elements of network layers 1-3. Understanding these layers is important from a core routing and switching perspective.
- Understanding the fundamentals of firewalls, wireless controllers and access points.
- Learn about IPv6 and basic network security.
- Access to labs to try the configuration commands with use cases provided during the lab exercises.

CCNA Routing and Switching

CCNA Routing and Switching is yet another highly-regarded certification in the IT networking world, almost all networking engineers have this certification at the start of their networking career. If you are planning to be one of them, you can expect to learn how to implement, operate, and configure an enterprise network, learn about IPv4 and IPv6 networks and about LAN Switch and IP router, how they work, and how to configure them. You will also learn about WAN and other security threats to networks. Last but not least, it also teaches you to troubleshoot the network and about network devices related to routing and switching. Apart from the topics that you may have already covered as part of CCENT, you will learn some additional skills:

- You will be able to manage a mid-size LAN with multiple switches, VLANs, trunking, and a spanning tree
- Get a grasp on troubleshooting IP connectivity
- Skills related to configuring and troubleshooting **Enhanced Interior Gateway Routing Protocol (EIGRP)**, **Open Shortest Path First (OSPF)** in IPv4 and IPv6 environments
- You will be able to build WAN by defining its characteristics, functions, and components

Offensive Security Certified Professional (OSCP)/Offensive Security's Penetration Testing with Kali Linux (PwK)

This is one if the best cybersecurity training courses you can take. Offensive Security's training courses focus on offensive security, specifically the field of penetration testing. Due to the large number of specializations from the information security domain, the most suitable course for you depends on what you are interested in.

The Offensive Security, **Penetration Testing with Kali Linux (PwK)** course focuses on modern techniques used by penetration testers all across the globe, so it would be a great start for you.

Cracking the Perimeter (CTP) focuses on exploit development, web application, and WAN attacks, which are also useful for pentesters; however, PwK teaches you the core skills that are required to be a good pentester. CTP also requires advanced knowledge of different offensive techniques, so it is not recommended for beginners. If you feel you possess the required knowledge to take it, feel free to try the following CTP course-registration challenge: http://www.fc4.me/.

In addition to PwK and CTP, they also have a course devoted to wireless penetration testing, Offensive Security Wireless Attacks (WiFu).

Before registering for a course, we advise you to look through each course syllabus and decide which one covers what you are interested in. Each of the courses has a syllabus available online to see what topics are covered: https://www.offensive-security.com/information-security-certifications/oscp-offensive-security-certified-professional/. Some of the courses available are shown in the following screenshot:

ONLINE COURSE	DESCRIPTION	ASSOCIATED CERTIFICATION	DIFFICULTY LEVEL
OFFENSIVE® **security** **Most Popular** Penetration Testing with Kali Linux (PWK)	PWK is Offensive Security's flagship ethical hacking course, designed and written by the Kali Linux developers, introduces students to the latest ethical hacking tools and techniques, including remote, virtual penetration testing labs for practicing the course materials. Learn more.	OSCP	●●●○○
Cracking the Perimeter (CTP)	CTP takes all of the skills acquired in the PWK course and further hones them through an in depth examination of the vectors used by today's attackers to breach infrastructure security. Learn more.	OSCE	●●●●○
Offensive Security Wireless Attacks (WiFu)	WiFu teaches students the base concepts of wireless networking and builds upon that foundation to conduct effective attacks against wireless networks of varying configurations. Learn more.	OSWP	●●○○○
Kali Linux Revealed	Build a strong foundation to use Kali Linux in a professional capacity by mastering the penetration testing distribution in this free course. Learn more.	KLCP	●●○○○
Metasploit Unleashed (MSFU)	MSFU is an ethical hacking course that exposes students to the Metasploit Framework, its tools and various ethical hacking features it has to offer. This course is considered to be an ethical hacking starter kit and a perfect way to start on the pathway to certification. Learn more.	N/A	●○○○○

Offensive Security's Penetration Testing with Kali Linux (PwK)

OSCP is one of the most recognized and respected certifications for info security professionals. To become certified, you must complete Offensive Security's PwK course and pass the 24-hour hands-on exam. For hands-on experience, each student receives access to a virtual penetration testing lab where techniques learned within the course can be practiced. The OSCP examination consists of a virtual network that contains targets of varying configurations and operating systems. At the start of the exam, the student receives the exam and connectivity instructions for an isolated exam network that they have no prior knowledge of or exposure to.

CertNexsusCybersec first responder (CFR)

By taking an approach where an understanding of the anatomy of an attack is developed, the **CyberSec First Responder (CFR)** cybersecurity certification ensures individuals have the high-stakes skills needed to serve their organizations before, during, and after a breach.

A CyberSec First Responder is the first line of defense against cyberattacks that can cost an organization valuable time and money. The CyberSec First Responder cybersecurity training and certification program will prepare security professionals to become the first responders against cyberattacks by teaching students to analyze threats, design secure computing and network environments, proactively defend networks, and respond/investigate cyber security incidents:

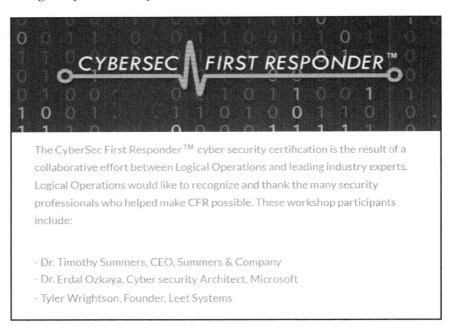

The CyberSec First Responder ™ cyber security certification is the result of a collaborative effort between Logical Operations and leading industry experts. Logical Operations would like to recognize and thank the many security professionals who helped make CFR possible. These workshop participants include:

- Dr. Timothy Summers, CEO, Summers & Company
- Dr. Erdal Ozkaya, Cyber security Architect, Microsoft
- Tyler Wrightson, Founder, Leet Systems

To learn more about the certification, visit `https://certnexus.com/cybersec-first-responder-cfr-continuing-education-program/`.

There is also an end user training course called CyberSafe. But this course is aimed more toward end users.

The NIST cybersecurity framework

The US Department of Commerce's **National Institute of Standards and Technology (NIST)** created the NIST Cybersecurity Framework in response to a Presidential Executive Order, *Improving Critical Infrastructure Cybersecurity*. The framework, developed in collaboration with the industry, provides guidance to organizations on ways to better manage and reduce cybersecurity risk. The NIST Cybersecurity Framework Core presents key cybersecurity outcomes identified by the industry as helpful in managing cybersecurity risk. The Core comprises four elements: functions, categories, subcategories, and informative references. The following diagram shows the five stages of the NIST cybersecurity framework:

The NIST Cybersecurity Framework

Identify

The activities in the Identify Function are a foundation for effective use of the framework. Understanding the business context, the resources that support critical functions, and the related cybersecurity risks enables an organization to focus and prioritize its efforts, consistent with its risk management strategy and business needs.

Here are the outcome categories:

- Asset Management
- Business Environment
- Governance

- Risk Assessment
- Risk Management Strategy

Here are some related cyber courses:

- EC-Council Certified Ethical Hacker
- CompTIA Cybersecurity Analyst
- Certified Information Systems Auditor
- Certified Information Security Manager
- Certified Information System Security Professional

Protect

The Protect Function supports the ability to limit or contain the impact of a potential cybersecurity event.

Here are the outcome categories:

- Access Control
- Awareness and Training
- Data Security
- Information Protection Processes and Procedures
- Maintenance
- Protective Technology

Here are some related cyber courses:

- CompTIA Security+
- CompTIA Advanced Security Practitioner
- CompTIA Cybersecurity Analyst
- Cisco Security
- EC-Council Certified Security Analyst

Detect

The Detect Function enables the timely discovery of cybersecurity events.

Here are the outcome categories:

- Anomalies and Events
- Security Continuous Monitoring
- Detection Processes

Here are some related cyber courses:

- CompTIA Cybersecurity Analyst
- Cisco Security Courses

Respond

The Respond Function supports the ability to contain the impact of a potential cybersecurity event.

Here are the outcome categories:

- Recovery Planning
- Improvements
- Communications

Here are some related cyber courses:

- EC-Council Computer Hacking Forensics Investigator
- CyberSec First Responder: Threat Detection and Response
- Cisco Security

Recover

The Recover Function supports a timely recovery to normal operations to reduce the impact from a cybersecurity event.

Here are the outcome categories:

- Recovery Planning
- Improvements
- Communications

Here are some related cyber courses:

- Certified Information Security Manager
- Certified Information System Security Professional
- CompTIA Advanced Security Practitioner

Summary

This chapter focused on knowledge check, particularly related to certifications. There are many eLearning platforms that have opened and all offer competitive courses and certifications upon the successful completion of each course.

Certifications will offer learners some advantages in the job market that applicants that only have degrees will not get. Certifications show employers that you take initiative, show that you are highly skilled in a certain niche, equip you with in-demand skills, market your skills, and can kickstart a cyber security career for people with non-IT degrees. Choosing the certification to take and the vendor must always be done with caution. Before picking a course, you should evaluate the vendor's reputation, the credibility of the certification, the duration of the course, the feedback from previous learners, the level of support that learners are offered, and market demand.

In the next chapter, we will explore the various aspects of security-intelligence resources that can be publicly and commercially consumed to enhance organizational security.

Further reading

Check out the following resources for more information on the topics covered in this chapter:

- https://www.trushieldinc.com/top-3-reasons-you-need-cyber-security-awareness-training/
- https://altimetersolutions.com/importance-of-cybersecurity-certifications/
- https://hirevergence.com/importance-of-cybersecurity-certifications/
- https://www.whitedust.net/the-importance-of-cybersecurity-certification-training/

Security Intelligence Resources

10

Cybersecurity is a buzzword right now. While it could be assumed to be a high-level, technical, and complex undertaking, in reality, it is just a few precautions that everyone in an organization can take to keep safe. It is not the burden of the IT department to keep everyone, as well as all devices, networks, and systems, safe. Most attacks are not even caused by direct attacks to networks, devices, or systems. Humans are the weakest link in the cybersecurity chain, and taking a few extra security precautions could shield the company from losses. This chapter will provide some of the resources that users in the organization can utilize to achieve this. It will be helpful for all types of users, both technical and non-technical. It will inform the average non-technical users of the security precautions they should take so as not to expose themselves to security threats. It will also give technical IT users a reference point to check the security of their organization or to learn more about the solutions that they need to implement to offer more security to users and digital assets owned by the organization.

This chapter will discuss the following topics:

- Checklist resources
- Cybersecurity advice and reliable information sources
- Cybersecurity courses
- Cybersecurity threat-intelligence resources

Checklist resources

Cybersecurity checklist websites are aimed at giving users a quick rundown of what to check to ensure that they are not exposed to threats. They also guide users on the steps to take to further protect themselves. This chapter has identified the following comprehensive checklist resource.

Security Checklist

The Security Checklist (`https://securitycheckli.st/`) is an online platform that all users can refer to for a comprehensive checklist of all the things they need do to be less prone to attacks. It is focused on protecting privacy and preventing exposure to malware and phishing attacks. The Security Checklist is composed of the following items:

- **Password managers**: There is a big problem in creating unique passwords for all services that you have an account with. Most users reuse the same passwords and this exposes them to more threats; once one account is compromised, hackers can access your other accounts. Many attacks involving the theft of credentials have resulted in such files being sold on black markets. Buyers will try to use the credentials to access other accounts linked with the username. This website offers several options of password managers that users can download and install on Windows, macOS, iOS, Android, and Linux. It also provides reading resources about password managers to help users understand their functions.
- **Creating strong passcodes**: The next item in the checklist is having a strong passcode. This website gives guidelines on the minimum length and composition of passwords. It also tells users to disable TouchID and FaceID when traveling. It refers users to several websites with in-depth information on how passcodes are broken, how they can be changed on iOS and Android, and how to disable TouchID and FaceID.
- **Two-factor authentication (2FA)**: Third on the list is the 2FA, which is focused on adding another layer of security to the usual login credentials. 2FA is briefly discussed and guidelines on how it should be set are given.
- **Encryption**: The checklist features encryption as a security technique to help you remain secure. Encryption is briefly discussed, where the resource explains that encryption prevents data from being read if a thief ever steals your computer or phone. It provides resources that can be used to learn how to encrypt iOS, Android, Windows, and macOS devices.
- **Freezing one's credit**: Due to the many security breaches that have led to the loss of data belonging to billions of users with different companies, the site informs you that you should assume that your SSN, credit report, and other personal details are known by hackers. To prevent hackers from opening new lines of credit using this information, the site encourages users (in the US) to enable a freeze on credit report checks on all bureaus.

- **Changing DNS to 1.1.1.1**: Unbeknownst to many users, a lot of the content they access on the internet is facilitated by DNS, which serves the role of translating domain names into IP addresses. However, DNS is highly insecure and it has been established that service providers log and sell data that passes through it. You can switch to using DNS tools that are security and privacy-focused. Cloudflare offers the 1.1.1.1 DNS address that still does domain-name resolution but is faster and more secure than the normal DNS provided by service providers. The site offers sites you can use to learn more about switching to the secure DNS.

- **VPNs:** Internet connections are not always secure and are prone to man-in-the-middle attacks. In addition, protocol analyzers, such as Ethereal or Wireshark, can be used to capture traffic flowing in a network and identify the sites being visited. VPNs solve this problem by offering a secure internet connection that is encrypted so that all the data you send or receive cannot be read by people snooping on a network. The resource provides six trusted VPN providers: IVPN, Encrypt.me, ExpressVPN, NordVPN, ProtonVPN, and Private Internet Access. Most of these are available on all operating systems.

- **Webcam covers and privacy screens**: There are websites that contain malicious scripts that can open your webcam without asking for permission and take pictures or videos. It is also possible to turn off the light indicator that shows that a computer's webcam is active. In addition, surfing in public places exposes you to shoulder-surfing, where malicious people simply watch and steal sensitive data when you enter it into a website or system. The site proposes two solutions: webcam covers and laptop privacy screens. Webcam covers make it impossible for hackers to see anything when they hijack the webcam and the privacy screen is a filter that blocks visibility of a screen outside of 60 degrees.

- **Privacy-first emails, browsers, and search engines**: The website warns that many service providers track and fingerprint devices for the purposes of advertisements. They offer the following alternatives:
    - **Browsers**: Brave, Safari, and Firefox
    - **Search engines**: `duckduckgo.com`
    - **Email providers**: ProtonMail, FastMail, and Tutanota

- **Reviewing app permissions**: There is an increase in the number of apps that have been requesting excessive permissions to sensitive data that is not required for their primary functionalities. Others have been granted permissions that allow them to act as espionage tools. The most abused permissions are location, microphone, camera, contacts, and messages. Besides apps, there are services that request access to social media accounts but access data that is not relevant to the functions they offer. For instance, a Twitter follower count service might have gotten access to reading messages in your inbox. Part of the security checklist informs users that they should revoke excess permissions from apps and services. The checklist provides resources that guide Android, iOS, Windows, and macOS users on how to manage the permissions they have granted to apps. In addition, the checklist offers resources that can be used to opt out of services that read data from social media accounts.
- **Social media privacy settings**: A lot of personal information can be obtained on social media networks without much hassle. Hackers often start an attack against a specific target by doing reconnaissance to find out as much information about them as possible. Social media platforms are littered with excessive personal information, such as birthdates, physical addresses, and names of family members. Social media platforms often have privacy controls which most users ignore or do not bother checking.
- **The security checklist**: A number of resources are given that explain how to make changes to multiple privacy settings on different social media.
- **Education on phishing attacks**: Hackers do not solely depend on using exploit tools and advanced software to breach accounts. They, at times, just request access from users under false pretenses. Many phishing attacks are being conducted via mail where users are being tricked into sharing sensitive credentials with people who claim to be from legitimate companies. In many cases, the targets are given malicious links that contain exact clones of login pages to some commonly used websites. Once the users enter their details, the hackers proceed to use the details on the correct websites and steal money or data.
- **Keeping devices updated**: The last item in the checklist informs users that they must keep their software and apps up to date. While it might be easy to know when updates are available for apps or computers, it might not be so obvious for other devices, such as routers. Furthermore, users are not always actively patching software when updates are available. The checklist gives links to authoritative sites that explain why, when, and how users should install updates.

Cybersecurity advice and reliable information sources

Another important category of cybersecurity intelligence is getting credible alerts about new attacks and advice on how to guard against becoming a victim to cybercriminals. The following are some of the sites that offer this information:

- **Krebs on Security** (https://krebsonsecurity.com/): Provides details on cybersecurity news and investigations into cybercrime and related incidences. The website offers lots of updated information regarding happenings in cybersecurity. For instance, at the time of writing, the top post explained how Google was able to stop all phishing attacks against employees as of 2017. As detailed in the post, the company simply got rid of passwords and instead offered employees physical security keys and one-time access codes. The relevance of the post was that Google was going to share this solution with the public by allowing Android phones to serve as physical security keys. However, the implementation would be limited to only Google-linked services. Another relevant post was the admission of a breach by an Italian firm, but two years after the incidence happened. The breaching involved the theft of personal data belonging to more than 2,000,000 customers. Buca di Beppo, the breached company, downplayed the claims for two years. Nevertheless, the company later admitted to having been hacked. However, that came a bit late since customers' data had been posted and sold on black markets.

  The site is relevant for people who want to read more about the latest cybersecurity news and learn about new security tools released into the market by companies. All posts are thoroughly researched and well-informed. The intelligence gathered can be used by cybersecurity professionals to secure their organizations further, while average users learn more about the dynamics of cybercrime and the importance of having adequate cybersecurity measures.

- **Naked Security** (https://nakedsecurity.sophos.com): This website is owned by Sophos, a leading cybersecurity company that offers several security products and services. The website provides detailed cybersecurity news with a focus on informing readers about new cybersecurity tools and how they can be implemented. It also alerts users about new cybercrime incidences and how they can protect themselves against becoming victims. At the time of writing, the most recent post detailed a privacy invasion technique of spy cams in hotel rooms. The post explained how to detect spy cameras in hotels and how to scan the network in hotels to find spy cameras. The names of spy devices will tend to differ from those of normal devices. The post said that, using the IP address of the suspicious device, you can scan the open ports and find out whether it has **rtsp (real-time streaming protocol)** or **rtmp (real-time messaging protocols)** services running. However, readers are cautioned that this alone is not enough or a sure way to find spy cameras in a network. The website is quite detailed and in all the posts, users can learn something new about cybersecurity.

- **Dark reading** (https://www.darkreading.com): A news and advisory website that is targeted at technical readers. The site publishes stories relevant to cybersecurity, informing readers about the skills they should have or the trends they should be aware of when implementing cybersecurity solutions. At the time of writing, one of the top posts detailed the essential skills cybersecurity experts need to have. The posts tend to be detailed but segmented in multiple pages. Nevertheless, the site provides advice for both beginners and experts in cybersecurity and thus is a valuable intelligence resource.

Cybersecurity courses

Due to the dynamic changes in cybercrime, cybersecurity professionals, or those aspiring to be, must keep up to date with skills that are needed in the market. In addition, they must also widen the scope of their knowledge to be conversant with many threats and security solutions. There are websites that offer free training to those willing to learn more on cybersecurity, which we'll look at now.

SlashNext

This cybersecurity intelligence resource is focused on one of the biggest challenges that organizations are facing today: phishing. Even after spending lots of money and other resources in putting up layers of security, companies are still being breached by cybercriminals through their own employees. Phishing has become a nightmare and has claimed many victims.

For instance, the attack on Yahoo that led to the theft of sensitive information of all of its 2,000,000,000 users was attributed to phishing. Many other companies have been the victim of phishing attacks, where employees simply surrender login credentials, send money, or click malicious links, causing their devices to be infected. SlashNext states that phishing can be initiated via emails, free software on the web, browser add-ons, online chat forums, social media, messages, and popups in browsers. After making the initial contact with the target, the hackers will use all the techniques at their disposal just to win the trust and thus hack the target. SlashNext offers a 30-minute informative webinar on the new types of phishing, why existing solutions are not able to contain the threat, and how organizations can use real-time threat intelligence to help stop phishing attempts before they become successful against employees.

Springboard

Springboard offers a cybersecurity basics course that is aimed at those looking to do a refresher or start learning about cybersecurity. Learners are given a 38-hour training session that is broken into nine modules. By taking the course, you gain a fundamental understanding of cybersecurity and can develop your skills further by specializing in a few areas.

Cybrary

Since 2015, Cybrary has been offering free cybersecurity training. The training is broken down into several courses, which you can take as nano-degrees. The advantage of the site is that it gives learners toolkits, practice labs, and practical tests. It is ideal for beginners, intermediates, and experts in the field.

US Department of Homeland Security

This is quite a notable addition to the list of free training sources. The United States is a preferred target for cyberattacks and most of its citizens are not aware of the basics of cybersecurity. The website offers free training to all who are eager to learn more about cybercrime and cybersecurity. Since many attacks against US companies have been industrial espionage, the courses provided on the department's training website are focused on industrial environments. The course is designed for beginners in cybersecurity but experts can take it to specialize in preventing threats against industrial systems. The trainees are given certification upon the successful completion of a course.

There are many other websites that offer cybersecurity training. However, many of the free academies do not offer quality teaching materials and do not give certifications. Three of the sites listed here do offer certifications and all of them have quality information. Therefore, they are invaluable sources of cybersecurity intelligence.

Cybersecurity threat-intelligence resources

By now, you have read about and learned how to improve yourself in cybersecurity. Let's now explore the various threat-intelligence resources to further our knowledge base. This section will take you through **Structured Threat Information Expression (STIX)**, **Trusted Automated Exchange of Intelligence Information (TAXII)**, **Oasis Open Command and Control (OpenC2)**, **Traffic Light Protocol (TLP)**, and **Cyberanalytics Repository** by MITRE (**CAR**). With the knowledge of the aforementioned resources, you will be better equipped to identify threats and vulnerabilities.

Structured Threat Information Expression (STIX)

Structured Threat Information Expression, commonly known as STIX, is a special language format to exchange threat intelligence related to cyberattacks. STIX is open source, and free to be used by anyone. STIX allows us to share threat intelligence from any point of view, such as suspicion or compromised information (IoC). It also allows us to represent clearly with objects and detailed relationships between them with threat information. STIX is generally shared in JSON format, but can also be represented visually for any analyst to take advantage of the information. The information shared can be easily integrated with security-analytics tools. STIX has 12 domain objects to define a threat element (more information can be found at `https://oasis-open.github.io/cti-documentation/stix/intro`):

- **Attack Pattern**: Allows us to describe how threat actors attempt to compromise any target by providing information about the type of **Tactics, Techniques, and Procedures (TTP)**.
- **Campaign**: Describes the grouping of attacker behavior for a particular set of malicious activities and attacks that are observed over a period of time against very specific group of targets.

- **Course of Action**: Defines what action is to be taken to prevent or respond to an attack.
- **Identity**: This object helps define individuals, organizations, or groups, as well as classes of individuals, organizations, or groups.
- **Indicator**: It can contain a pattern of threat information that can be used to detect suspicious or malicious cyberactivity.
- **Intrusion Set**: Describes attacker or adversarial behaviors and resources grouped together as a set, and its common properties are assumed to be orchestrated by an individual threat actor.
- **Malware**: Information about malicious code and malicious software, which can be used to compromise the confidentiality, integrity, or availability of a victim's data or system.
- **Observed Data**: Contains information observed on a system or network (for example, a source or destination IP address).
- **Report**: This object may contain threat information related to the description of a threat actor, malware, attack techniques, or contextual data.
- **Threat Actor**: This object can carry information about any individuals, groups, or organizations assumed to have malicious intent.
- **Tool**: Any information about software packages that can be used by adversaries to perform an attack.
- **Vulnerability**: Vulnerability or bug information of a software that can be directly used by a hacker to compromise a system or network.

Here is a sample JSON structure of STIX:

```
{
"type": "<any ond the 12 objects>",
"id": "object--xxxxxxxx-xxxx-xxxx-xxxx-xxxxxxxxxxxx",
"created": "yyyy-mm-ddThh:mm:00.000Z",
"name": "<Attacker group name and target>",
"description": "<Description of the campagin can be given here>"
}
```

Trusted Automated Exchange of Intelligence Information (TAXII)

The **Trusted Automated Exchange of Indicator Information (TAXII)** is a standard way for message exchanges that provides a sharing mechanism of actionable cyber threat information between different organizations and product/service boundaries. TAXII defines concepts, protocols, and message exchanges to exchange cyber threat information for the detection, prevention, and mitigation of cyber threats. Broadly, TAXII covers two primary services of sharing models:

- **Collection**: This is an interface to access a repository of **Cyber threat intelligence (CTI)** objects provided by a **TAXII server**, which further allows a producer to host a set of CTI data that can be requested by TAXII clients and servers to exchange information in a request-response model (more information can be found at `https://oasis-open.github.io/cti-documentation/taxii/intro`), shown as follows:

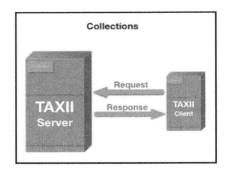

- **Channel**: This is maintained by a TAXII server. Channel allows CTI producers to push data to many consumers and consumers to receive data from many producers. TAXII clients usually will exchange information with other TAXII clients in a publisher-subscriber model, shown as follows:

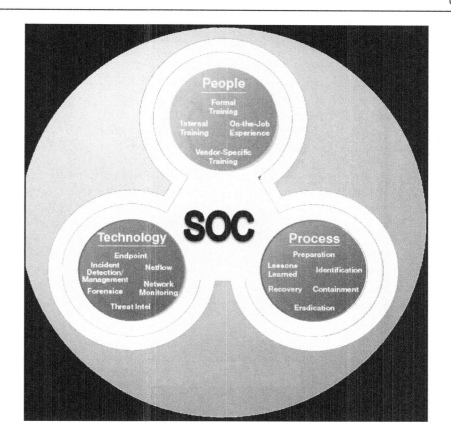

OASIS Open Command and Control (OpenC2)

OASIS **Open Command and Control (OpenC2)** is a technical committee that focuses its efforts on artifacts that are generated by the OpenC2 community forum. The OpenC2 TC was chartered to draft documents, specifications, or other artifacts to support the needs of cybersecurity commands and control in an industry-standard manner. The Technical Committee also leverage any preexisting standards to a great extent and practically identify gaps pertaining to the command and control of technologies that provide or support cyber defenses (https://www.oasis-open.org).

Traffic Light protocol (TLP)

The **Traffic Light Protocol** (TLP) was created in order to facilitate the sharing of information. TLP is a set of designations used to ensure that sensitive information is shared with the appropriate audience. It employs four colors to indicate expected sharing boundaries to be applied by the recipient(s), and the different degrees of sensitivity and the corresponding sharing considerations to be applied by the recipient(s). TLP only has four colors; any designations not listed in this standard are not considered valid by FIRST.

TLP is a simple and intuitive schema to indicate when and how certain sensitive information can be shared, for more repetitive and effective collaboration, but on the other hand TLP is not to be treated as *"control marking"* or classification. TLP is optimized for easy adoption, human-readable, person-to-person sharing; it can also be used in automated sharing. The source who is sharing the threat information is responsible for making sure that the recipients of the TLP information have complete understanding of the sharing guidelines of TLP. In case the recipient wants to share the information further, they must obtain explicit permission from the owner of the information. Here are the TLP definitions that can be used to tag information while sharing (for detailed usage, please visit `https://www.us-cert.gov/tlp`):

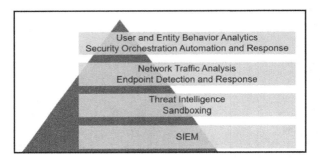

Cyber Analytics Repository by MITRE (CAR)

The **Cyber Analytics Repository** (CAR) is a repository based on analytics of **Adversary Tactics, Techniques, and the Common Knowledge** (ATT&CK) threat model as developed by MITRE. The analytics stored in CAR include information such as an explanation of the thought process of the analytic of a subject, information about the primary domain (for example, host, network, process, external), available references to ATT&ACK (`https://attack.mitre.org/`) techniques, and also a pseudocode and unit test that can be used to implement and test the analytic. You can find more details for further research and reading at `https://car.mitre.org/`.

IntelMQ by ENISA

IntelMQ is a platform for the security teams in any CERT, CSIRT, or other security operations. This platform is a community-driven initiative by the Incident-handling Automation project by ENISA, CNCS (National Cyber Security Centre—Portugal), CERT.AT, CERT-EU, and CERT.BE for collecting and processing security feeds by leveraging a message-queuing protocol. IntelMQ is focused on reducing the complexity of system administration, writing new modules for new data feeds, using a common format for sharing by JSON, integrating with common existing tools, providing flexibility to store information in popular log collectors, such as Elasticsearch and Splunk. This platform also offers the flexibility to create custom blacklists for your own use and to share threat intel by the HTTP RESTFUL API. Full details on its usage and an implementation guide can be found at `https://github.com/certtools/intelmq`.

Recorded Future

Recorded Future (`https://www.recordedfuture.com/`) is an advanced SaaS-based product. This platform combines the automatic collection and analysis of threat intelligence from open source, dark web, and other technical sources into a single solution. Recorded Future uses advanced technology, such as **natural language processing** (**NLP**) and machine learning, to process, enrich, and deliver threat intelligence in real time. This platform has the ability to contextualize threat intelligence to provide proactive threat information for developing a security strategy. The ability to crunch and process huge volumes of threat-intelligence data with machine learning helps analysts reduce their time to come to a conclusion. You can access the threat-intelligence data from Recorded Future in their web-based platform, which can also be integrated with a wide range of cybersecurity solutions. It will help you to get wide visibility of the threat landscape you are in and enrich alerts for your security teams. Recorded Future also provides integration with multiple deep analysis products, incident response tools, intelligence platforms, network detection products, SIEM, SOAR, threat hunting, vulnerability management tool, and ticketing systems.

Anomali STAXX

Anomali STAXX (`https://www.anomali.com/community/staxx`) is a tool for sharing threat intelligence from STIX/TAXII sources by connecting to STIX/TAXII servers; this gives you access to search and configure your own threat feeds based on your specific needs. It also allows you to import threat-intelligence data into Anomali STAXX and then upload selected intelligence data to other STIX/TAXII servers. This platform provides a very easy and interactive interface to skim through threat-related information. Anomali platform helps you collect threat intel feeds from OSINT and ISACs.

Because of the huge volume of threat intelligence that is collected from multiple sources, the STAXX platform provides analysts with a normalized and enriched threat context to use in security operations and incident response. The tool also assists in identifying the most viable threat for your organization by applying its own scoring methodology for each threat, giving you the historical context of the identified threat. Anomali STAXX has great capability to integrate with existing SIEM and EDR solutions to help you in security operations.

Cyberthreat-intelligence feeds

As you know by now, cyberthreat intelligence focuses on providing actionable information on adversaries to build a proper cyber defense against attacks.

Knowing the right resources will help you to speed up your research as well as get the right advice from the industry. Check out these resources (listed in alphabetic order):

- `AlienVault.com`: Multiple sources including large honeynets that profile adversaries.
- **Cyveilance.com**: Unique feeds on threat actors and indications of criminal intent.
- `EmergingThreats.net`: A variety of feeds.
- `FireEye.com`: **Dynamic Threat Intelligence (DTI)** service.
- `Hacksurfer.com` (**SurfWatch**): Insights tailored to your business.
- `InternetIdentity.com`: Threat feeds from their big data solution, ActiveTrust.
- `RecordedFuture.com`: Real-time threat intelligence from the web.
- **Advanced security with Intelligent Security Graph** (`https://www.microsoft.com/en-us/security/operations/intelligence`): Advanced analytics link massive amounts of threat-intelligence and security data to provide you with unparalleled threat protection and detection.
- `Secureworks.com`: Provides feeds and also instruments networks.
- `Symantec.com`: DeepInsight feeds on a variety of topics including reputation.
- **Spytales.com**: Everything there is to know about the past, present, and future of spies.
- `Team-Cymru.com`: Threat intelligence plus bogon lists.
- **TheCyberThreat**: Our Twitter feed. High-level but comprehensive and curated.
- `ThingsCyber.com`: The most critical lessons in cyber conflict and cybersecurity, relevant for your defense today.

- `ThreatConnect.com`: Created by Cyber Squared and focused on information sharing.
- `ThreatGrid.com`: Unified malware analysis. Now part of Cisco.
- **ThreatIntelligenceReview.com**: Updated reviews of threat-intelligence sources.
- `ThreatSTOP.com`: Block botnets by IP reputation.
- `ThreatStream.com`: Famous team. Multiple sources in interoperable platforms.
- `ThreatTrack.com`: Stream of malicious URLs, IPs, and malware/phishing-related data.
- `Verisigninc.com`: iDefense feeds that are highly regarded by some key institutions.

Summary

This chapter focused on valuable resources for security intelligence. We looked at three broad resources: security checklists, news or advisory sites, and cybersecurity training websites. The security checklist discussed was thorough and takes the user through the A-Z of security. It is aimed at ensuring that they protect themselves and their devices from hacking, espionage, scams, and privacy infringement. The checklist has identified some of the security tools that users need to have to ensure that they secure their devices. It has also highlighted some of the security changes that users should take regarding the exposure of personal information on social media. The chapter looked at the trustworthy news sources, which double as cybersecurity advisers. The websites reviewed provide well-researched information about cybersecurity incidences in the real world and they break down how the incidences happened and how they can be prevented. For instance, one website featured the privacy issues of hotel rooms having spy cameras. It explained a relatively easy way that a tech-savvy person could track the spy cameras through the use of network and port scans. Finally, the chapter looked at cybersecurity training resources and highlighted four resources. The first one offers training on phishing while the others offer a wider variety of courses with certifications. All the discussed resources are invaluable to anyone with interest in cybersecurity either as a practitioner or for the sake of securing themselves from attacks.

Further reading

Check out the following resources for more information on the topics covered in this chapter:

- http://slashnext.com/
- https://www.nativeintelligence.com/resources/links
- http://www.intelligence101.com/99-of-the-best-intelligence-resources-some-youve-probably-never-heard-of/
- https://www.microsoft.com/en-us/security/operations/security-intelligence-report
- https://www.liferaftinc.com/resources/

11
Expert Opinions on Getting Started with Cybersecurity

To make this book more valuable and help you to excel on your cybersecurity journey, I reached out to some industry experts and asked them how they started their career in cybersecurity and what they would recommend to you to allow you to improve.

I spoke to industry experts from Fortune 500 companies such as Microsoft, Standard Chartered bank, SAP, and FireEye, and experts from Oxford University, Charles Sturt University, army veterans, active cybersecurity consultants, architects, hiring managers, speakers from Black Hat and other tier-1 security conferences, and cybersecurity firm owners, as well as law enforcement professionals. Hopefully, this chapter will help you in your career.

Ann Johnson

Corporate Vice President, Microsoft

> *"Our teams must be as diverse as the problems we are trying to solve."*

The preceding statement is not an empty platitude, and it is not something that should be trivialized or over-hyped either. We are facing a battle against cybercrime that is impacting all aspects of our lives, including governments, financial systems, food supplies, water supplies, critical infrastructure, and healthcare. Large-scale cyber events, such as those witnessed in the past several years, threaten our very way of life. So, the question becomes, how did we get here? More importantly, where do we go from here? What can you, as a candidate, do to pursue a career in cybersecurity?

To explain, let me take you on my personal career journey. I graduated from college with a dual major in political science and communication, and an ambition to attend law school. I was accepted into law school and had obtained a scholarship for tuition and fees, but I was burdened financially from my undergraduate work and was also concerned about food, housing, healthcare, and so on. I made a decision to pursue a career rather than attend law school. Jobs in Northern Utah were scarce in the late 1980s for a graduate who didn't have a directly applicable degree, that is, one in accounting or medicine, and I ultimately moved to the Los Angeles area. I had one short-term position as an executive assistant in a medical firm, and then found my calling in technology.

My calling came by way of a newspaper ad for a floor salesperson at a wage of $17,000 USD per annum. I knew a bit about computers—as in, I could use one—and I knew I could talk to people, so a career was born. I attended every vendor training available and was diligent in studying and developing my skills. I was fortunate to have two early career mentors who encouraged my success and taught me everything they knew. I took on assignments related to operations, sales, network architecture and installation, computer repair, storage, partner engagement, customer engagement, and so on. I learned and absorbed all I could. At the time, mainframes and mini-computers dominated the industry, and PCs and client-servers were becoming a thing. Storage systems were massive near-line devices, and the biggest concern for a CIO was a rogue phone line in a data center. There were very few formal CISO positions, and security folks were generally of two types: investigators and network professionals. I entered security somewhat accidentally, but according to a plan.

In 1999, I was based in Chicago and working as a healthcare specialist for Data General. Data General was acquired by the EMC Corporation. I explored my options post acquisition and decided to make a change. The change was inspired by the hardware token I carried for authentication. I was fascinated by the technology, and I pursued a company called RSA Security and was ultimately hired as a PKI specialist. I not only had to look up the term, I had to study and develop an understanding of PKI, which I did. So, in 2000, a new career began—I was still in tech but in a highly specialized, but very nascent, field called cybersecurity (InfoSec at the time). CISOs were a thing by then—in very large organizations—and 2FA was used by about 20% of corporate employees (yes, that was all).

Since 2000, I have once again committed myself to self-study, learning, and growth—developing a deep understanding of the underlying technology of cybersecurity and the methods, modes, and motives of threat actors. I have also come to an understanding that there are simply too few people in cybersecurity roles. We used to joke, circa 2000, that people spent more on their annual coffee budgets than on their IT security budgets. If they had a firewall, a router, and an antivirus solution, and high-value users were using 2FA, everything was covered as far as most organizations were concerned. They were not prepared or adequately budgeted for the hyper growth in anytime, anywhere connected devices; the explosion of mobile devices that are as powerful as legacy servers; cloud-based technologies; the explosion of nation-state funded threat actors; or the explosion of malware and cybercrime as an industry. Universities and colleges were delayed in offering a cybersecurity-based curriculum, relying on a lot of network-based courses to cover the topic. Cybersecurity professionals were largely still from network or investigative backgrounds, and the industry was collapsing under the weight of too many disparate tools and too-many-point solutions.

By any measure, there are currently about 1 million open cybersecurity roles globally that all say something akin to *"must have 10 years' experience, STEM degree...."* We are becoming a self-fulfilling prophecy as an industry. We claim we want diverse backgrounds and skills, and we have too many job openings; we want to reduce complexity, but we continue to hire the same profiles, bemoan the lack of talent, and choose a single-point solution to add to our growing list of solutions because it solves a specific problem.

This group thinking, as an industry, has limited our options for hiring a diverse set of talent and for deploying the required solutions and technology to solve problems. For example, research shows us that diverse teams make better and faster decisions 78% of the time. Yet, we ignore this in the interest of quickly filling roles and a fundamental lack of desire to train the next generation of cybersecurity professionals due to our immediate need to protect our infrastructure.

As a self-taught infrastructure professional, who also taught myself cybersecurity via vendor and industry training immersion, I am a strong advocate for bringing in new voices from a wide range of backgrounds and different perspectives to drive meaningful change in the industry and to stay one step ahead of the bad actors. In addition, our tooling must modernize. We must fully realize the capabilities of tools such as machine learning to get a handle on the trillions of threats we see daily. We must also operate in partnership with public organizations, private companies, peers, and competitors. We must act like a community; an industry. We must also account for the stress of being a defender who is often working extraordinarily long hours in an understaffed environment.

So, where does this all leave us? It leaves us with an industry that has some opportunities to improve. We have the tools, we have the technology, we have available pools of talent, but we must have the will. We must have the will to take risks; we must have the will to accept that change is needed. We must have the will to hire a wide variety of people from diverse educational and societal backgrounds. We must create a community that takes care of its members and empowers people to be their absolute best. We don't actually have a choice; cybercrime is here to stay. What is needed now is a cybersecurity industry that acts as a community to bring the best tools, people, and partnering together as a robust solution. We can do this through investment in education programs at the grade school-level through to the high-school level, by investing in organizations that fund scholarships and mentorship programs for diverse individuals, through programs that invest in training transitioning military members and retraining displaced workers. We can actually bring cybersecurity to the broader population by simplifying the lexicon of the industry and making it less intimidating. We can mentor broadly, and we can speak publicly and frequently on the need for change and the steps required.

Given the need to evolve as an industry, what can you do as a candidate? I described my history here as a way to encourage you to be creative and to self-learn throughout your whole career. As a candidate, you need to work to describe your skills in a way that translates them to the cybersecurity landscape. Are you an experienced teacher? We need learning materials to explain complex concepts in simpler terms. Are you a psychology major? We need to understand the motives of attackers. Are you in law enforcement? We need to complete investigations. Are you a business analyst? We need to comprehend vast amounts of data. And if you are a programmer, network engineer, or database architect, there is a natural place for you in security—leverage your existing skills and learn new ones. Take risks and be part of the change that cybersecurity needs to fulfill its mission of securing global enterprises and governments. Seek out mentors and learn from them. Act now to join a quickly growing and highly exciting industry.

Who is Ann Johnson?

As Corporate Vice President of the Cybersecurity Solutions Group at Microsoft, Ann Johnson oversees the go-to-market strategies of cybersecurity solutions for one of the largest tech companies on our planet. As part of this charter, she leads and drives the evolution and implementation of Microsoft's short- and long-term security solutions road map with alignment across the marketing, engineering, and product teams.

Prior to joining Microsoft, her executive leadership roles included CEO of Boundless Spatial, president and chief operating officer of vulnerability management pioneer Qualys Inc, and vice president of World Wide Identity and Fraud Sales at RSA Security, a subsidiary of the EMC corporation.

Dr. Emre Eren Korkmaz

University of Oxford

What is the place of the general public in the new tech revolution?

Rapid technological progress in **artificial intelligence (AI)** is about to transform existing business models. Companies are beginning to use AI to help manage their human resources, attract and promote the loyalty of clients and customers, and increase transparency in their supply chains. Companies are also using AI to automate decision-making processes about their employees, customers, and suppliers.

This process began with companies using big data analytics to increase transparency in supply chains and continued with companies using cloud-based systems and AI to process the enormous amount of data collected globally from thousands of workplaces. Efforts to develop AI and blockchain (https://blog.sweetbridge.com/managing-supply-chains-on-the-blockchain-a-primer-1f7dc293e3d9?gi=8bee415e5b5a) to improve supply chain traceability are still pretty new, and the focus so far has mainly been limited simply to ensuring that products can be traced from lower tiers of the supply chain to supermarket shelves. There are even fewer initiatives that focus on sustainability (https://deepmind.com/blog/deepmind-ai-reduces-google-data-centre-cooling-bill-40/), and these have largely been directed toward environmental sustainability (https://www.eli.org/vibrant-environment-blog/environmentalism-next-machine-age); so far, little attention has been paid to the potential of AI to address labor and human rights issues. However, it is clear that AI will have a real impact in these areas and that it will directly affect the existing relationships between corporations, their suppliers, workers, and customers.

Thus, AI can analyze a vast amount of data very quickly and offer a summary judgment that can be used to inform decision-making (https://link.springer.com/article/10.1007/s13347-017-0263-5). However, a primary concern in this context is the extent to which AI analysis can be relied upon to produce objective judgments (https://link.springer.com/article/10.1007/s13347-017-0285-z) that do not simply reproduce and legitimize existing discrimination or inequalities (https://www.telegraph.co.uk/technology/2017/08/01/algorithms-future-must-not-allow-become-shield-injustice/). This concern has prompted discussions about the accountability and transparency of algorithms. And there have been efforts to understand how to mitigate the potentially discriminatory and unfair decisions of algorithms in a range of important areas of life, such as, say, applying for a bank loan or seeking justice.

Revolution for corporations?

Corporations are increasingly benefiting from digital expertise to manage their global production by tracking every move within the supply chain in real time. A companies' application of AI to their operations provides better visibility and predictability; however, these efforts don't yet incorporate human rights into their design at the moment.

As technology companies involved in the development of AI target global corporations as their clients, they don't necessarily focus on the interests and expectations of workers or local businesses. The use of AI to monitor production could massively increase the power of corporations vis-à-vis their suppliers and workers, resulting in the potential surveillance of workers by their employers. UNI Global Union's Future World of Work initiative offers 10 principles for ethical AI (http://www.thefutureworldofwork.org/docs/10-principles-for-ethical-artificial-intelligence/) and informs AI designers and companies of the importance of worker inclusion with the aim of safeguarding workers' interests and maintaining a healthy balance of power in workplaces.

In addition, if algorithms (focusing on visibility and traceability, based on real-time information, being received from thousands of workplaces operating in various countries) begin to manage suppliers in an increasingly competitive market, the constant comparison of different countries and workplaces to increase profits will likely increase the pressure on prices, delivery times, and productivity. This would create enormous stress and vulnerability for those suppliers. Local businesses (suppliers) would then transfer all that pressure onto their workers, who would be the real losers of the process.

The current mainstream business model, where companies seek to lower prices at any cost to be competitive, has caused *"a race to the bottom"* for their suppliers, who are generally located in the Global South, by increasing the productivity of the labor force and decreasing wages. This model (https://www.ethicaltrade.org/blog/modern-slavery-and-child-labour-its-all-about-choice) has intensified the exploitation of children through child labor, enabled instances of modern slavery, and undermined health and safety conditions.

As a result, unions and NGOs have taken many steps to support sustainable and fair business and increase respect for human rights in supply chains. Human rights due diligence, promoted by the UN's *Guiding Principles on Business and Human Rights* (https://www.unglobalcompact.org/library/2), is one expectation of companies as part of their responsibility to respect human rights. This approach allows all stakeholders to collaborate in order to determine the actual and potential risks that harm employees within a workplace or an industry. Instead of a one-sided decision-making process, this approach is action-oriented and calls on all parties to negotiate to address potential and actual risks and to resolve and mitigate the harm caused by them.

These models offer important lessons for companies utilizing AI to manage their relationships with suppliers and employees. If technology companies developing algorithms and training machines ignore all the accumulated experience in this field, they risk destroying existing relationships between global corporations, suppliers, and workers, and erasing human rights by offering unimaginable power to corporations.

The expected results of technological progress depend on users' approaches, and the use of AI to manage supply chains could have a positive impact. It is important that companies and civil society consider two questions:

- How can we teach machines about human rights and labor rights? (`http://www.siia.net/Press/SIIA-Releases-Ethical-Principles-for-Artificial-Intelligence-and-Data-Analytics-with-Support-from-the-Future-of-Privacy-Forum-and-the-Information-Accountability-Foundation.`)
- How can suppliers and workers/trade unions influence the machine learning process? (`http://www.thefutureworldofwork.org/docs/10-principles-for-ethical-artificial-intelligence/.`)

The answers to these two questions will determine the content of ethics by design. If AI internalizes accumulated knowledge about business and human rights and allows workers and local businesses to track its decision-making process, then it could promote labor rights (`https://www.bsr.org/our-insights/blog-view/remedy-against-the-machine-tech-and-human-rights`).

For instance, one of the demands of the UNI Global Union is that workers must have the right to access, influence, edit, and delete data that is collected on them via their work processes. Also, global trade unions and corporations should include the role of AI into their areas of collaboration. Additionally, multi-stakeholder initiatives that are alliances of global corporations, trade unions, and NGOs should pioneer this process to act as watchdogs for AI practices (`https://www.theguardian.com/technology/2017/jan/27/ai-artificial-intelligence-watchdog-needed-to-prevent-discriminatory-automated-decisions`).

A recent report by the House of Lords called *AI in the UK: ready, willing and able?* (`https://publications.parliament.uk/pa/ld201719/ldselect/ldai/100/100.pdf`, *Chapter 2*, page 58) states the following:

> *"It is important that members of the public are aware of how and when artificial intelligence is being used to make decisions about them, and what implications this will have for them personally."*

What about governments?

Over the last 2 years, many countries have released their official strategies on AI (https://policyatmanchester.shorthandstories.com/on_ai_and_robotics/index.html). This trend started with the US in 2016, followed by the United Kingdom (UK), Germany, France, the EU, Russia, Japan, China, and the United Arab Emirates (UAE).

These official strategies have many issues in common (https://assets.publishing.service.gov.uk/government/uploads/system/uploads/attachment_data/file/652097/Growing_the_artificial_intelligence_industry_in_the_UK.pdf). However, they also focus on specific aspects of the technological revolution based on their comparative advantages (https://ec.europa.eu/growth/tools-databases/dem/monitor/sites/default/files/6%252520Overview%252520of%252520current%252520action%252520Grow.pdf). For instance, the US places more importance on data-driven innovation; the UK concentrates on the financial sector and health services; Germany focuses on manufacturing, including smart factories and autonomous cars (also known as **Industry 4.0**); Japan aims to improve robotics; and UAE deals with AI in the public sector. Russia and China pay more attention to domestic surveillance and strengthening their military capacities.

One shared concern of these official documents is the fear of *missing the boat* as technological progress brings rapid changes in society that are likely to directly affect the global balance of power, military strength, economic wealth, and social structures (https://researchbriefings.parliament.uk/ResearchBriefing/Summary/POST-PB-0027).

For example, in the review of the UK's official strategy (https://assets.publishing.service.gov.uk/government/uploads/system/uploads/attachment_data/file/652097/Growing_the_artificial_intelligence_industry_in_the_UK.pdf), Wendy Hall and Jérôme Pesenti define this concern in terms of not being dominated by other countries. The solution also suggests a desire to dominate other countries, by taking advantage of leadership in the new technological revolution, and such an approach does not include any regulations or references to human and labor rights.

Thus, all these global powers focus on the areas in which they have a comparative advantage so as not to lose their superiority, or permit others to overtake them in these areas—with little regard to the human rights risks of these actions.

The common features (https://royalsociety.org/~/media/policy/projects/data-governance/data-management-governance.pdf) of these strategies suggest close cooperation between state, industry, and academia. For instance, states have all pledged to allocate billions of dollars in future investments and research projects on AI, and have offered substantial incentives both for global corporations and start-ups to invest in their countries. They are also encouraging universities to open new departments and research centers dealing with different aspects of the technological revolution and create new PhD and post-doc positions to attract the world's best brains.

In addition, authorities have promised to take the necessary measures to adapt the workforce to changing conditions, upgrade skills, and develop a curriculum for students to prepare themselves for dramatic changes in the labor market. Multi-stakeholder AI commissions (https://assets.publishing.service.gov.uk/government/uploads/system/uploads/attachment_data/file/702810/180425_BEIS_AI_Sector_Deal__4_.pdf) are formed to audit and monitor the process and deal with the expectations of stakeholders on a day-to-day basis. Since data is crucial for the development and training of algorithms, national data centers/trusts (https://assets.publishing.service.gov.uk/government/uploads/system/uploads/attachment_data/file/702810/180425_BEIS_AI_Sector_Deal__4_.pdf) are in the process of forming in order to verify and share data with stakeholders and prevent competitor states from accessing and manipulating the process.

The weakest side of these strategy documents is an inability to suggest any clear approach to the different sections of society, primarily workers and small and medium-sized enterprises. These strategies contain short sections regarding ethical concerns, but they are generally abstract, repeating similar concepts such as accountability, transparency, and complying with ethical rules. But official strategies should go beyond these wishes.

A clear approach to working with different stakeholders is crucial because governments are allocating millions of dollars to promoting AI systems and the planned actions listed will be conducted through close cooperation between corporations, universities, and states without any clear, legally binding ethical and social principles. For instance, what are the social and ethical preconditions and review processes for corporations to receive this government funding for developing AI systems? Without clearly mentioning legal requirements for accessing funding and for auditing processes, terms such as *being people-centered* and *worker-friendly technological progress* will remain wishful thinking.

In addition, while the strategies touch on the potential for AI systems to promote economic growth and wealth, there is no mention of fair income distribution. Some of these documents stress (https://assets.publishing.service.gov.uk/government/uploads/system/uploads/attachment_data/file/702810/180425_BEIS_AI_Sector_Deal__4_.pdf) that SMEs will have access to good quality data and benefit from the services and research findings of universities to promote their businesses, and that necessary measures will be taken to avoid unemployment (https://www.ijhrdppr.com/book-review-martin-ford-rise-robots-technology-threat-mass-unemployment/) through career support and skills training for people who are employed in jobs that are at risk (http://www3.weforum.org/docs/WEF_Future_of_Jobs.pdf). Finding jobs to avoid unemployment is important, but there is no mention of labor rights or decent working conditions. What kind of employment (https://theconversation.com/automation-robots-and-the-end-of-work-myth-89619) will be promoted (https://arxiv.org/pdf/1802.07228.pdf): short-term, self-employed, precarious working conditions, or decent working conditions with a living wage, freedom of association, and the right to bargain collectively?

So, the common approach of these strategy documents and guidelines on employees and SMEs could be defined as *wait and see*. It is clear that the consequences of the technological revolution (https://www.brookings.edu/blog/brookings-now/2018/05/23/artificial-intelligence-will-disrupt-the-future-of-work-are-we-ready/) cannot be fully determined or even imagined yet, so this might mean we are stuck with general concepts and wishes. On the other hand, policy-makers could set out a clearer, more detailed approach. There is already extensive literature on the gig economy, the ethics of AI (https://www.openglobalrights.org/as-artificial-intelligence-progresses-what-does-real-responsibility-look-like/), and debates on protecting people from discriminatory decisions made by algorithms in human resources (https://www.openglobalrights.org/artificial-intelligence-can-be-a-boon-for-businesses-but-can-it-protect-workers/), supply chain management, the judiciary, and the police. This is not only a debate about the future of work and society; it is a process that we are already living through and experiencing, making it imperative that new and ongoing debates, concerns, and demands be considered.

These government strategies set out the expectations and interests of large corporations (https://theconversation.com/automation-robots-and-the-end-of-work-myth-89619) and reflect a states' political, economic, and military strategies. However, AI strategies should not only reflect existing competitions, rivalries, and the future strategies of corporations and states. Members of society more broadly should have a say in what kind of future they would like to live in and how they would like to benefit from the technological revolution.

Therefore, at the dawn of a new technological revolution that is set to transform global supply chain management, it's high time we launch a debate about the role of AI in industrial relations. This is not just in order to stay true to the creed, that is, ethics by design (`https://www.bsr.org/our-insights/blog-view/human-rights-by-design`), but also as a requirement of innovation. Debate will help us evaluate and develop existing approaches, such as human rights due diligence, as promoted by the UN Guiding Principles on Business and Human Rights, so we can continue to make progress in this area. In this way, all social partners—including employers, workers, and other related entities, such as NGOs or state authorities—will have greater scope to collaborate in order to assess current and potential risks to employees within the workplace and take steps to mitigate them.

Who is Emre Eren Korkmaz?

As an academic at the University of Oxford, my research and consultancy areas cover new technologies (AI and blockchain) and international development with a focus on sustainability and human rights due diligence in the global supply chain, business and human rights, modern slavery and forced labor, and the decent employment of migrants and refugees.

I have worked as a consultant for various companies and NGOs, and initiatives such as the Ethical Trading Initiative, the Business and Human Rights Resource Centre, the Fair Wear Foundation, Amfori, and Anti-Slavery International on the decent employment of refugees and immigrants (particularly Syrian refugees in the Turkish garment supply chain of global corporations) and modern slavery issues.

I have been invited to many events of various industry stakeholders and organizations, such as the OECD, ILO, EU, BSR, and Amfori to deliver keynote speeches and training.

Robin Wright

Chief Architect, Cybersecurity, Microsoft

What was your career in before making the switch to cybersecurity?

My career has always involved some form of security and I have evolved as the industry has evolved. My career in IT security has spanned 34 years and has followed a natural interest and passion in the area.

Tell us about your journey transitioning from your primary career to cybersecurity as a career.

I have been very fortunate to have a career where my passion lies. I began with physical security electronic warfare in the **South African Air Force (SAAF)** and then embraced many roles in commercial IT. My natural interest and curiosity in computers and how they work has always incorporated security and challenged me to stay one step ahead of attackers.

Why did you choose a career in cybersecurity?

As an industry (and, more specifically, Microsoft), we saw an increase in cyber attacks together with a change in trends. Personally, I was interested in honing a specialized skill set and saw cybersecurity as both a business opportunity and an area for personal investment and growth.

What did you do differently than your peers when choosing cybersecurity as your career?

How I differed from my peers was my interest in security. I was continuously reading about it and completed my ISC ISSP certifications to broaden my knowledge. As an enterprise security architect, I integrated that learning into my job.

Can you please share your views and thoughts for those who want to be part of the cybersecurity industry?

The cybersecurity industry is seeing an increased demand for both generalized and specialized skills. It is not a vendor/product-specific skill that is sought after but rather a broader understanding and knowledge set. The landscape is continuously changing and evolving so it attracts individuals who can problem-solve and apply their learning to new challenges.

In your opinion, how is your old career helping you or influencing you on your cybersecurity journey?

I have evolved as the industry has evolved—I have always been in security and cybersecurity.

What would you like to suggest to our readers who want to start a career in cybersecurity, and how can they can do so?

My suggestion is to build a solid base that allows you to expand in this diverse environment. Firstly, explore—read security blogs, follow industry experts, follow vendor-specific websites, and then determine where you want to focus. It is also essential to do something that interests you and drives your passion.

Do you suggest that someone should be an expert in one vertical of cybersecurity or should they be an expert in every domain of cybersecurity? What is your opinion from an industry perspective?

Everyone should have a common body of knowledge. I always recommend the ISC ISSP certification. Choose a vertical but adopt the T approach, where the top of the T gets wider as you progress in your career and you gain depth in your vertical/specialty (the bottom of the T).

The cybersecurity landscape is ever-changing and extremely dynamic, how do you keep yourself updated? What are your suggestions for our readers?

I do several things to keep myself current. Daily, I review different blogs, Twitter feeds, and user groups. I also subscribe to RSS feeds and attend conferences and webinars. Here are a few key links:

- https://www.darkreading.com/Default.asp
- https://thehackernews.com/
- https://azure.microsoft.com/en-us/blog/topics/security/
- https://www.microsoft.com/en-us/security/operations/security-intelligence-report

In your view, what is more important, having a security certification, getting the relevant security training, or gaining hands-on experience through a job?

A combination of all three. There needs to be a balance. Certification gives you credibility, but you definitely need experience that's been gained on the job and through training. You should master your domain by training on tools and continue to develop your skill set. Another crucial area is the sharing of cyber intelligence and threats.

We all agree to the fact that cybersecurity is a non-negotiable factor of today's industry. As an industry leader, in your opinion, what are those new frontiers where cybersecurity will be needed in the near future?

Looking forward, there are two key parts. Today, we see that many organizations haven't got the fundamentals right, so it makes them soft targets for cyber attacks. Secondly, they need to focus on security hygiene—modernizing IT infrastructure, privileged access management and privileged identities, patch management, and reducing the surface attack area. As we go into the future, we are going to see an increase in multi-channel attacks that are going to be more difficult to defend against. We are going to see an increase in the adoption of AI and cloud-security providers and a move away from bolt-on security to built-in security. Traditional security controls will be challenged to deal with the evolution of cloud-based security and zero-trust security.

Who is Robin Wright?

Robin's current role is chief architect of cybersecurity for Microsoft Services, worldwide. He has over 34 years of experience in IT security and cybersecurity, with 17 years in Microsoft Services. As chief architect, he is responsible for the technical and capability strategy of Microsoft Services and the alignment to the Microsoft Product Groups and the Cybersecurity Solutions Group.

Before moving to the chief architect role, Robin was the service practice lead for the Cybersecurity Global Practice for EMEA and APJ Time Zones for 5 years. He has been responsible for building the Microsoft Services Cybersecurity Business in EMEA and APJ and supporting Microsoft Enterprise customers in the realm of cybersecurity.

In 2000, Robin joined Microsoft Services South Africa as a security consultant. While in the South African subsidiary, he worked primarily with customers and partners, striving to ensure that they gained value from Microsoft infrastructure and security solutions and technologies. Before joining Microsoft, Robin held multiple roles in the military and commercial space, in positions as varied as technician to company director.

Ozan Ucar and Dr. Orhan Sari

Founder and Chief Technologist of Keepnet Labs/Content Developer

What was your career in before making a switch to cybersecurity? Tell us about your journey transitioning from your primary career to cybersecurity.

Since high school, we were told to build up cybersecurity as a career, but we had no idea where to start as students. We read many texts and consulted some acquaintances to gather information regarding a career in cybersecurity and got some standard pieces of advice from the school counselor. However, during those years, developing a career in cybersecurity was complicated, because there were not many credible sources to get advice from. The lack of clarity, guidance, and real interest in cybersecurity continued to persist. So, we did not start our career as cybersecurity specialists. Ozan was occupied with studying math and getting an academic degree, and Orhan was on his way to being a professor of social sciences. However, we realized that we had an interest in cybersecurity and were exhibiting potential skills. Thus, we made a shift on our path to develop a cybersecurity career in which we managed to explore, learn, achieve formal qualifications and certifications, get university degrees, and eventually accomplish a position in cybersecurity.

The primary reason for us choosing cybersecurity as a career was due to a lack of experts in cybersecurity in businesses, as well as because it was a growing area. Cybersecurity is critical to the framework of any modern business. Today, every organization needs professionals in cybersecurity. Since there are many components and roles within cybersecurity, we especially focused on email security, because we realized that most breaches start with a single email.

Before Keepnet came into this process, we went through some other processes. In particular, Ozan, the founder and the CEO of Keepnet, took advantage of the experience by getting lots of practice and a background in shaping the Keepnet project. Before Keepnet was founded, Ozan developed a new-generation security wall with the first company he was cofounder of, Coslat Security systems. This company was focused on the detection and prevention of network-based attacks. After 2 years of gaining expertise at Coslat, Ozan transferred his shares to perform a new venture, leaving Coslat active in business with over 2,000 customers. Ozan continued his career at the BGA Information Security Academy as a manager, where he ran over 39 unique projects on cybersecurity, mainly on penetration testing, forensics, and incident response. With his experience and success in the cybersecurity business and markets, which gave him the opportunity to strictly follow the trends and easily apply appropriate solutions for cybersecurity, Ozan was able to see the risks ahead in information security. He started the Keepnet Labs project, which offers solutions to prevent email-based cyber attacks.

Then, with the assistance of the Keepnet team, we cooperated and developed a suite of solutions that prevented email-based cyber attacks such as phishing, fraud, malicious content, and attachments, and it continues to preserve safety.

Why did you choose a career in cybersecurity?

We chose a career in cybersecurity because the cybersecurity market was a flourishing industry with swiftly growing business opportunities, because the technology was improving and cybersecurity threats resulted in a demand for qualified manpower. It was clear to us that the world would face a shortfall of cybersecurity experts, not to mention that the salaries were also on the rise.

Even today, companies need skilled cybersecurity employees. According to research by ICS, 47% of people said that they were struggling to find qualified personnel in cybersecurity. Companies have said the shortfall of cybersecurity professionals is having a significant impact on their customers and 45% said it's causing more cybersecurity breaches.

Companies using digital technology put themselves at risk of cyber attacks. To lessen the risk and vulnerabilities, many organizations look for cybersecurity experts to protect their organization against complicated cyber attacks. Also, the shortage of more cybersecurity specialists becomes obvious when you look at the news. Every day, there is a new data breach and a hacking case appears, and most organizations understand that they need to do more to guard themselves against cyber attacks.

Moreover, the high salaries and bonuses of cybersecurity jobs were attractive to us; however, it was the love of the technology that attracted us to this field: the field was exciting, entertaining, interesting, challenging, relevant, and meaningful for us.

Furthermore, with its expanding scope and range, cybersecurity bestowed growth potential for our career and learning opportunities. We knew that we would learn new things over and over. We would work with brand-new technologies that were exciting. Those were the things that encouraged us to start a career in cybersecurity.

With the development of technology and its components, you begin to see various models of issues that cybersecurity experts can control. So, we wanted to challenge these problems and address these issues by identifying, recognizing, and understanding them. No kind of job provides this experience like utilizing the latest in technology, facing quick changes, seeing the creativity in many aspects, and participating in the never-ending struggle between good and bad. This was another reason we chose our career in cybersecurity.

We knew that we could help make the world a better place to live in. Because everything cybersecurity specialists do is intended to bring goodness to the world, to protect people from bad guys who would hurt them.

What you did differently than your peers when choosing cybersecurity as your career?

Cybersecurity is securing the **integrity, confidentiality,** and **availability (ICA)** of information. It is the capacity to protect against and recover from accidents and from attacks by criminals. Protecting information is vital for any business. We wanted a career in a field that will always be a top priority for businesses.

Moreover, as technology continues to evolve, so does cybersecurity. Therefore, unlike most of our peers, who built their careers on more traditional jobs, we chose cybersecurity as our career because technology never stops evolving; it dynamically changes.

Share your views and thoughts for those who want to be part of the cybersecurity industry.

Cybersecurity centers on protecting computers, networks, and data from illegal or unauthorized access. It has become more significant because every establishment today, such as governments, corporations, and even people, store or process data using cyberspace. However, data breaches occur almost every week. Organizations are now becoming more aware of the potential threat and they allocate greater resources for services that help mitigate such risks.

Due to the risks mentioned here, the cybersecurity market is one of the fastest growing markets in the business sector and has the potential for huge economic opportunities because steps need to be taken to prevent the escalating number of cybercrimes that organizations encounter every day.

It is obvious that the world is becoming ever more connected. Billions of smart machines and tools are producing huge volumes of data, which provides a critical opportunity for organizations to optimize their operations in a digital environment that both creates important opportunities and also important barricades; that is to say, getting digitized also brings potential risks for organizations. Mainly due to the evolution of **Internet of Things (IoT)** devices and new business models that largely depend upon digitization, as well as more complex systems and the interconnectivity of devices and information, the susceptibility to cyber attacks has become much broader, while there are gaps in the security systems of organizations.

As cyber threats have grown, spending on cybersecurity awareness training and defense platforms has increased. Currently, the security awareness training market exceeds 1 billion USD in annual revenue (globally) and is growing by approximately 13 percent per year. Vendors in the Gartner report account for around 650 million USD in annual revenue. By 2027, the market size is predicted to be 10 billion USD per year. Moreover, the major drivers of this market include stringent government regulation on data privacy and increasing cyber threats. Regulations and standards such as GDPR, PCI DSS, ISO/IEC 27001 and 27002, the **Federal Information Security Management Act (FISMA)**, the Gramm-Leach Bliley Act, the **Health Insurance Portability and Accountability Act (HIPAA)**, the Red Flags Rule, NERC CIP, CobiT, US state privacy laws, the Australian Government InfoSec Manual, PAS555 Cybersecurity Risk: Governance and Management, and Turkish Government Law #6698 on the Protection of Personal Data all require security awareness programs. This situation also gives a market opportunity for cybersecurity start-ups, as the *Cybersecurity Market* report illustrated that the cybersecurity market is expected to grow from 137.85 billion USD in 2017 to 231.94 billion USD by 2022, at a **Compound Annual Growth Rate (CAGR)** of 11.0 percent.

Security awareness training for employees is the most underspent sector of the cybersecurity industry. However, 91 percent of breaches start with a spear phishing attack. Therefore, the security awareness sector will become fundamental to cyber defense the strategies of Fortune 500 and Global 2000 corporations by 2021, with small businesses following shortly after that.

What would you like to suggest to our readers who want to start a career in cybersecurity, and how can they do so?

To start a cybersecurity career, you don't need a background in it. However, many people beginning their career in cybersecurity come from related areas, such as systems or information administration.

There are lots of positions available, such as junior penetration testers, for example, who have little work experience, and can acquire knowledge and learn while on the job. Still, experience is a significant advantage, even though you might not have enough skills. Thus, to start a career in cybersecurity, taking an internship or volunteering for an organization is necessary.

Besides this, you should be reading blogs about cybersecurity trends as much as you can to see the most up-to-date developments in the industry and stay up to date with the freshest cybersecurity tips, as well as follow cybersecurity industry professionals on social networking platforms such as Twitter and Facebook, since many of them produce some useful tips and points on social media by engaging in discussions and responding to questions. Engaging with people and building relationships with them is a great way to get into the industry. Therefore, go to face-to-face meetings wherever possible, or use LinkedIn for networking. Also, find conferences to participate in, because they are great places to start relationships.

To gain an edge in your career in cybersecurity, you should also be qualified, which will depend on your career path. You might need to concentrate on the following certifications:

- Network+ Certification
- Security+ Certification
- Certified Ethical Hacker certification
- **Certified Information Systems Security Professional (CISSP)**
- **Licensed Penetration Tester (LPT)**

Do you suggest that someone should be an expert in one vertical of cybersecurity, or should they be an expert in every area of cybersecurity? What is your opinion from an industry perspective?

Since cybersecurity is a broad domain, you can pursue your career path according to your own interests, because specializing in one area will give you an interest in going deeper and becoming more professional in your approach. For instance, at Keepnet Labs, we specialize in protecting businesses through the life cycle of email-based attacks. Specializing in protection against an email-based attack has led to us creating unique solutions in the market. People who want to build a career in cybersecurity can specialize in the following areas:

- Application security
- Forensics and incident response
- Information security
- Disaster recovery
- OS security
- System security (user level)
- System security (kernel level)

- Explicit encryption
- Explicit decryption
- Web security
- Browser security
- Malware analysis (static/dynamic)
- Network security
- Wireless security
- Android security
- IoT security
- Endpoint security

The cybersecurity landscape is ever-changing and extremely dynamic; how do you keep yourself up to date? What are your suggestions for our readers?

Overlooking cybersecurity advancements, trends, and reports can distance you from serious updates that could impact your cybersecurity career. Also, data breaches are more prevalent today, and the best way to stay ahead of cybercriminals is to know about the latest scams and how to fight them.

To stay up to date, you should read news and blogs online about data breaches and cybersecurity trends daily. There are plenty of platforms that provide information on cybersecurity. Just do a Google search to get them. For instance, Keepnet Labs creates weekly cybersecurity briefings to keep users informed about cybersecurity news and developments, with tips on how to keep people safe from cyber attacks. It is possible to get these briefings automatically by subscribing to the newsletter platform on Keepnet.

Also, it is important to follow experts on social networking websites such as Twitter, LinkedIn, and others, and routinely examine the news and reports for points on data security.

In your view, what is more important: having a security certification, getting relevant security training, or gaining hands-on experience through a job?

Many young people who choose cybersecurity careers are network engineers or network administrators. However, to be a cybersecurity specialist, you do not have to have these backgrounds; anyone with the skills and experience can build a career in cybersecurity. For instance, to start a career in cybersecurity, you don't have to have a computer programming degree. Nevertheless, you need both experience and certification for a business career. Businesses are aware of the need to have skilled employees when hiring, so they give great importance to certifications on cybersecurity as one way of picking their candidates.

To start a cybersecurity career, we agree that individuals need to have basic certifications. However, gaining hands-on experience through a job is more important, as people experience theoretical assumptions on a practical level, which will yield more perspicacity than certifications will deliver. Thus, as I mentioned earlier, to start a career in cybersecurity, taking an internship or volunteering for an organization is necessary.

We all agree with the fact that cybersecurity is a non-negotiable factor of today's industry. As an industry leader, in your opinion, what are those new frontiers where cybersecurity will be needed in the near future?

Cybersecurity is thoroughly connected to the fate of information technology and the advancements in cyberspace and the digitization of the world. Taking into account the evolution of cyberspace today, it is obvious that the industry will grow bigger in our individual and business lives.

With the development of IoT devices and other technologies, many critical systems today are interconnected and run by different machines. This situation will grow, the bond between devices will be even tighter, and solutions will be more computerized and automated. IoT devices particularly will be an element of practically every aspect of our lives.

However, the complexity and interconnectivity of these machines and systems affects their level of susceptibility. When we look at the big picture, big financial organizations and government institutions can be targets for hackers, despite the fact that they will continue to develop ways to defend against cyber attacks. Big financial organizations will be targets because they are accessible from every location in the world, and an attacker with the motivation of financial gain can attack from a distance. Also, governments will be at risk from enemy states who could launch cyber attacks anonymously on institutions of the target country to infiltrate the entire network or system for various purposes.

Hacktivists, terrorist groups, and states who are active in cyberspace due to the evolution of technology can pose a danger to the cybersecurity ecosystem, with different motivations. Cybersecurity defence systems will need to become more smart and sophisticated to cope with the new threat vectors appearing every day.

At Keepnet Labs, what criteria do you look for before you decide to hire talent?

Cybersecurity jobs are in high demand, and selecting the candidate with the best ability can be a hurdle. Once we get applications, we consider some important factors when selecting talent.

Experience is the primary determinant for us to consider cybersecurity talent. If applicants have expertise in related fields, they will stand a reasonable chance of success within our company, since they have proven that they have been successful before. It is essential for us to decide between an applicant with experience over someone without experience.

However, we know that experience, practice, and knowledge are not everything. Candidates who show potential can sometimes be more valuable than people who are more experienced on paper. Therefore, when interviewing candidates, we may meet people who look promising, but don't have experience. They may be new university graduates or people who graduated at the top of their class from an authorized university in the field. Those candidates haven't proven themselves at work yet but they have high potential.

One of the other criteria we look for is an applicant's skill base. Because, if applicants don't have the appropriate abilities, they have to get job training. For instance, we may require some certifications, such as CEH, CRISC, CISM, or CISSP.

Besides raw skills, we also look for soft skills such as communication skills, work ethics, and being a team player.

When hiring new talent, we also evaluate their dedication to developing their career in cybersecurity. We look for employees who are going to be faithful to our company, and who will see the job as a chance to develop their career and be a valuable asset to Keepnet at the same time.

Furthermore, one of the best methods to get the best talent for the job is hiring interns, because we can monitor their progress and skills and get to know them much better than in any interview.

Why should people join Keepnet? What career development opportunities do you provide?

We have developed unique and new-generation technologies that protect businesses throughout the full life cycle of email-based cyber attacks. We have developed a full spectrum suite of cybersecurity defense, threat monitoring, security management, and user awareness products that encapsulate an integrated approach to people, processes, and technology, thus reducing the threats in all areas of cyber risks.

We are committed to continuous innovation and the expansion of our suite of security products in order to meet the needs of a dynamic and rapidly growing networked population in a constantly evolving cyber-threat environment. Therefore, it is a great opportunity for individuals who would like to develop a career in email security.

Our cyber defense strategy adopts three holistic elements: people, processes, and technology:

- **People**: We focus on the human factor, using engaging, structured content to raise cyber awareness and engender active defense behaviors
- **Process**: We support the development and management of user security awareness plans, monitor user compliance and key performance indicators, and embed cybersecurity as an intrinsic part of corporate culture
- **Technology**: We scan and isolate malicious attachments and email content and provide system administrators with one-click management across the enterprise

Our internal corporate strategy creates a stimulating and innovative environment where the Keepnet team has the opportunity to continually enhance its skills and creativity while contributing to growth.

Keepnet Labs' solutions deliver a full-spectrum approach to mitigating phishing risks by doing the following things:

- Analyzing phishing attacks using AI and third-party integration for identification, notification, and the deletion of suspicious emails
- Safely simulating phishing attacks using a broad range of real-world models
- Automating malicious email management through one-click removal
- Providing education modules with third-party training platform integration
- Supporting user training and recording of training outcomes and compliance
- Delivering integrated cyber-intelligence reporting
- Cloud and on-premise implementation options

Our flexible technology implementation model means that we can scale from the smallest SME to the largest corporate organization using both cloud and on-premise implementations.

The *as-a-service* model is particularly attractive to smaller organizations without in-house security capabilities, as Keepnet Labs provides both the platform and the operational management of alerting, user training management, phishing simulations, and security reporting.

For larger organizations who may choose an on-premise implementation, we provide full support capabilities, including heuristic and threat intelligence-based updates to reflect the dynamic nature of the threat perimeter.

Keepnet Labs improves the overall organizational security posture and mitigates cyber risks by doing the following things:

- Real-time analysis and management of email-borne threats
- Threat simulation designed to test an organization's security
- Offering timely threat intelligence via a realistic, but safe, phishing simulation
- Supporting security awareness training programs

Unique patent-pending technologies

Keepnet Labs has two patents pending and is differentiated from other solutions by the following things:

- Its unique model of threat simulations, which allows organizations to safely test their email technical security perimeter
- Its user-initiated analysis and automated investigation and incident response
- The automation of hazardous email removal from all user inboxes
- The integration of user training
- Compliance with simulated phishing attacks and training materials

Keepnet Labs' competitors do not provide integrated solutions for each phase of email-based attacks, meaning that organizations need to implement multiple technology platforms to address these elements.

Keepnet covers all phases of email threats with unique solutions that are designed for each specific phase of the email attack chain and thus can stop an email-based attack before it propagates.

The multi-layer approach is shown in the following diagram:

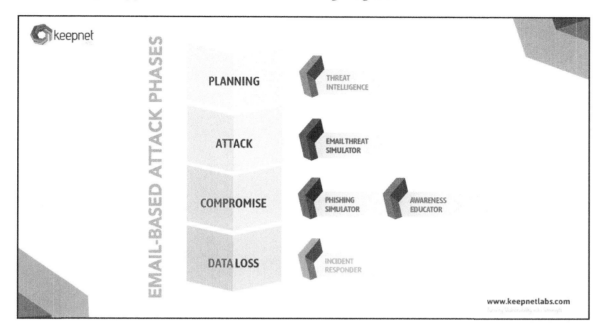

This multi-layer approach is the key innovative differentiator between Keepnet Labs and other competitors in the market.

The **Email Threat Simulator** and **Incident Responder** features are patent pending.

Keepnet Labs has five platform modules working hand in glove to provide a market-leading, holistic solution. The modules are **Phishing Simulator**, **Awareness Educator**, **Email Threat Simulator**, **Threat Intelligence**, and **Incident Responder**:

- **Incident Responder**:
    - Allows a user to report suspicious emails with one click via our Outlook add-on
    - Sends email content to our suspicious email analyzer for header, body, and attachment analysis
    - Creates a variety of attack signatures for alarm generation or blocking active security devices

- Integrated third-party service licenses—VirusTotal, Zemana Anti-Malware, Trapmine and Roksit DNS Firewall, Carbon Black, FireEye, Splunk, QRadar, ArcSight, and others
- Automated incident investigation on the client's inbox and active responses

- **Email Threat Simulator**:
  - Regularly tests your technological investments (such as firewalls, anti-spam, and anti-virus) by using simulation logic to mimic the attack vectors targeting organizations like yours through your email services
  - Techniques include email harvesting, domain squatting, vulnerability scanner, client-side attacks, malicious attachments, ransomware samples, misconfiguration, browser exploits, and file format exploits

- **Cyber Threat Intelligence:**
  - Scans the web, searching for signals and data that may represent a breach of your data security and therefore a threat to your business
  - The constant vigilance afforded to you by the Threat Intelligence module shortens the time between the potential data breach and a defensive response

- **Phishing Simulator:**
  - Simulates phishing attacks in a benign environment
  - Tracks user responses and reports
  - Quantifies vulnerabilities
  - Facilitates a proactive response
  - Customizable, scheduled, and self-service

- **Awareness Educator:**
  - On-demand cybersecurity awareness training
  - Automated in response to a failed phishing simulation
  - Comprehensive training content covering all current threat types and learning styles
  - Serious gaming integration
  - Granular reporting for total visibility

Who is Ozan Ucar?

Ozan is the founder and chief technologist at Keepnet Labs. He lives in London.

He has been innovating in the cybersecurity space since 2006, and in 2008 he cofounded Coslat Security Systems, a new-generation firewall technology that detects and prevents network-based attacks.

In 2010, he cofounded BGA Security, which offers a wider range of cybersecurity services to major corporate clients in his native home, Turkey, including cybersecurity training, penetration testing, forensics, and incident response. The company has grown to a team of 40 people and is one of the most respected cybersecurity companies in Turkey. In 2017, Ozan left his position as managing partner of BGA Security to focus on the development of Keepnet Labs' range of cybersecurity products.

Ozan holds international accreditations including **Certified Ethical Hacker (CEH)**, **Certified Security Analyst (ECSA)**, **Licensed Penetration Tester (LPT)** (Master), and Master Penetration Tester, **Turkish Standards Institution (TSE)**. He is well-respected within the industry and has attended over 60 national and international conferences as a speaker. He has collaborated on two books about cybersecurity and regularly blogs and comments on industry themes.

Chaim Sanders

Security Lead at ZeroFOX

What was your career in before making a switch to cybersecurity?

Unlike many professionals in the current field, I started my career in the cybersecurity industry.

Tell us about your journey transitioning from your primary career to cybersecurity.

By the end of high school, I had established my aptitude for computing, and security in particular. Like many students in such a situation, I was advised to seek a degree in computer science. Upon arriving at university, I was surprised to find out that they had started a dedicated computing security degree that very year. Given my passion for the subject, I enrolled in the new program which, after graduating, led to my career in cybersecurity.

Why did you choose a career in cybersecurity?

In short, passion. I had always been interested and practiced the topic before I realized that it could become a lucrative career.

Share your views and thoughts for those who want to be part of the cybersecurity industry.

The industry is not for the weak-willed. As a professor, I occasionally happen upon students or parents who will talk chiefly about the opportunity for compensation. While there is certainly money in the field, it is important to remember that cybersecurity is a constantly evolving industry that requires tremendous effort to master and subsequently remain up to date with. Without this investment of time and energy, failure—or at least failure to advance—is a very likely possibility.

What would you like to suggest to our readers who want to start a career in cybersecurity, and how can they do so?

Cybersecurity is a fantastically interesting and entertaining field that is just now starting to mature. Unlike other careers, its relative youth means that there is always plenty to learn, and new tools and techniques are becoming public daily. My suggestion is to get involved in the cybersecurity community. More than most industries, security provides for an open and nurturing community that is there to both teach you and empower you as you develop.

Do you suggest that someone should be expert in one vertical of cybersecurity or should they be an expert in every domain of cybersecurity? What is your opinion from an industry perspective?

Becoming an expert in one field is a common occurrence; however, the most successful security practitioners have a well-laid foundation of the principles and are able to speak to and, if needed, pivot to other areas within the industry. More generally, I find that most successful members of our industry have a limited few areas where they don't focus, rather than restricting themselves to just one vertical.

The cybersecurity landscape is ever-changing and extremely dynamic, how do you keep yourself updated? What are your suggestions for our readers?

Staying up to date should be an outcome of your love of the topic. This can involve reading the news, books, conferences, training, and more. I find that the more engaged with the community you can be, the easier it is to stay on top of advances.

In your view, what is more important: having a security certification, getting the relevant security training, or gaining hands-on experience through a job?

Without a doubt, hands-on experience is the most useful background to have when it comes to any job. Think about security as if it were driving. While sitting through a driver's education course and getting a driver's license is part of the equation, they simply indicate that you have the minimum set of capabilities to drive a car. It is the years of practice and experience that make you a good (or a bad) driver.

We all agree to the fact that cybersecurity is a non-negotiable factor of today's industries. As an industry leader, in your opinion, what are those new frontiers where cybersecurity will be needed in the near future?

I think we will continue to see a place for the traditional offensive and defensive security engineering positions. However, there are some areas that we, as an industry, have underperformed in. Two of the weakest areas are data analytics and development. Often, these two go hand-in-hand, either working on automating complicated problems or making new products. We can be sure that there will be continued growth and demand for these skills. The other area that is just starting to really take shape is a more involved role for technical security individuals in legal and policy matters. This is being driven both by recent regulations around privacy, such as GDPR, but also by third parties that require basic levels of technical security controls and auditing, such as via SOC2.

Who is Chaim Sanders?

Chaim Sanders is a professional security researcher, lecturer, and tall person. When he is not busy being overly cynical about the state of computing security, he teaches for the computing security department at the Rochester Institute of Technology. His areas of interest include eating food bathed in butter, and web security. Lately, his research has been focused around defensive web technologies. Chaim's sarcasm-driven approach to security provides a unique vantage point that helps him to contribute to several open source projects, including ModSecurity and OWASP Core Rule Set, where he serves as the project leader. You can find his personal website at `http://www.chaimsanders.com/`.

Yuri Diogenes

Senior Program Manager at Microsoft Cybersecurity Engineering, Cloud and Artificial Intelligence Division

The cybersecurity journey—where do I start?

If, in the past, the struggle to get into the information security (because it wasn't really called cybersecurity) field was due to lack of information, today, we have exactly the opposite: a tsunami of information. In the past, you just couldn't really find anything; it was almost like a dark market, and now it is fully mainstream. I believe that today's situation is much better from a self-learning perspective, as today you can easily create a lab environment to simulate attacks on your own machine, or in a cloud-based environment. Books are widely available, free online materials are usually of good quality, and there are far more target security certifications. So, if everything seems so good, why is it still so hard to start working in this field? I could give many reasons, but I will start with the two main ones: the level of competition and the (infamous) previous experience in the job. Let's see what can be done to overcome those.

An information security career has many ramifications, from a very specialized pentester to a security analyst who needs to know a variety of topics about security. This means that the first step that you should take is to perform a self-assessment and decide where you want to go in your career. What do you like to do and how can you advance in that particular field? This is an important point because, often, a professional decides what they will do based solely on the market's demand. Blindly following this rationale can be dangerous, because you might end up working in a field that you don't like, and that will have a negative impact on how you grow in your position. As a result, you will not evolve and, sooner or later, you will start looking for another job. Regardless of what pays more, you must be passionate about what you are going to embrace in your next career move. Some security professionals are already in this situation, having to work in an area of this field where they don't feel passionate; the rationale is the same: find your next career move by doing this self-assessment and discover what motivates you. Nowadays, everyone talks about *hacking, ethical hacking, cybersecurity,* and other terms. Don't let the buzz distract you; understand deeply what you want to do and pursue the right path for your next move.

Once you decide which path you will take, evaluate what you already have to offer. In general, there are three core components that you must assess regarding the field that you are going to work in:

- **Experience**: Do you have the required experience in that field?
- **Professional certification**: Do you have the professional certifications that are required for the job that you are looking for?
- **Degree**: Do you have a degree that will be helpful in that field?

This self-assessment is very important to allow you to understand your strengths and weaknesses. The goal is to ensure that, once you detect your weaknesses, you start working on a plan to fill those gaps. If the result of this self-assessment shows that you need a specific certification in order to be more competitive, then you already know what to do: study and obtain the certification.

A survey performed by SANS in 2014 shows that experience is a key factor for a better salary in the information security field. The same survey also reveals that certification is a critical component for career success in the information security arena. What should we conclude from this? Having both is the best scenario for a security professional. While experience is, for the most part, directly related to the jobs that you had in that field, you can also obtain experience by attending training conferences and helping your community. Initiatives such as Security BSides are available in many locations around the world. You could propose a presentation for one of their meetings or you could volunteer to work at their meetings. By engaging yourself in communities like this, you will gain knowledge and you will also expand your network.

I've been teaching the bachelor of science in cybersecurity and the master of science in cybersecurity at EC-Council University since 2015, and every year I have a good mix of students who are already in the market and ones who are brand new. What they have in common is that they are all pursuing a university-level degree in the field. I'm truly a believer in studying to your foundational knowledge about something, and getting credentials to validate your skills; credentials will be the most useful in this market. Keep in mind that credentials via certification or degrees do not give any guarantees that you will rapidly get a promotion (if you are already in the field) or a job in the field. What you need to understand and focus on is that there are things you have control over (pursuing a better education in the field) and things that you don't have control over (getting a job, for example). By doing your homework, you increase the likelihood of a positive outcome, so make sure you do your homework!

Now that you understand the general considerations regarding which path you should take, how to choose it, and the generalist/specialist dilemma, it is important to build your security foundation. If you are new to this area and you want to know what you should learn about security, the best advice is to obtain a vendor-neutral certification, such as CompTIA Security+. The current exam (SY0-501) is very broad, because it covers subjects such as BYOD, SCADA, Incident Response, and other topics that are relevant for anyone who wants to either start working in security or boost their security career by obtaining a vendor-neutral certification.

One of the advantages of starting with a broad certification in the security field is that you can decide which area you want to focus on in if you want to specialize in something; for example, after obtaining this certification, you might conclude that you want to invest more time and effort into becoming a computer forensics analyst. If that's your choice, you could start with **GIAC Certified Forensic Analyst (GCFA)** or EC-Council's **C|HFI (Computer-Hacking Forensics Investigator)**. The reasons that will lead you to choose one certification over another can vary; it could be job requirements, financial restrictions, and so on. It is important to research and to verify what certification will aggregate more valuenot only on your resume, but also your own knowledge. What you learn throughout the preparation phase is vital, because if you are going to spend hours and hours studying for an exam, you better like the subject and be very passionate about what you are about to embrace.

If IT is already a very dynamic field, information security is even more challenging, because it changes on a daily basis and one change can cause collateral damage in different areas. Be aware that these challenges can be overwhelming but they are also full of opportunities to highlight the quality of your work. As with anything you do in life, progressing in this field becomes easier if you are passionate, self-driven, and have discipline to pursue your vision of what you want for your career. Make sure that you participate and network with other professionals, because this will help you to identify areas that you can explore further and will offer real-world scenarios that you might not be exposed to if you are working on your own.

Last but not least, follow this simple advice and stay hungry for knowledge:

"The more I learn, the more I realize how much I don't know."

- Albert Einstein

Who is Yuri Diogenes?

Yuri Diogenes is a senior program manager at Microsoft C+ AI Security CxE Team, working with Azure Security Center, and Azure Sentinel. He is also a professor at EC-Council University for its master's degree in Cybersecurity programs and bachelor of science in cybersecurity.

Prior to working in this team at Microsoft, he worked as a senior content developer for Azure Security Center. He started in the content team in 2011, initially working as a technical writer for the Windows Security Team. Prior to joining this organization at Microsoft, he was a senior support escalation engineer at the CSS Security Forefront Team.

He has a master of science degree in cybersecurity intelligence and forensics from UTICA College, an MBA from FGF Brazil, and a post-graduate from UGF Brazil. Some of the IT industry certifications that he currently holds are CISSP, E I CND, E I CEH, E I CSA, E I CHFI, CompTIA, Security+, CompTIA Cloud Essentials Certified, CompTIA Network+, CyberSec First Responder, CompTIA Mobility+, CompTIA CySa+, CASP, MCSE, MCTS, and MCT. He is also a senior member of the ISSA, Fort Worth Chapter, and a writer for the ISSA Journal.

Dr. Ivica Simonovski

University of St. Cyril and Methodius

What was your career in before making the switch to cybersecurity?

Compared to today's cyber-teen generation, I spent my childhood counting fighter jets and tomahawks that were flying across the Balkan sky daily, praying the given coordinates were precise, guiding the tomahawks to the right targets. I took my first steps in the field of security at the Military Academy General Mihailo Apostolski, Skopje, Macedonia, studying aviation. As the first generation that was trained and educated according to NATO standards, luck turned its back on us. Due to the transition of the army and security structures, the entire generation of graduated lieutenants changed course from the military to civilian life. I started studying political science at the Iustinianus Primus Faculty of Law at the University of St. Cyril and Methodius in Skopje, where, in 2011, I successfully defended my doctoral dissertation in the field of politics and security. Earlier, in 2008, I started my career as an independent intelligence officer in the Financial Intelligence Office, a position I'm still active in today. My main duty is to analyze suspicious transactions related to money laundering and terrorism financing, as well as the implementation of international restrictive measures. Within the scope of my duties, I am a member of the National Committee for Countering Violent Extremism and Counter-Terrorism in the Republic of North Macedonia, the working group for *Chapter 24 - Justice, Freedom, and Security*, which has an obligation to harmonize domestic legislation with European legislation.

Tell us about your journey transitioning from your primary career to cybersecurity.

"It is not the strongest of the species that survives, nor the most intelligent, but rather the one most adaptable to change."

- Charles Darwin

Knowing and discovering the way in which criminals use cyberspace in order to generate proceeds of crime has imposed the need for its study. Only through such an approach can you understand the psychology of criminals, why and for what purposes they use cyberspace, what methods of attacks they use, and how they choose their targets. Naturally, I started independently by studying legislation, researching the norms and standards, as well as investigating cyber crime cases. I have to admit, the internet has played a major role in this. Afterwards, together with my esteemed friends, associates, and colleagues, we established the **Cybersecurity Corporate Security and Crisis Management Initiative (C3I)** in Skopje, through which we accomplished several projects concerned with building a cyber resilient society. C3I started cooperating with private institutions, especially financial institutions, through education and printing instruction materials intended for clients in order to inform them about the risks and threats of cyber crime and ways to protect themselves. There is a saying that if you are not able to share your knowledge outside, then you will not be able to share it at home either. I was elected an honorary member of the nonprofit organization Cyber Security Research Center – Global in Istanbul, Turkey, which is a unique research center focusing on the effects of cybersecurity threats on societies. For 4 years, I have been a lecturer at the Academy of Banking and Information Technology, where financial workers are educated and introduced, among other things, to cyber crime and security.

Why did you choose a career in cybersecurity?

Internet technologies become continuously more advanced, and so do the ways in which criminals utilize them for their illicit and illegal activities. Among these technologies, digital currencies are transforming the criminal underworld. They are also a powerful new tool for criminals and terrorist financiers to convert, remit, and conceal illicit funds from law enforcement authorities. There is a clear consensus that digital currencies pose a money laundering and terrorism financing threat. A small number of cases have already shown law enforcement agencies that money laundering and terrorism financing can easily take place inside virtual environments, offering high levels of anonymity and low levels of detection, removing many of the risks associated with real-world money laundering and terrorism financing activities. On the other hand, the introduction and distribution of new products into the banking system is an open field where criminals have found a solution to commit criminal activities and abuse.

The most common risks to a financial institution that offers e-banking services and users of e-banking services are internet fraud, harmful software, **Advanced Persistent Threat (APT)**, payment card fraud, and DDoS attacks on critical financial information infrastructure. These actions represent offenses in which the offender may acquire illegal profit. In order to conceal the source of illegal property (usually in the form of cash), the perpetrator puts the cash into the financial system and pursues a process of money laundering. The role of public and private partnership, which means cooperation between the private sector and law enforcement, is of great importance in the early detection of suspicious persons or transactions that deviate from daily operations. A public-private partnership must set up an ambush. They wait for terrorists and their supporters to make the smallest mistakes in order to reveal their identity and purpose. We always need luck to not get hacked, but hackers need it only once to break into a system.

My first task is to prevent cyber crime by setting up standards and legal framework, and thus building a cyber crime-resistant society. My second task is to detect, identify, and lead investigations related to cyber crime, money laundering, and terrorist financing.

What did you do differently than your peers when choosing cybersecurity as your career?

As I have said, I haven't made a full career switch, but a career update. I have never stopped my schooling and research. The study of an unknown subject (cybersecurity) required dedication, love, and desire to discover new things. By doing this, you acquire new knowledge that will make you more recognizable and competitive in the job market.

Can you please share your views and thoughts for those who want to be part of the cybersecurity industry?

Whether we like it or not, the environment itself imposes the need to keep pace with the development of technology, and therefore cybersecurity. Cybersecurity is a wide area. Certainly, depending on your background, you need to determine which area of cybersecurity you will be researching. To be more successful, focus on the area that will help you upgrade your career.

In your opinion, how is your old career helping or influencing you on your cybersecurity journey?

As I described, trying to understand the psychology of criminals in order to discover why and for what purposes they use cyberspace, and creating cybersecurity based on that, imposes the need for it. I will mention again that there is no old or new career here, but an upgrade of my old career. From a practical point of view, as a financial analyst, you will never find a criminal who, through cyber crime, acquired proceeds while using virtual wallets, currencies, and channels for transferring proceeds of crime.

What would you like to suggest to our readers who want to start a career in cybersecurity, and how can they do so?

The first thing they need to do is explore cybersecurity and focus on the area they feel will be able to help them with their career. Of course, further education should be carried out systematically, from studying norms and standards to exploring practical functionalities and ways of functioning. I am speaking from the aspect of detecting the financial crime that takes place in cyberspace, which, according to all surveys, is common among cyber criminals. Certainly, the main aspect is discovering the weaknesses of the internet and technology products, such as smartphones, tablets, computers, POS terminals, ATM machines, e-banking, and so on. Of course, all of these products and services are used by people. Do these products offer full protection of users' personal information, and how can personal information be stolen and misused (identity theft, phishing, pharming attacks, and so on)?

Do you suggest that someone should be an expert in one vertical of cybersecurity or should they be an expert in every domain of cybersecurity? What is your opinion from an industry perspective?

I already mentioned that cybersecurity is a wide area. It is not possible to be a cyber expert in the financial and the military field at the same time; these are two different areas. Perhaps upgrading the platform is common, but later they will have to redirect to the area they feel is most suitable for them, that is, in which they can build a career as a cyber expert. The development of cybersecurity is so dynamic that it is virtually impossible to explore both areas simultaneously. Or, in a nutshell, tomorrow makes a distant past of the present day in terms of the development of technology and the opportunities that emerge from it.

The cybersecurity landscape is ever-changing and extremely dynamic; how do you keep yourself updated? What are your suggestions for our readers?

The area of cybersecurity is a constantly evolving one, which raises the question of whether infinity is the limit. It requires continual reading and researching, following new trends and practices. This will enable you to observe and detect cyberspace's weaknesses, which can be used by criminals for their purposes. If conditions allow it, it is necessary to participate in seminars, conferences, workshops, and forums in which the main topic is cybersecurity.

In your view, what is more important: having a cybersecurity certification, getting the relevant security training, or gaining hands-on experience through a job?

Could you drive your car without a driver's license? Yes, if someone teaches you how to drive. But would you be able to recognize traffic signs, and would you acquire driving etiquette? No, because you need to pass the tests. It's the same with cybersecurity. Theory without practice is not functional. Practice without theory is not innovative. This means both are necessary to make a whole. I always say to my students that non-formal education today is just as important as formal university education. The formal education will give you the basis, but practice in correlation with non-formal education will direct you in a certain area of cybersecurity.

Can you give us an example of an organization that needs cybersecurity even more than others?

Definitely, yes! I will speak from the aspect of the financial sector as it is the sector most abused by criminals in order to generate proceeds. Virtual currencies have further slowed down the process of detection, monitoring, freezing, and confiscation. Therefore, the focus of cybersecurity within the financial sector is directed toward these aspects. Well-known cases such as **Carbanak**, **Mariposa**, and many others, where banks and their clients were directly threatened, only stress the need for enhanced cybersecurity in this sector. An additional problem is the lack of awareness of the risks posed by cyberspace. This is especially true for companies that are export- and import-oriented. Following investigations, they are the most affected at the moment. Their correspondence with foreign partners is often intercepted and modified by criminals, causing financial damage.

Who is Ivica Simonovski?

Doctor of political science at the Faculty of Law, University of St. Cyril and Methodius – Skopje, Republic of North Macedonia, Dr. Simonovski has almost 12 years' experience in the Financial Intelligence Unit as an independent intelligence officer. He is also a lecturer at the Academy of Banking and Information Technology – Skopje, Republic of North Macedonia.

He is the cofounder of Cybersecurity, Corporate Security, and the Crisis Management Initiative – Skopje, Republic of North Macedonia, and is also an honorary member of both the Cybersecurity Research Center and the Cybersecurity Research Center, Istanbul, Turkey.

Dr. Simonovski writes and briefs extensively on these subjects. He is the author and coauthor of papers published in national and international science journals. He is also the coauthor of *Countering the Financing of Terrorism in the International Community*, published by Peter Lang GmbH, Switzerland.

During his career, he has been a lecturer at the NATO Centre of Excellence – Defence against Terrorism in Ankara, Republic of Turkey, and the George C Marshall European Centre for Security Studies in Garmisch, Partenkirchen, Germany.

Dr. Mike Jankowski-Lorek

Database and Machine Learning Expert

Recommendations to cybersecurity beginners

Every year, there is a growing number of news stories about data breaches, cyberattacks, corporate cyber espionage, hacktivism, or cyberterrorism threatening organizations all around the world. That news is not only spreading across specialized websites, news channels, podcasts, or digital newspapers related to information technology, but reaching mass media, which is making cybersecurity a hot topic among everyone. So, it is not a surprise that more and more young students, as well as employees, want to have a career in cybersecurity.

IT employees are already in high demand as it is—adding in the element of security makes them even more sought after. According to ISACA, a nonprofit information security advocacy group, there is a global shortage of 2 million cybersecurity professionals already in 2019. Combine this with the predictions of the US Bureau of Labor Statistics that the growth rate for information security positions will be 37 percent greater than the average of other positions and we have practically zero-percent unemployment for those who choose this career path!

At CQURE, as one of the leading providers of specialized services in IT infrastructure security, business applications, and consulting and advisory services, with more than 10 years of experience, we noticed that trend a few years ago and started our own CQURE Academy, where we turn new adepts into security experts through a set of authored training.

Moreover, as a responsible organization gathering a group of enthusiastic and charismatic experts, we share our security knowledge, tools, examples, experience, and fun with others at the most important conferences all over the world. It has been during those events that, multiple times, we have been asked what the best way is to start a journey into the exciting world of cybersecurity. How can you boost your career? How do you follow the trends and learn about new threats and ways of mitigating them?

To answer those questions, you need to ask yourself what the current state of your knowledge and expertise is. Are you a rookie with no basic knowledge in computer science, or are you currently working in the IT field? It is important to realize that an academic background must not necessarily be related to engineering or information technology, although in most cases, that helps to understand how technology is used and to get a better perspective of the overall process of digital transformations in organizations.

So, what does it take to be successful in cybersecurity? It is all about having the right mindset, skills, and knowledge.

First comes the mindset. As a child, did you ever wonder how toys worked and try to disassemble them, or try to make modifications that would make them go faster, or do tricks that the maker did not design them for? Yes, that's probably what all of us did; yet some of us are lucky enough to be doing those same things in our work life. Whenever we get a new piece of software or we are in a new environment and someone is trying to convince us that it is secure or how it works, we simply don't take it for granted! There is no way we will pass by a chance of looking behind the scenes: checking the source code, testing different payloads, or sniffing the network traffic. If you ask someone *"Can it be done, hacked, or bypassed?"*, just don't take *"no"* for an answer.

This mindset, in general, will drive you through these new cybersecurity areas, and it is always inside us when we want to crack something, and we always want to be up to date. These two things drive us pretty much every day to discover something new.

If you are one of those people who likes to follow the news and likes to know more and more every day, and when there is something new coming up, you are like *"Oh, I didn't know that; let me dig in,"* then that's definitely an appropriate mindset. And, don't worry—it's not something that you can only be born with; obviously, it's something that you need to work on.

You must also pay attention to the details and be systematic and persistent. It takes lots of time, learning, and practice to advance in cybersecurity, as this field requires knowledge from many different areas.

This brings us to the second and third requirements, which are skillset and knowledge. While pursuing a cybersecurity career, you should become familiar with multiple domains:

- Hardware and software architecture
- Programming languages
- Cryptography
- Networking
- Operating systems

This is, of course, just a glimpse of what you should build a strong basis of for further development; a glimpse into many possible specializations as a security analyst, architect, pentester, auditor, secure software developer, and so on.

I myself started my career as a software developer, just to become a system and database administrator, and finally moved toward security. Every time I switched to a new job role, I was thinking how this position requires me to get broader knowledge from even more disciplines than the previous one; that is, until I found myself in the security space, where, now, I'm convinced there are no limits to the number of topics you can learn and benefit from.

Remember that, at first, you don't need to be an expert in any domain, and you probably will never become a cryptographer or a hardware designer, but for every security professional it is crucial to understand and connect many completely different parts of infrastructure and computer science.

From our experience, we have seen that the biggest breaches and successful attacks occur mostly through a combination of multiple misconfigurations, mistakes, and events chained together that, separately, do not pose a huge threat. It's the same with plane crashes—a single failure will not bring an airplane down, but a combination of many unforeseen factors may have catastrophic results. Our goal as security experts is to think out of the box and connect many dots together before someone else does.

CQURE specializes first and foremost in Windows-oriented environments, so we have been asking ourselves what the necessary sets of hard skills are that a security specialist working in this environment should have. We came up with 10 groups of these:

- Windows internals
- Managing identity and access in Windows systems
- Managing infrastructure services
- Securing Windows networks
- Application whitelisting
- Practical cryptography
- High availability
- Scripting and automation
- Monitoring and troubleshooting Windows systems
- Pentesting

When going into Windows security, you should start with the basics and core information in order to understand how your operating system really works, understand threads, processes and services, memory management, and how code is executed. Next, move to one of the key aspects of security—identity and access management—to get insights into permissions, access control, object protection, and system privileges.

After that, you'll be ready for core Windows infrastructure services, including DNS, DHCP, Active Directory Domain Services, Internal Public Key Infrastructure, and even the popular database server, Microsoft SQL Server. You should understand what the purpose of each of these is and the key security concepts related to them, as well as what the common mistakes made by administrators are and what to look for when you perform audits or penetration tests. These are the same things that attackers look for.

Network security and understanding the most important protocols used in Windows networking and common services is the next goal for you to achieve. Focus on protocols used to transfer data such as TDS, SMB, and FTP, and those that are related to name resolution and remote authentication.

When you already know how to work with Windows Server and its core services, it's time to focus on hardening workstations, as most common kill chains start by compromising the user's workstation. Understanding how malware avoids detection, spreads, and takes control of your system will be crucial for you. You also need to know how to prevent it from even starting by implementing successful application whitelisting and code-execution prevention techniques. You'll need some practical cryptography knowledge and to find out how to protect your precious data with BitLocker drive encryption. Moreover, get to know how Windows protects your secrets, passwords, and other content with DPAPI. Here, we are true experts, as CQURE Team was the first to fully reverse engineer the Windows Data Protection API and we made a few surprising discoveries!

You should already know how to ensure the confidentiality and integrity of your data and systems, but there is still more to learn, as the last component of security is availability: how to ensure that your systems are still working during or after an attack. You should be able to understand virtualization, failover clustering, and other technologies. At this point, don't forget about disaster recovery and how to prepare for the worst.

The next part of the skill set is making your day-to-day working life easier. You need to know how to become a real scripting and automation ninja. This will reduce the number of mistakes you make and give you more time to learn new stuff. You must understand how to use PowerShell, write your own scripts, use just enough administration for delegation, and automate everything with Desired State Configuration and Group Policy Objects.

Finally, we have the monitoring and troubleshooting of infrastructure. Proper monitoring and getting correct insights from your infrastructure without unnecessary noise will assure that an intruder will be detected quickly and easily stopped, or, in a worst-case scenario, after a breach, you will know how it happened so you will be better prepared next time.

Additionally, we would like to add penetration testing as a necessary skill group that's not only related to Windows. It represents knowledge about operating system internals, combined with various tools to exploit system services, vulnerabilities, and misconfigurations.

While we have been working with our customers and delivering other specialized masterclasses focusing on just one topic, we realize the need to define this kind of fast track to get new practitioners into the cybersecurity sector as it is expanding rapidly, fueled by the growth in demand from businesses who want to feel secure. We created an online 30-day intense course to give a really good set of ideas, insights, and core knowledge in all the aforementioned skillset groups. Up until now, this has been a great success and we are proud that many of our trainees have started successful careers and are progressing in the cybersecurity world.

So, you already know how you should frame your thoughts and what you should learn and practice. Now, there is the question of how to do it. First of all, find what your best way of learning is. Is it online training, an instructor-led on-premises class, or maybe reading books and watching video tutorials? It's up to you, but remember: you must practice thoroughly. Build your test environment or rent one in the cloud and get hands-on lab experience.

A great way to stay up to date with the newest technology or threats is to follow multiple security researchers, experts, and companies on Twitter, LinkedIn, Facebook, and YouTube. CQURE and our team members are contributing to the cybersecurity community on all social media, constantly sharing our knowledge directly from the battlefield against cyberattacks.

If you would like to know about useful books, I would recommend *Windows Internals* by Mark Russinovich, because it is a book that describes internals in a way that every cybersecurity professional should know. Although, at first, it might be difficult to keep up with the content, going slowly through the book and learning everything that you need to fully understand it will guide you to cybersecurity mastery.

In the end, it's a lot of work and it's a never-ending story. Yet, acquiring the right curiosity-driven approach will help you gain the right skill set, as in cybersecurity knowledge, the sky is the limit. Stay CQURE!

Who is Dr. Mike Jankowski-Lorek?

Mike designs and implements solutions for databases, networks, and management areas, mainly for Microsoft platforms. As for his day-to-day work, he works as a solution architect, designing and planning database-related solutions and software.

He is interested in big data, high availability, and real-time analytics, especially when combined with machine learning and AI or natural language processing. He is currently finishing his PhD thesis.

Judd Wybourn

Cybersecurity Consultant, Microsoft

The road to cybersecurity

Much like the adage *"the road to hell is paved with good intentions,"* so too can be the journey of a budding cybersecurity professional. The ability to adapt to varying environments and circumstances is key to anyone who is seeking to go down the path of a cybersecurity professional. The biggest learning factor through my career path in the security profession is that security can normally be trumped by a business's need to perform! This is normally a big blow to any individual that has the passion to secure a business, only to be halted at the next meeting, project review, development discussion, or just plain corridor talk, for many varying factors.

When I started along my journey, there were many things I had to learn, and I had to double- and triple-check to make sure I was getting it right. This industry has changed from a *no* business to a *let's make this work, however, securely* business. Whether you are talking to technicians, architects, managers, directors, or even end users, none of these people will quite understand the passion behind your convictions to get a product or environment as secure as possible – that is, until disaster strikes or it is looming in the background.

Knowing the limits

My first bit of advice would be to know yourself, and to know your own limits. There are plenty of individuals in the cybersecurity industry, and I haven't met one who knows everything. This field is miles long and plenty deep, all depending on which path you choose. The many facets of the industry can be very rewarding if you know what you enjoy and what will keep you going. Puzzles, challenges, mystery, intrigue, and even romance, can all be expected in this field, a cliché never the less out of a novel or even a movie, yet all these things can be experienced in a moment or over a period of time.

Forensics, compliance, breaching, testing, analytics, or even design, are all pieces of a larger puzzle that encompass this vast subject called cybersecurity. The question that most people ask when they hear about what I do is *"How can I get into that?"* or *"What should I study to do security?"* Many a time, I have been left pondering the correct answer to give, only to think about my journey to this career path. This can be a discussion that goes on for minutes or hours as I sit and describe all the exciting options that cybersecurity has to try to guide you in the right direction. Sometimes, it's a simple question of, do you prefer to read or watch movies? And, out of the those, what is your favorite genre?

This is a general guideline of where you could see yourself within the field of cybersecurity. The following are some of the exciting roles and brief descriptions that can await you, just to name a few:

- **Application security:** A continually growing field, with exciting challenges and tremendous rigor. This can have you thinking about software integration, development life cycles, vulnerability management, or simply how security will feature in the application itself. The ability to learn as the world changes around you and how to adapt to those changes will see an individual soar in this field.
- **Cloud security:** With all things moving to the cloud, the call to have better controls and security around this will be on the up and up. This is no longer a pipe dream, and the ability to make sure that all requirements are met for varying frameworks, laws, and customer requirements is a big must. IoT will be your best friend and will definitely challenge you.
- **Cryptography:** Does your mind work at a mile a minute? Can you make up secret languages, or decipher them quickly? Then this is where you would want to be. In a world where your PlayStation 3 can be clustered and used to break encryption (Dumitrescu, 2009), the need for better encryption and encryption methodologies are always welcome. This career path can see you working in top-secret organizations or defense contracts.
- **Forensics:** Your typical *who dunnit* scenario or murder mystery. Whether you go corporate or law enforcement, your ability to solve puzzles will be key. Sometimes, it will be as easy as spotting Waldo in a snow field standing alone, or as tough as trying to find him in at a Father Christmas convention. Your ability to do things methodically and with due diligence will be a great asset to you as you could be called to testify as a witness.

- **Information security:** Protection information while it is a rest or in motion can be called for in many regards, whether it be Yahoo's data breach of 3 billion accounts in 2014 (Armerding, 2018) or some small database from the local medical practice. Information is sacred to someone and can have dire consequences if it's in the wrong hands. Various industries have varying standards on how to protect information. Financial, personal, or just trade secrets, it could be your responsibility to make sure that it remains safe and secure from leaking. This could even mean that you deploy technologies to prevent leaks from occurring from within an organization.

- **Mobile security:** Nearly everyone in a corporate environment has a mobile device. These devices are powerful handheld computers that can be used to steal information, infiltrate a meeting, or just plain cause malicious harm to its end user. Companies require their staff to be productive while mobile, but not at the expense of information or access. Where alarming numbers of mobile devices are being left in taxis in the UK alone (Peyer, 2014), the potential of any of those devices to contain company data is very high. You would need to know how to secure and segregate company data versus private data on a single device and be prepared to wipe the device remotely if possible.

- **Network security:** Your initial start to this part of the industry can be slow, as many people will not let a rookie loose on their production environment. With different vendors in this space, you will have options to venture through, but as you master this technically, your expertise will be sought after and consulted upon for design and security considerations. Firewalls with deep packet inspection, direct access, VPNs, and even detection and prevention mechanisms of the data traversing in, out, and around your network could be controlled by you. You would be an information traffic cop, if you will.

- **Penetration testing:** You know the bad guys we are trying to protect systems from? Well, it would be your role to simulate those guys within known or unknown environments to try to ascertain whether there are known weaknesses on a system that could be exploited. Thinking on your feet to try and break into a system and get the data or the highest level of privilege possible would be your goal. You could use your smarts and code an exploit or simply your charm to get onto the system. However you do it, it is up to you, but the goal is getting access! As a penetration tester, you will help by finding gaps in the security already established for systems and thereby inform organizations or other security individuals about said gaps so that they can be mitigated before the system goes live.

- **Risk management:** This is about recording and tracking all known security risks to an organization. Even though this may not sound exciting, it is key to understand the potential threat or losses that could occur due to open risks. What is the likelihood of such an occurrence happening? Research and industry knowledge will be key here. This role is tied to business continuity and consultation on most security incidents.

- **Security analysts:** Breaches, false positives, events, and pages of data is what will await you here, for example. Trying to determine where a malware originated from, who coded it, or whether it was just a hoax. As an analyst, you can be part of the **Security Operations Center** (SOC) or an incident response team. Understanding data flow, methods of compromise, or just what looks abnormal, your in-depth knowledge will point you in the direction of potential or existing threats. This can very much be a detective role with a cowboy outlook, stopping bad guys at the source.

- **Security auditing and compliance:** Are you the kind of person who loves following the rules, and enjoys making sure that others do too? Well then, this role will suit your needs. Different frameworks, legislation, and standards are adhered to or must be followed through most industries and organizations. Things such as the Payment Card Industry for dealing with credit or debit cards, VISA, MasterCard, and Amex will adhere to the standards and require anyone issuing their cards to do the same. You will make sure that these frameworks are being followed and adhered to, making sure that the minimum level of security set by those standards, frameworks, or legislation is being used within the organization. It is when the rules are not being followed that the auditing comes in and brings this to the attention of the directors. Auditors can do manual or automated checks to help find these discrepancies.

- **Security operations:** This is your man-on-the-ground role. You may need to implement a fix to mitigate a problem penetration testers have found, close a gap discovered by an auditor due to non-compliance, or find a solution to reduce a risk that has been plaguing the risk management team. Welcome to the firefighting team. This role will keep you busy, and your learning curve will be exponential and rewarding. Though you might never be a master of a specific listed field, you can certainly excel in other ways. Things such as identity management, technical controls, centralized management, and deployment techniques could all stand you in good stead along your path. You will eventually deal with all of the cybersecurity roles to a certain degree. Your broad knowledge will have you challenging even physical security concerns.

The listed roles provide a glimpse of the skills or mindset you might require to fulfill those roles. Bear in mind that these roles could be fluid and ever-changing, adapting to the times and the situation you are in. Remember what I said at the beginning of this chapter: have the ability to adapt. Keeping that in mind, the industry has a lot of certifications to help aspiring cybersecurity professionals. The problem, is which ones should you take and how will they help you? This is another question that is asked of most cyber professionals, and there can be many opinions on the matter. I also know of many individuals that are not certified in any of the well-known certifications, but are, however, still very knowledgeable in their areas of expertise.

I would suggest that, depending on your level of knowledge of the industry, number of years in the industry, years of study, and, of course, knowing your probability to fall into a certain role, that you investigate the known certifications houses and see what offerings they have from beginner to expert level. See which appeals to you or where you would like to focus your interest. Also, look to the job boards to see the role you are looking for and what the certification requirements are, if any. Some certifications have a practical requirement, which requires you to demonstrate the knowledge that you have learned in a simulated environment over a standard test. Where possible, practice building labs with friends or family that have the same interests and learn; you will be surprised at just how much you will know after you rebuild that lab for the tenth time due to an incorrect security setting, or a failed simulation.

In my case, I had already been in the **Information Communications Technology (ICT)** industry for 10 years before my interests led to cybersecurity. Although security was always something in the back of my mind, it became more imminent when threats where causing late-night work and presumed on-call work. Viruses such as the ILOVEYOU virus in 2000, which brought down email systems, or the Conficker worm in 2008 and Stuxnet in 2010, really tested the resolve of cybersecurity teams.

Its through scares such as these and the needs of the organization I was in at the time that drove me to look to names in the industry and follow principles. When tackling any identity-related security, I always looked at principles of least privilege as a starting point, and, subsequently, the segregation of duties. Having a military background really helps with this line of thinking; however, it does not always translate well into every organization. Saying that, it reiterates my previous statement that flexibility is key.

Frameworks really helped to build the ground roots of my understanding, and each one can be quite different. When starting out, I shot straight for the US **National Institute of Standards and Technology (NIST)**, and this gave me a broad depth of knowledge that led me to find out about more frameworks to use, which were industry-specific. This included the likes of PCI DSS for all payment card handling, HIPPA for US health care and information handling, and PIPA for the handling of personal information in South Africa. Much like the foundation of a house, a framework can provide you with some of that foundation. However, these are just foundations; certain aspects can differ for various reasons.

The next step is to look to big names in the industry. Bruce Schneier was one of the first that I found that was useful, especially around the topics of cryptography. Then, many others will come to light and you will soon see whose style of writing and insights you enjoy. Try to follow these people on social media and visit their blogs and websites if you have that information. That said, the internet is full of information and helpful sites. Sign up to some threads around your topics of interest to see what's happening around the world. But, beware—you can soon find yourself inundated with information and not know what to read. Stick to reputable sources and keep it relevant to your needs.

Knowing your threat helps you to better focus on what would be required to protect the system. So, in those terms, when I was tasked with looking after certain bits of the business, I would focus all my attention on the means of delivering that software, the hardware it was on, and the methods of accessing it. To better understand the vectors of attacks, I learned to think like an attacker and went and learned about hacking. I achieved a Certified Ethical Hacking (EC-Council, 2019) certificate, and that was my first cybersecurity certification. My next goal was to achieve my CISSP (ISC2, 2019), as this was seen as the flagship certification to have in the industry. This was great to achieve at the time, as I had already had a lot of experience to my name. I also completed my masters degree in computer security just to enhance my educational background. The quest for learning in this field is always vast, and never dull. There is always something to find, even if it means you find out that it's a subject you don't like.

I have used my skills in different organizations and in different roles, each very different and fulfilling. I'm constantly learning and still, to this day, have a passion for the cybersecurity field. I always have a drive to protect the innocent from the dark side of the internet, as many, many people can be naive. Where possible, I like to make my knowledge available to those people, to help them understand the role of cybersecurity. I like talking to parents so that they can protect their children. The World Wide Web is just like the real world and has scary places to visit, and I always like to say that it has made the oldest crimes available in the newest ways; that is, you can rob a bank from the other side of the world without leaving the comfort of an armchair.

In closing, if asked would I do this again, my answer would yes be a thousand times over, as I love it very much. It is a great profession to be in and will be needed as long as the world progresses to move forward, where information will be valuable to someone at some time.

Who is Judd Wybourn?

Judd is a cybersecurity professional with over 20 years' experience in the ICT industry. He has a master's in computer security and various industry certifications. He currently works at Microsoft as a Cybersecurity Consultant, delivering solutions to customers. Judd has a big passion for protecting children on the internet and when he has the opportunity, he speaks about it to children, parents, and professionals alike.

Onur Ceran

Chief Cybercrime Inspector, Turkish National Police (PhD candidate)

What was your career in before you made the switch to cybersecurity?

My career started in the police, and that's where I am today. Actually, I was assigned to the Cyber Crime Department, because of my academic and personal studies, but that was not my choice.

Tell us about your journey transitioning from your primary career to cybersecurity.

I studied at the Police Academy and Computer Education and Instructional Technologies Department (at Gazi University, Turkey) simultaneously. My career started in the Turkish National Police in the IT Department in 2006. I worked at that department as an office supervisor. My responsibilities were managing all the infrastructure, including Active Directory, the network, the firewall, and so on. I was also attending basic computer skills courses for police officers as an instructor. At that time, I recognized that all kinds of crimes started to contain some kind of IT traction. For a simple example: at that time, bingo was as popular as gambling. It was being played in facilities that were formally operated as entertainment venues. The problem for gamblers was it was very difficult for them to remove all the evidence, because of its heavy weight, in the event of a police raid. After that, they started to use information technology. They were picking numbers using an application running on a remote computer and reflecting them onto a wall. It was easy to remove all of the material that could be called evidence.

The terms *pure cyber crime* (such as hacking) and *cyber-enabled crime* (such as online romance) were on the way. The first thing we, as police, are told is that *"it is more important to prevent a crime before it happens than investigating after it happens."* I recognized that cybersecurity was not just about technical issues; it is inter-disciplinary. Human factors, awareness, economics, and management are all related to it. So, then I got my MSc degree in information systems (at the Middle East Technical University, Turkey). Then, I was assigned to the Cyber Crime section and started to investigate. In 2015, I was assigned to the Cyber Crime Prevention Division at the General Directorate of the Turkish National Police. I started to attend meetings and courses on how to enable cybersecurity. At that time, I got another bachelor's degree at the International Relations Department (at Anadolu University, Turkey), recognizing the importance of establishing good relations internationally for information exchange for cybersecurity. I am a PhD candidate now and about to finish my thesis about cybersecurity awareness. To sum things up, my career is going the same way as it started, but has evolved into cybersecurity over the years.

Why did you choose a career in cybersecurity?

As I mentioned, cybersecurity is an inter-disciplinary area. You should take into consideration many issues while working in it. It also has a parallel evolution with the technology. The rapid development of technology causes changes in cybersecurity. I mean, your knowledge of a topic becomes old very quickly, so you have to read and practice more. It also prevents work from becoming monotonous. I like these types of challenges.

What did you do differently than your peers when choosing cybersecurity as your career?

I did not just focus on technology itself but also security. Security is managed against attacks on different areas of life. The reasons for attacks also differ. Sometimes, targets are governmental systems because of an international contention, sometimes, targets are financial departments because of money, and sometimes, targets are just innocent people, just for *"fun."* There is no silver bullet for preventing cyber attacks, such as firewalls, password policies, and so on. Hence, I am trying to study all the related topics.

What would you like to suggest to our readers who want to start a career in cybersecurity, and how can they do so?

I want to explain this in detail. I have been playing the **baglama** (a Turkish traditional musical instrument that is just like a guitar in appearance) for almost 20 years. My parents bought a baglama for my eldest brother in order for my uncle to teach him how to play it. He was not willing to play the instrument, but I was willing to play it. Then, I started to play it by imitating my uncle's finger movements. I was just following the sequence of finger-presses on the frets. I learned a few songs to play and expanded my repertoire. My desire to play baglama and daily practice made me play it better. But there was a problem. In order to learn a new song, I was dependent on my uncle. Because if I wanted to learn a new song he was playing, I had to imitate his finger movements. After that, I noticed musical notes. A friend of my mother, who is a music teacher, taught me how to read notes and apply them to the baglama. I was no longer dependent on my uncle. I could play new songs by reading notes. After spending more time practicing, I was able to write notes for songs that I heard and played by myself. Years after, I learned the **short-neck baglama**. The one I learned to play was a **long-neck baglama**. A long-neck baglama has 23 frets; on the other hand, a short neck baglama has 19. The chord layout is also different. At first, I thought, *I can play every song with my instrument, so why would I need a different one?* But after listening to performers using short-neck baglamas, I recognized that it was easier to play a song where I needed to move my fingers very quickly. I changed my mind and bought a short-neck baglama. The notes' positions were different, but it still had the same notes. The mathematics of both instruments was the same. The only thing I had to do was practice. Although it is not easy to play a song for the first time, by applying notes and doing some practice, now I can play baglama professionally. Now, I am almost 35 years old, and I can also play guitar, oud, violin, side-flute, and some percussion instruments. But I am not a professional player. (For the readers who do not believe me, please visit my YouTube channel and don't forget to subscribe and click on the **Like** button for the videos that you like.)

The period that I spent learning the baglama is almost the same with learning any other topic—and I think all of us have a similar story. There is a similarity between being a good baglama performer and being a good cybersecurity expert. But when they are compared, to be a cybersecurity expert is something like being an orchestra itself. In my opinion (there may be different opinions in literature), a **cybersecurity expert** is a top leader.

As a simple example: if you examine the job advertisements of big companies, you can see that the job titles are *vulnerability researcher, malware analyst, security engineer, penetration tester,* and another 30 or so on top. I think these job titles are each like a musical instrument in an orchestra. Working as a cyber-crime investigator and studying cybersecurity for academic purposes, I can determine the necessary topics:

- **Desire to learn**: A person who wants to work in a cybersecurity field should be a life-long student, even if they have got every certificate in the field. Information technologies are evolving rapidly and knowledge about one technology, which was just learned yesterday, can be old tomorrow. It took almost 38 years for 50 million people to have a radio at home. But it took just 9 months for Facebook to reach 100 million subscribers. According to statistics for the last quarter of 2018, Facebook has 2.32 billion subscribers, and taking into consideration how many times Facebook has changed its user interface and infrastructure, has added new features, and opened new platforms from its establishment, it is easy to see that there is no limit to what we can be faced with and what we should learn about cybersecurity.

A person who wants to work in the cybersecurity field should continuously read academic papers, books, and journals that relate to this field; articles on forums and the writings of people who have proved to be good in the field, from their social media accounts and personal web sites (the list can be expanded). This will allow you to both be updated and to be able to search for the correct keywords by becoming familiar with new technical terms and jargon.

Another important topic is to learn *why to* instead of *how to*. Anyone can learn how to configure a router by just imitating an administrator. But in the case of an update on a user interface (I am not talking about changing the router itself), you cannot handle *how to* configure it. You can easily adapt, even if the router has changed, if you learn why the configuration is done that way.

If you lose your desire to learn and try to learn *how to* instead of *why to*, you won't be able to switch from the *long-neck baglama* to the *short-neck baglama*. You'll get bored playing the same songs, and in the end find yourself getting cross with the instrument.

- **English:** This topic is so clear that it does not need to be explained. While writing these opinions, I searched on Google Scholar using the keyword `cybersecurity`. It returned 22,700 results from 2015 to the current date. But when I repeated the search with the same keyword in Turkish, it returned just 323 results within the same time period.
  English is just like musical notes that enable you to play any song that you hear. If you do not know how to read notes, you will always be dependent on another who shows you how to play a new song.

- **Computer sciences**: As I tried to mention, cybersecurity is a top priority and it does not sound proper to me when someone says *"I am a cybersecurity expert,"* because you cannot be an expert in all sub-fields of cybersecurity. But there will be some topics that a person is very good at and some areas in which the person is not familiar with a sub-field of cybersecurity. My recommendations for beginners would be the following:
  - **Data management and file structures:** Whatever sub-field we choose to be an expert at within cybersecurity, we always work with some kind of data. The basic questions that we should be able to answer are how a system defines data, computes it, where and how store to it, find it when needed, and destroy it when it's not needed. We will face all these questions in every sub-field of cybersecurity.
  - **Algorithms and programming:** We can examine this issue from two different perspectives. First, creation: processing and exchanging data becomes possible with an algorithm running through programmed software. The importance of knowledge of algorithms and programming in order to find vulnerabilities in information systems, networks, or software itself is so obvious. Secondly, you will be using some software dedicated to a sub-field of cybersecurity. Sometimes, you will face situations where that software won't be enough or even exist for what you are working on. For example, you might face some cases where you need to visualize data for someone who is not from a technical background, or the software that you are using (nowadays, a lot of software allows you to run your own code with it) doesn't meet your needs completely. Hence, even if it is limited, being able to write your own code takes you one step further.

- **Data communications and networking:** How does the internet work? What protocols provide security? Understanding networking is a core aspect of cybersecurity. As an example, IoT is very popular and defines a network of devices, such as vehicles and home appliances, which allows these things to connect, interact, and exchange data. If you don't understand the basics of networking, how can you analyze what data is sent from your IoT device? How can you secure the right protocol without knowing how it works? We will also face all these questions in every sub-field of cybersecurity.
- **Math and Statistics:** You will hear the *"computers work with ones and zeros"* discourse from anyone who is interested in IT. The way I say this is *"like every system in the world, information technologies work with math."* You can apply math from four basic operations to integral calculations in cybersecurity. In order to calculate how much MB your x bit data is, you use four basic operations, and in order to classify your log data, you can use a discriminant function.

If you learn the basics of playing, you can be a professional musician. Then, you can also play other instruments or be a part of an orchestra, where you can play in harmony.

- **Hands-on:** It is really hard to learn about any sub-field of cybersecurity without doing hands-on activities. You can find billions of YouTube videos or free PDF books online about the subject. But you should not confine yourself to just watching or reading. You can easily find tools for free or create your own lab for hands-on activities. If you want to learn web programming, then just install a web server, one database, and an editor, and by writing `<?php`, take your first step. If you want to learn about networking, then install simulation software and start dragging and dropping computers, routers, and network cables onto the stage. If you want to just calculate how many MB your x bit data is, then take a paper and a pen and start writing four operations. Don't be afraid.
If you do not take the pick in your hand and strike the strings, you cannot create a sound with a baglama, even if you watch thousands of videos on how to play.

Can you please share your views and thoughts for those who want to be part of the cybersecurity industry?

Actually, I can just share some of my experiences regarding who is working or will work in the cybersecurity industry:

- If you face a cybersecurity problem, don't always think that it is a technical problem and has a technical solution. Some (maybe many) of these issues are related to human factors. We can examine this issue from two different perspectives:

    - Attackers, who want to access systems without authorization, disrupt or destroy them, try to achieve their goals by using humans, who are the weakest link in the system. Research shows that 90% of cyber attacks start with a fraudulent phishing attempt, because a human firewall has many holes. Human behavior on information systems is affected by age, personality, and so on, and attackers examine these to reach systems. This makes it easier to access systems by using human rather than technical processes, which shows the importance of awareness in cybersecurity.

    - If there is an error in a system, don't panic, thinking that your system is under attack. I encountered an interruption on a local area network just because of a cleaning staff member seeing a connector lying on the ground (it was connected to a wire to a network face-plate socket on the wall). They unplugged it while cleaning and tried to fix it by plugging it into a free network face-plate socket on the wall, which caused a loop in the network.

- Never forget that we who are working in the cybersecurity field need to be one step ahead of attackers. Whatever design you make or policies you apply, thinking that you have taken everything into consideration, you will always miss something out. We will create systems and someone will disrupt it deliberately or accidentally. If systems could process as stably as they were created, then no antivirus software would need any updates.

- Days when you face resistance against your security policies will come. For a simple example, you will face a staff member/manager who doesn't want to use a password that must contain at least one uppercase letter, one lowercase letter, one digit, one special character, be at least eight characters long, and should be changed every 6 months without matching the previous ones. Sometimes, you will refuse to change the policy but, unfortunately, sometimes you will not. Whatever you do, just document it. Otherwise, when things go bad, the first person who will be accused is you.

Who is Onur Ceran?

Onur is working for the Turkish National Police as a chief inspector at the Cyber Crime Department. He is trying to make people security-aware, by attending cybersecurity awareness programs as a lecturer, and also fight against the bad guys in cyber-space. He holds the following qualifications: Police Academy (BSc), Computer Education and Instructional Technologies (BSc), International Relations (BSc), Information Systems (MSc). He is also about to finish his Doctor of Philosophy (PhD) in cybersecurity awareness. His research area is cybersecurity, cybersecurity awareness, information technologies, systems, data mining, adaptable learning, collaborative learning, e-learning, and m-learning. He has articles published in national and international journals and books.

He has attended many workshops, conferences, symposiums, and panels as a speaker to talk about cybersecurity. He has attended many courses to train law enforcement officers, and has represented his country on projects and in meetings about cyber-crime and investigations.

He is married to the most beautiful girl in the country and has a lovely son.

Neil Rerup

Chief Architect at Enterprise Cyber Solution Architects

What was your career in before making the switch to cybersecurity?

Prior to becoming a security architect, I was a technical sales engineer focusing on IT solutions. I was in that field from 1988 to 2000, and it was in that role that I was introduced to IT. My first company decided to start selling network test equipment and I was tasked with understanding the tools. But, without even understanding what a network packet was, that was hard. So, I learned about network protocols and my career in IT took off. I have always been learning about new IT technologies and, as a result, I have always been ahead of the curve.

Tell us about your journey transitioning from your primary career to cybersecurity.

I've been in IT since 1988, back when networking was getting started, but long before the internet came about. This was back when a router was used rather than a firewall and firewalls were just specialized routers. My initial introduction to IT security, as it was called then, was when Checkpoint came out with its layer 7 firewall, which introduced the concept of tracking where packet communication originated from.

I became a security architect in 2000, when EDS made me its very first security person in Canada. As a result, I've worked on pretty much every major project in Canada, and many in the US.

Why did you choose a career in cybersecurity?

Actually, IT security chose me. At the time, I was the senior NOC analyst for EDS supporting BC's Provincial Learning Network (PLNet), the largest public network in North America. But my job description had one phrase that said "...*and responsible for security.*" Well, at the time, EDS had a CEO by the name of Dick Brown who had this habit of sending out emails from various parts of the world saying how well the team in that location was doing.

One of our other projects' account managers had approached me about doing a security assessment of their servers, to which I said, "*sure.*" Having never done that before, I looked around EDS's world for the proper way to do security assessments. Around that time, Dick Brown sent one of his emails and I decided to jokingly respond to it. I wrote back, saying "*Thanks, Dick, for the email. By the way, where can I find out how to do security assessments?*" I didn't expect any response, but life surprises you. Dick forwarded my email to the VP who had just set up the IT Security team in Hearndon, Virginia, to support the NSA, CIA, and another three initialism organizations of the US government. That VP flew up to Vancouver to meet with me and, surprise surprise, I became EDS's very first security person in Canada (even before there was executive support for that).

What did you do differently than your peers when choosing cybersecurity as your career?

Becoming the very first security person in Canada for EDS meant that I was put onto every major project that EDS had. I did the security for the Bank of Canada's bond-selling outsourcing project. I secured the ScotiaBank's HR outsourcing project. I designed the security for the city of Calgary's web portal, back when web portals were just taking off. So, what did I do differently than my peers? Well, everything.

I was involved in the implementation of the first Federation solution at GM. I was the security architect for the Vancouver Winter Olympics. I've worked on security for the Smart Meter infrastructure for BC and worked with NIST's NCCoE creating reference architectures for the utility space. In short, I've been where very few security architects have gone.

And I've done this by focusing on the architecture component of security architecture. The vast majority of security architects are security people who deal with architectures. I am an architect who specializes in security. As a result, I'm a lot more versatile than most.

Can you please share your views and thoughts for those who want to be part of the cybersecurity industry?

Well, basically, I believe that security people now have forgotten why they are in existence. They believe they are gate keepers of the organization they work for and, as a result, put up roadblocks to most projects. They have forgotten that they are *not* the core business of the organization and, as a result, will often be viewed as people to be avoided, if at all possible. They tell people why they *can't* do something rather than giving them solutions so that they can move forward.

If you want to go into cybersecurity, keep in mind that, while you may find issues with what someone is doing, it's far better to provide a proper course of action than to simply just say *"no."*

In your opinion, how is your old career helping you or influencing you on your cybersecurity journey?

I have trained numerous security architects through the years and I have found, without fail, that the best architects (regardless of what domain they are in) come from the sales side of things. This is simply because they know to ask questions before proposing solutions. People that come from the technology side of things tend to jump to solutions before asking questions and understanding requirements. So, from my old career, I thank the fact that I learned how to ask questions.

What would you like to suggest to our readers who want to start a career in cybersecurity, and how can they do so?

My biggest suggestion is to find out more about what is going on before jumping to conclusions or solutions. I remember the first time I was working in an operations center and I saw what I thought was some sort of hacking attempt. I was excited and jumped to all sorts of conclusions, none of which turned out to be real. Take your time to understand what is going on and don't let your emotions run away with you.

Do you suggest that someone should be an expert in one vertical of cybersecurity, or should they be an expert every area of cybersecurity? What is your opinion from an industry perspective?

Going vertical or going horizontal all depends on what you want to do with your career. Remember that the further up you go, the more your expertise becomes a combination of business and technology. The higher you go, the more you focus on the business aspects and the less you focus on technology. If you want to become an expert in one specific area, that's fine. Just keep in mind where you want to end up.

Oh, and that doesn't mean that you have to try and move up the corporate ladder. I have a friend who I worked with originally at EDS, and he taught me that not everyone wants to move up the ladder. I could never do what he loved to do, which was Level 1 Help Desk. But that's what was right for him. Understand what you want to do and what you enjoy and go from there. Don't assume that what you want is the same as what others want.

The cybersecurity landscape is ever-changing and is extremely dynamic; how do you keep yourself updated? What are your suggestions for our readers?

The nature of what I do has evolved over time simply because the nature of security has changed. Originally, it was called IT security, then it became information security; now, everyone calls it cybersecurity, and that is simply because the breadth of security has changed as technology has expanded.

What I have learned is that you don't focus on the technologies. Technologies constantly change, and no one will always be an expert in every technological area. But if you see patterns of how to do your job, document them and then follow them. For example, the process of creating a design is the same, regardless of the technologies involved. So, try to get really good at following the processes you have. Remember, every solution is a combination of **people**, **process**, *and* **technology**—not technology alone. If you remember that, it becomes easier.

In your view, what is more important: having a security certification, getting relevant security training, or gaining hands-on experience through a job?

That's a chicken-and-egg question. When you first get into the field, every HR person is asking for your certifications. But after a few years, your resumé will speak louder than any certification you could have. You need certifications when you first go into a field, but then it's the experience that you pick up that moves you forward.

When I first got into security, back in 2000, I got my CISSP (I was something like 2,410, which tells you how few of us there were). I then got my CCNA (Cisco), CNA (Novell), MCSE, and CCSA (Checkpoint). But I let them elapse by 2005, simply because my resumé was so much better. I haven't had a certification since then. But I wouldn't have gotten started without them.

We all agree that cybersecurity is a non-negotiable factor of today's industry. As an industry leader, in your opinion, what are those new frontiers where cybersecurity will be needed in the near future?

I think that there are technologies out there that presently do not have network connectivity, but that will have. We commonly call that the IoT. As technologies become more and more connected, you will see more and more need for cybersecurity. But that's only part of the story.

Remember, every solution has three components (people, process, technologies). To just talk about technological changes is to miss the vast majority of changes coming. Every role will start to have cybersecurity built into them. Remember, security isn't the responsibility of any one person or team. It's the responsibility of all individuals. Making sure individuals understand security is going to grow in leaps and bounds.

From the process side of things, there's a real need to ensure that security is integrated into *all* processes in such a way that processes speed up, while at the same time ensuring that security becomes integrated into the way we do things. So, the audit and the operations side of cybersecurity will grow.

But one area that people forget is **governance**. I believe that there is a fourth component to all solutions, and that is governance. And I believe that the time will come when products that are networked will have to meet some sort of industry standard. Not ISO 27001, but something different (maybe ISA99—who knows?). But if you look at anything electrical, it has to meet CSA and UL standards of safety. I think the same thing will occur with cybersecurity.

Who is Neil Rerup?

I lead an architecture firm that provides architectural services (enterprise and solution) to enterprises across North America. I, personally, am an enterprise architect who came out of the world of cybersecurity. I have worked on a number of projects for enterprises around the world and have worked in various architecture domains, including security, networking, and applications.

My clients have been in various market segments, including, but not limited to, utilities, government, finance, forestry, automotive, special events, and retail. I've acted as an enterprise architect (providing strategy creation services and architecture leadership) to solution architects (creating solutions and performing architecture assessments).

My company focuses on providing fixed-fee *Security Architecture as a Service*. We are moving our clients away from a time and materials business model to one where they are purchasing the delivery of a security architecture deliverable using our standardized template and process.

Girard Moussa

Director, SAP

What was your career in before making a switch to cybersecurity?

My first job out of university was as a network engineer setting up switches and routers for customers. The company I was working for back then was also selling Checkpoint firewalls, and I was soon drawn into the security world! So, in reality, I was fortunate enough to start in cybersecurity in 2000, long before it was called cybersecurity!

Why did you choose a career in cybersecurity?

Cybersecurity is fascinating; it is like being on the superheroes team fighting the villains! It is continuously changing and never, ever boring. It sits horizontally across IT and recently it is discussed at board level and by CxOs across the globe. If you are someone who likes to learn and develop, then the cybersecurity field is definitely one to consider.

What you did differently than your peers when choosing cybersecurity as your career?

I started off briefly in the networking field and built a strong foundation in routing and switching, which really helps when you transition into a security technical role, as it provides you with a strong foundation that will make it easier to understand the different cybersecurity solutions and better troubleshoot any issues. I also sought to get certified in my first few years. I focused on the Cisco and Checkpoint certifications from a technical point of view and on the CISSP to provide me with knowledge so that I could have better discussions with CISOs. In 2003, I was one of the first CISSPs in my region, and this really provided me with a strong boost to my career. Of course, it's not all about the certifications and knowledge. You need to augment it with hands-on experience and practice. As I was working for a systems integrator, I was installing and configuring firewalls and other security solutions day in and day out.

There was a lot of self-learning. I remember spending sleepless nights reading up on Linux and Solaris as I had to configure servers and harden them to install the Checkpoint firewall. I invested a lot of time and effort in my learning and certification. Till this day, I love learning new stuff and since I am no longer in a technical role, I am now in sales. I love sitting down with smart technical people and having a discussion with them, asking them to break down certain concepts to a level where someone such as me can understand—cybersecurity for dummies.

Can you please share your views and thoughts for those who want to be part of the cybersecurity industry?

If you are reading this, then you are probably interested in cybersecurity. It is a fascinating field and yet so mysterious. Tell anyone that you are working in cybersecurity and their eyes will light up and they will start asking you *is it true ...* questions, such as *"Is it true our phone manufacturer can spy on us via our camera?"* or *"Can a hacker hack my Facebook password in seconds,"* and so on. No matter who you are talking to, they will be interested in listening to what you have to say. As a career, it is one that will always have you coming back for more. I have been in the cybersecurity field for 19 years, on and off, and I still enjoy every bit of it. The conversations I have had have really changed over the years, from protecting your organizations, the perimeter, to protecting users and data and mobile devices—and it doesn't stop there. You will definitely not have a single boring day if you choose to pursue a career in cybersecurity.

In your opinion, how is your old career helping you or influencing you on your cybersecurity journey?

I started out my career in networking, quickly moved into cybersecurity, and spent 6 years in a cybersecurity-focused role. I then moved into a sales role with less focus on cybersecurity. I then moved back into a cybersecurity-focused sales role after an 8-year gap. However, throughout those 8 years, I was always passionate about cybersecurity, and even when working for Cisco and Google, I always identified solutions that related to cybersecurity and led discussions with customers on those solutions. I had the knowledge and experience in this field, and this provided me with a lot of credibility and trust with customers, even though I was a sales guy! The 8 years outside of cybersecurity helped me to better appreciate security, since even when I was selling cloud applications at Google, guess what the first question would be? *"Is the cloud secure?"*. When I would try to sell a large end-to-end network at Cisco, one of the top questions would be *"How do we secure it?"*. So, no matter what role we play in the IT world, cybersecurity is going to be left, right, and center. My foray into the non-cybersecurity world made me appreciate cybersecurity even more and get a better idea of what customers have in mind when they say security. For some it is privacy, for others it is information security and governance, and for others it is even physical security, as in bodyguards and CCTV!

What would you like to suggest to our readers who want to start a career in cybersecurity, and how can they do so?

These days, you are fortunate to have a lot of resources, courses, and official university courses on cybersecurity. So, it all depends on which level of your career you are at and what you want to do in the future. You need to decide whether you want to be technical, pre-sales, governance, or maybe even sell cybersecurity (as I do). And then you can delve deeper into each area. The CISSP is still a great certification, I hear, and there are definitely a lot of other certifications out there. Find one that makes sense for you and pursue it.

Do you suggest that someone should be an expert in one vertical of cybersecurity, or should they be an expert in every area of cybersecurity? What is your opinion from an industry perspective?

The jack-of-all-trades and master of none! That is never a good thing, unless you are just a hobbyist. If you want to build a career out of anything, you need to focus. Cybersecurity is definitely a very wide domain these days. I would strongly urge you to get a holistic understanding, not very deep, across the domains and then choose one area to focus on and go deep into that area. The area you choose might be related to the solutions you are working on now, or that you want to work on in the future. But you can never learn one area in isolation. If you want to focus on IoT cybersecurity, as an example, you cannot just learn IoT cybersecurity and that's it. You will need to understand a lot about cybersecurity at a high level, and in some areas even at a deeper level, before tackling IoT. And the beauty with learning is that you don't have to stop there—you can learn more and learn different things. So, after a few years in IoT cybersecurity, you might decide that you want to do ethical hacking for the next few years. Put your learning hat on, leverage everything you have learned so far, and build on top of it.

The cybersecurity landscape is ever-changing and extremely dynamic; how do you keep yourself updated? What are your suggestions for our readers?

If you have been reading my answers so far, you will have noticed that I am all about learning. Keeping yourself up to date is just another way of learning. And luckily, today, regardless of how you like to consume knowledge regarding cybersecurity, there are endless resources out there, from websites to podcasts, videos, and tons of contents from cybersecurity vendors such as the *Cybersecurity for Dummies* free PDF from Palo Alto Networks. You can subscribe to newsletters, read websites such as `darkreading.com`, and listen to a podcast on your way to work. Another favorite method of learning for myself is to talk to my colleagues and friends in the cybersecurity world and ask them what's the latest, what they are working on, and so forth. You learn so much from speaking to other people.

I also do the same with my customers; they are out there talking to dozens of vendors every day, so I am always curious to know what the latest trends are from them and then go back and research them online. Attending conferences and trade shows can be valuable as well, as long as you take the time to talk with people and understand what they are doing and why their solutions are important. **Always Be Curious** (**ABC**), whether that translates into reading more or asking people around you more.

In your view, what is more important: having a security certification, getting the relevant security training, or gaining hands-on experience through a job?

Honestly, all three! We have a lot more time on our hands, even if we are busy, to fit in all three. Security certification is like a course: you go through it for a period of time and then get certified. So, it will keep you busy for days, weeks, or months, but then it is over and it will have been time and effort well spent. In terms of security training, those are usually very expensive, so if you get a chance to attend one sponsored by your company, make sure you do. Even if you believe you won't learn a lot of new things, you only need to learn a few new things. If you come out knowing 10 percent more than you did before attending the course, that is amazing! 10 percent more in 4-5 days! However, if you are technical or training to be in the technical field of cybersecurity, then nothing beats hands-on experience at work. Offer your services for free if you are a student, just so you can learn. When I was at university—a long time ago—I worked for free at a computer shop, just to learn how to take PCs apart and put them together, and then set them up again. I learned more in the first few weeks on the job than all the reading I had done in the past 5 years!

We all agree that cybersecurity is a non-negotiable factor of today's industry. As an industry leader, in your opinion, what are those new frontiers where cybersecurity will be needed in the coming future?

Cybersecurity is already embedded in everything we do as people and as organizations. Whether you are using Face ID to unlock your phone or sending an email to your manager, several layers of cybersecurity are at play to make sure each interaction is secure. As we all know, devices are all getting connected to the internet, and devices are already talking to one another and to us humans. Every aspect of our lives is being automated or turned into an on-demand service, whether it is catching an Uber to work, getting your car refueled, watching a TV show, or walking into your house. All these services will need to be secured, and attackers will always try to illegally access those services, devices, and information. Our children need to be educated about cybersecurity, and so do our parents and grandparents.

Cybersecurity is going to go hand in hand with any future technology, whether it is quantum computing, VR, or flying to the moon. So, there are no limits to where cybersecurity is going, but I can guarantee you this: if you pursue a career in cybersecurity, you will definitely have a lot of fun, and your skills will always be in demand, even if AI tries to take over the world, as we will need cybersecurity experts to protect us from the AI!

Who is Girard Moussa?

As an experienced IT professional, I've helped companies execute their business goals and grow revenue exponentially across the Middle East and Turkey.

I have over 19 years of IT business experience and have successfully established and run start-up businesses for large multinationals in the region, including Microsoft, Cisco, Google, and Splunk.

My focus and commitment is to leverage my sales and leadership skills to help our clients achieve their goals while ensuring my organization is achieving exponential growth.

Kaushal K Chaudhary

Executive Director IT and IS

What was your career in before you made the switch to cybersecurity?

I was heading an IT project in the Indian Navy before I switched over to cybersecurity.

Tell us about your journey transitioning from your primary career to cybersecurity.

While launching an application over a naval network in the Eastern Naval Command, the challenge was to protect information from unauthorized access. Knowing full well the implications of any loopholes, I decided to first educate and test the network myself before even seeking any external help. So, I learned ethical hacking and got myself certified by the EC Council. Then, I trained my team and secured the network before launching the application. I found the career to be very challenging, demanding, and fulfilling. As I was one of very few certified ethical hackers, I got support from my command to carry out security audits of many units. This gave me a solid foundation for my career in cybersecurity in the corporate world after my naval service.

Why did you choose a career in cybersecurity?

It was a transition phase from a manual to an automated work culture. The pace of digitization was picking up, and many channels of communication were opening. The security of data and communication was the prime challenge in the success of these products. I found the field of cybersecurity to be very demanding and fulfilling.

What did you do differently than your peers when choosing cybersecurity as your career?

Before taking help from any external vendors in securing my application and network, I thought of educating myself fully on risk and mitigation control. This gave me a complete understanding of the challenges and helped me get the most from the external vendors and experts. I volunteered for many initiatives that were required for a secure network. In this regard, my paper on indigenous firewalls was well appreciated by DRDO. The completion of this project under my guidance and appreciation by DRDO brought me to the limelight and gave me many opportunities to excel in my career in cybersecurity.

Share your views and thoughts for those who want to be part of the cybersecurity industry.

With the quick pace of digitization and the proportional threat of data theft or disruption, the cybersecurity industry is getting more traction than any other industry. Whereas security expenses used to be considered an avoidable cost, it has now become an essential element in any initiatives on digitization. Hence, there has been a paradigm shift toward the cybersecurity industry.

In your opinion, how is your old career helping you or influencing you on your cybersecurity journey?

For any career journey to be successful, basic knowledge and hands-on practice of the underlying technology is an essential ingredient. My old career gave me the opportunity to build up this foundation.

What would you like to suggest to our readers who want to start a career in cybersecurity, and how can they do so?

Thinking about cybersecurity is the first step. Then, in whatever way they are part of the digitization process, they should understand the underlying technology and the possible vulnerabilities. The gate to the next step will automatically be open.

Do you suggest that someone should be an expert in one vertical of cybersecurity, or should they be an expert in every area of cybersecurity? What is your opinion from an industry perspective?

After obtaining an understanding and expertise on network and endpoint security, they should look for vertical experience in one particular area, such as IoT, cloud security, or application security, and so on. From a job perspective, this would be preferred.

The cybersecurity landscape is ever-changing and extremely dynamic; how do you keep yourself updated? What are your suggestions for our readers?

There are many ways to remain updated. I am part of many groups and forums that are active on issues related to cybersecurity. I speak at these forums and listen to other experts. Speaking at such forums of experts and enthusiasts gives me the energy to learn more on the topic. Listening to experts provokes a thought process to learn more. Discussion groups are a good source of the latest information related to cybersecurity.

You should join or form such interest groups and start attending seminars on cybersecurity to remain updated.

In your view, what is more important: having a security certification, getting relevant security training, or gaining hands-on experience through a job?

Certification gives you the credentials for a job, whereas training and hands-on experience boost self-confidence. Hence, both are important for a career in cybersecurity.

We all agree that cybersecurity is a non-negotiable factor of today's industry. As an industry leader, in your opinion, what are those new frontiers where cybersecurity will be needed in the near future?

Cybersecurity is now part of everyday life and hence no frontier is left out. Because of the rapid automation of every aspect of life, be it in the health industry, transportation, or general governance, there will be an exponential increase in connected devices. The security of these devices is becoming one of the greatest challenges in the area of cybersecurity.

Who is Kaushal K. Chaudhary?

He has over 25 years of experience in developing IT and IS blueprints for organizations with short and long term strategies, in alignment with business objectives, encompassing IT operations, ERP implementation, help desk support, network and communication infrastructure management, vendor and service provider management, risk management, business continuity and disaster recovery planning, and compliance audits such as ISO 27001, PCI DSS, SAS70, HIPAA, SOX, and so on. He is a strategist, planner, and leader with the distinctive abilities to create value by forming effective customer relationships, coordinating with functional leaders, and mentoring teams.

He heads the IT and IS team as the group head of IT of the Lanco group of companies. He has an M.Tech.(CS-IIT), MBA, CISSP, CISA, ISO 27001 LA, ITIL, ISO 20000 LI, Dip in cyber law, and is the recipient of much appreciation from clients, employers, and industries, including having received the Greatest Corporate Leaders of India Award - 2013, the CIO100 Award - 2013, and the Top 100 CISO Awards - 2011 and 2013. He was given front-page coverage in the *CIO* magazine (September, 2013) and *InfoSecurity* magazine (August, 2013).

Will Kepel

Threat Intelligence Analyst, FireEye, Inc.

Why did you choose to move into the cybersecurity industry?

After graduating from CSU with a grad certificate in criminal intelligence, I landed a role as an intelligence analyst in the Child Exploitation Internet Unit of the NSW police force. I became fascinated by the cat-and-mouse game that played out between the technical strategies of offenders and the police. This is very similar to the dynamic between hackers and those seeking to protect computing assets. Additionally, the intelligence cycle itself is similar to the reconnaissance phase of a cyber attack. Shortly after leaving this role, I commenced my master's in information systems security (MISS) at CSU.

What did you do before moving into cybersecurity?

After working for the NSW police force as an intelligence analyst, I commenced a role as a content analyst at the Office of the eSafety Commissioner, which involved a take-down of child sexual abuse material online. This required tracing content to the hosting servers, and inspecting content for digital artifacts that could be used by police to protect victims and catch offenders. It was during this role that I commenced and completed my MISS.

What process (including a timeline) did you use to move into cybersecurity?

Before commencing the MISS, I completed the grad certificate in criminal intelligence at CSU in 2008, and in 2013 completed a Dip of Public Safety (Police Intelligence Practice). This study prepared me for the rigors of studying the MISS by distance, which I commenced in 2013.

It took me around 5 years to complete my MISS while working full-time. It took so long because I only undertook one subject per session, and also took a one-session break away from the course. This slow pace was necessary for me, as I did not come from a technical background, and so I did a lot more reading and preparation for each assessment task, which took considerable time. The session off from study was necessary to avoid burn-out. As a conclusion of my study, I began applying for entry-level roles in cybersecurity. I was extremely fortunate to have the assistance of IT masters at CSU, who announced my success at winning the MISS award for the highest graduating grade point average, to a wide pool of potential employers. It was only a matter of weeks after this email announcement that I received a number of invitations to interview. Shortly after, I accepted a position as a security consultant doing penetration tests.

What helped your move?

Performing well on my master's course was critical in securing a role. Additionally, being able to demonstrate an employment background in an analytical discipline also helped me past my lack of experience in technical roles. My strong academic background helped me perform well in the MISS, so my prior studies were also very important.

What hindered your move?

My biggest barriers to moving into a cybersecurity role were a lack of a computing undergraduate degree, and experience in technical roles. Every employer seems to want security experience, or IT experience at the very least.

The challenges of completing a master's level study in an unfamiliar field were also considerable. Studying by distance mode while working full-time in an unrelated field was very taxing. The first time I met one of my fellow students was at graduation. I never even met another student on the same course of study at exam time. This meant that I had no fellow students to bounce ideas off. Not working in IT also meant I had no one at work to seek guidance from.

Can you describe your current role?

I am currently employed as a cyber threat analyst for a multinational security company. In this role, I provide analysis to public and private sector clients regarding the threats posed by various threat actors. I provide intelligence on the **Tactics, Techniques, and Procedures (TTP)**, targeting patterns, favored malware, and so on, of different threat actors to drive clients to direct resources in order to combat the most likely sources and forms of attack. I am able to either work from home or the office.

With the benefit of hindsight, are you happy that you decided to move into the cybersecurity industry?

Since moving into the cybersecurity industry, I have never looked back. Being a growing industry, my opportunities are only likely to increase, and I'm not likely to be ever out of a job unless I choose to be. I am now able to work from home and take my children to and from school. I have never had more flexibility. I also have the opportunity to work in other countries if I so choose. The only thing that troubles me is the lack of gender diversity in the industry. Universities and employers need to become more creative to incentivize women to consider a career in the industry.

Do you suggest that someone should be an expert in one vertical of cybersecurity, or should they try to an be expert in every area of cybersecurity?

Although I'm still very new to the industry, I don't believe it's possible to be an expert in all domains of cybersecurity. You can become an expert of one or two domains, or even three (if you have no life), but I don't believe there is necessarily an employer demand for having knowledge of all domains. Roles are increasingly specialized, due to the time it requires to accumulate the skills and knowledge to even become proficient in a role, let alone master it.

In your view, what is more important: having a security certification, getting the relevant security training, or gaining hands-on experience through a job?

Employers seem to look for certifications that require a practical component. Multiple-choice certifications are often ridiculed, and I have found that it can be better to list no certifications than include these type of certifications on a resumé. Hands-on skills are highly valued, and should be acquired in any method possible. Universities could do a lot more to incorporate practical assessment tasks in their subjects, and market this to employer groups. I have known employers to favor a prospective employee's blog that demonstrates their hands-on skills over qualifications. They want to know that you can demonstrate the skills, not describe principles (unless you want to work in sales).

Is it feasible for students to move into the cybersecurity industry if they don't have experience working as a sysadmin or in a network support role?

It is feasible, but only for the exceptionally motivated. If you live by the mantra that *"P's get degrees,"* and have no sysadmin or network support experience, expect to be disappointed. I demonstrated with no sysadmin or network support experience that you can still master a body of knowledge with a lot of hard work. Also, demonstrating good writing skills in assessments is also important. I was actually requested to provide a sample assessment from my MISS in light of my lack of work experience. In my experience, short of having work experience, demonstrating the ability to acquire the knowledge through studies is the next best thing.

Who is Will Keppel?

I have recently joined FireEye as a threat intelligence analyst. I have 7 years' experience working in online investigations and intelligence analysis in State and Commonwealth government agencies.

I also have experience conducting penetration tests, vulnerability assessments, and physical security audits for both public and private sector clients.

Competencies: intelligence analysis, penetration testing, vulnerability assessment, and cybercrime investigation.

Martin Hale

CEO of IT Masters, Lecturer at Charles Sturt University

Background

In 2002, Microsoft and Martin Hale from the industry-based education company IT Masters approached **Charles Sturt University (CSU)** with the concept of building an industry-relevant master's degree. The target audience for the proposed master's was industry professionals who would study the degree online while working full-time, and the latest industry certifications would be an integral part of the master's.

The Master of Networking and Systems Administration was introduced in 2003 and the first of two cybersecurity masters' in 2006. In 2007, CSU became Australia's largest provider of master's degrees to Aussie IT Pros, and the latest enrollment figures show that the CSU has 115 percent more enrollments than the next largest university.

Getting a job in the cybersecurity industry

Up until approximately 5 years ago, I would have included **Cybersecurity Specialist (CSS)** in the same category as other specialist IT roles, such as information architect, or data architect and my advice to inexperienced applicants would basically have been *"good luck."* This is because employers would only consider experienced applicants for these roles, and the pool of potential positions was small.

However, the last 5 years has seen an explosion in CSS roles, which has meant that experienced people are either no longer available or leaving because they are being poached by other companies. This shortage has forced the employment of inexperienced and partially qualified applicants.

Process and timeline for getting a job in the cybersecurity industry

The first thing to understand is that CSS roles are high-end roles dealing with extremely complicated combinations of platforms, technologies, and threat landscapes. Even if CSS roles were not complicated, a mistake by a CSS has the potential to literally bring down a company, so employers will definitely only consider applicants with the right background and underpinning knowledge. The key underpinning knowledge is an understanding of how computer networks are structured, so my timeline for those wanting to get a job in the cybersecurity industry would be as follows:

- **Now:** Get a job in IT support. L1 IT support roles are a great learning platform for not just the technology but also dealing with users and management. L1 support positions are also the main pathway into the rest of the IT industry and because they have high turnover rates, there are lots of entry-level positions available.
- **In 12 months' time:** Get promoted into a network support, sysadmins position. Concentrate on positions with SMEs, because they are normally more diverse than large IT support shops, allowing you to learn and broaden your horizons and also give exposure to security. If you are going to a large IT section, make sure there is the opportunity to get widespread exposure and not be stuck supporting only a narrow subset of technologies.
- **In 18 months' time:** Start a comprehensive education or development program that covers all the major facets of cybersecurity. As pointed out earlier, CSS roles are inherently complicated, and you need to make sure that your program covers all the eight domains defined by the leading cybersecurity industry body—the **International Information System Security Certification Consortium (ISC2):**
  - Security and Risk Management
  - Asset Security

- Security Engineering
- Communications and Network Security
- Identity and Access Management
- Security Assessment and Testing
- Security Operations
- Software Development Security

What should I look for when selecting a cybersecurity education program?

Your choice of education program is extremely important. Some of the factors you should research before making your choice are as follows:

- **How much is on topic?** Employers are only going to be interested in what is relevant to the CSS, so make sure that most of the program you select is focused on cybersecurity
- **How current is the content?** The cybersecurity industry is evolving rapidly, and it is critical that the very latest developments are incorporated into the program
- **Does it include prep for cybersecurity industry certification?** This is not essential, but you can differentiate your resumé by adding less complex industry certifications, such as CompTIA's Security+ and EC Council's Certified Ethical Hacker

Attachment A describes how well Charles Sturt Universities' Master of Cybersecurity meets the preceding criteria.

- **In 24 months' time:** Start applying for cybersecurity roles 6 months after you commence your development program. Because of the chronic skills shortage, we have seen numerous examples where students have been employed while only part way through their degree.

Attachment A: The Master of Cybersecurity degree from Charles Sturt University

How much is on topic?

Depending on which electives you select, it is possible to study 100 percent cybersecurity in the Master of Cybersecurity degree from Charles Sturt University:

- *ITI581 Cyber Security Fundamentals* (`http://www.csu.edu.au/handbook/handbook19/subjects/ITI581.html`)
- *ITC578 Dark Web* (`http://www.csu.edu.au/handbook/handbook19/subjects/ITC578.html`)

- *ITE534 Cyberwarfare and Terrorism* (http://www.csu.edu.au/handbook/handbook19/subjects/ITE534.html)
- *ITC597 Digital Forensics* (http://www.csu.edu.au/handbook/handbook19/subjects/ITC597.html)
- *ITE516 Hacking Countermeasures* (http://www.csu.edu.au/handbook/handbook19/subjects/ITE516.html)
- *ITE514 Professional Systems Security* (http://www.csu.edu.au/handbook/handbook19/subjects/ITE514.html)
- *ITC595 Information Security* (http://www.csu.edu.au/handbook/handbook19/subjects/ITC595.html)
- *ITC571 Emerging Technologies and Innovation* (cybersecurity research project) (http://www.csu.edu.au/handbook/handbook19/subjects/ITC571.html)
- *ITE512 Incident Response* (http://www.csu.edu.au/handbook/handbook19/subjects/ITE512.html)
- *ITE513 Forensic Investigation* (http://www.csu.edu.au/handbook/handbook19/subjects/ITE513.html)
- *ITE533 Cyber Security Management* (http://www.csu.edu.au/handbook/handbook19/subjects/ITE533.html)
- *ITC593 Network Security and Cryptography* (http://www.csu.edu.au/handbook/handbook19/subjects/ITC593.html)
- *ITC568 Cloud Privacy and Security* (http://www.csu.edu.au/handbook/handbook19/subjects/ITC568.html)

By the end of the master's degree, you will have completed 1,200-1,500 hours of study in all the major facets of cybersecurity, except how to develop secure code.

How current is the content?

50 percent of the preceding master's degree is developed by industry-based cybersecurity experts who are working in the industry during the day. The other 50 percent is delivered by the university's outstanding pool of cybersecurity researchers.

Does it include prep for cybersecurity industry certification?

Preparation for the following certifications is included:

- *ITI581 Cyber Security Fundamentals* - Security+ (http://www.csu.edu.au/handbook/handbook19/subjects/ITI581.html)
- *ITE516 Hacking Countermeasures* - Certified Ethical Hacker (http://www.csu.edu.au/handbook/handbook19/subjects/ITE516.html)

- *ITE514 Professional Systems Security* - Certified Information Systems Security Professional (http://www.csu.edu.au/handbook/handbook19/subjects/ITE514.html)
- *ITE512 Incident Response* - Certified Incident Handler (http://www.csu.edu.au/handbook/handbook19/subjects/ITE512.html)
- *ITE513 Forensic Investigation* - Certified Hacking Forensic Investigation (http://www.csu.edu.au/handbook/handbook19/subjects/ITE513.html)
- *ITE533 Cyber Security Management* - Certified Information security Manager (http://www.csu.edu.au/handbook/handbook19/subjects/ITE533.html)

Studying Cybersecurity at Charles Sturt University, Australia

Who can pursue a career in cybersecurity?

Over the last couple of years, we have seen students from a wide range of backgrounds successfully transition into the cybersecurity industry. The one common thread with almost all of these students is that they have had a long-term *"interest in"* or *"passion for"* computing networking and security.

Is there an age limit to changing from a primary career to cybersecurity?

We have had students from their early 20s up to 50 years old.

Why should cybersecurity be chosen as a career?

The obvious answers are the wages and job security, but I think it would be a fascinating career because every day would throw up new challenges. The growing importance would mean that you have the opportunity to work with senior management.

What is ITM/CSU offering in cyberspace, and do you help your students find jobs?

We offer two master's degrees: a Master of Cybersecurity (https://futurestudents.csu.edu.au/courses/police-security-emergency/master-cyber-security) and a Master of Information Systems Security (https://futurestudents.csu.edu.au/courses/technology-computing-maths/master-information-systems-security).

The Master of Cybersecurity is designed for cybersecurity specialists, while the Master of Information Systems Security is designed for generalists with security as part of their job (for example, system administrator, IT manager, and so on).

However, our customers would not be impressed if we facilitated the poaching of their staff, so this service is restricted to students who are not already employed in the cybersecurity industry.

Share your views and thoughts for those who want to be part of the cybersecurity industry.

It's a fascinating industry that is on the cusp of becoming one of the major sectors in the IT industry. The growing sophistication of attacks and the devastating impact they can have on any company will mean that the CSS will become among the most important/valued employees in any company.

How is ITM CSU influencing a cybersecurity journey for their students?

Charles Sturt University (CSU) has (easily) the largest number of IT enrolments of any university in Australia, and cybersecurity is by far our largest IT research area. All of the students studying our Doctor of IT are studying applied research that is designed to make contributions to the international knowledge base.

What would you like to suggest to our readers who want to start a career in cybersecurity, and how can they do so?

See my recommendation pathway at the beginning of this document.

Do you suggest that someone should be an expert in one vertical of cybersecurity, or should they be an expert in every area of cybersecurity? What is your opinion from an industry perspective?

Students should definitely concentrate on a vertical because cybersecurity is far too wide for them to become an expert in every vertical. However, they should set up a development pathway that exposes them to all of the verticals so that they can work effectively and also have the option of moving between verticals.

The cybersecurity landscape is ever-changing and extremely dynamic, so how do you keep students updated? What are your suggestions for our readers?

- Obtain industry certifications such as CISSP, CEH, and Security+, and then update them as they get out of date
- Engage with cybersecurity industry associations

In your view, what is more important: having a security certification, getting relevant security training, or gaining hands-on experience through a job?

Nothing beats the learning gained from hands-on experience in the field. However, if experience in the field is not available, the next best option is a comprehensive education program that incorporates hands-on practice.

We all agree with the fact that cybersecurity is a non-negotiable factor of today's industry. As an industry leader, in your opinion, what are those new frontiers where cybersecurity will be needed in the near future?

I don't think I am qualified to answer that.

My work schedule is extremely busy; I cannot attend classes physically. Do you have a solution for that?

Both master's are only available online, and all of the students that are currently enrolled are studying part-time while working full-time.

How much does a master's course cost, for Australians and for international students? Are there any free courses?

The cost is AUD 3,250 per subject for domestic students and AUD 3,350 per subject for overseas students. Depending on how much credit you qualify for (https://www. itmasters.edu.au/am-i-eligible/), there are up to 12 subjects.

We have 10 free cybersecurity online courses (https://www.itmasters.edu.au/about-it-masters/free-short-courses/) that cover the first 4 weeks of one of our subjects. Passing exams in the course will qualify you for a certificate, and passing 3 exams will qualify you for credit into our Master of Cybersecurity degree.

See https://www.itmasters.edu.au/ and www.csu.edu.au for more information.

Ahmed Nabil Mahmoud

CISO, PGESCo

How can someone become a good information security professional?

Nowadays, organizations are looking for good security professionals, especially with the aggressive move to cloud technologies and full dependency on technology in all work aspects.

Based on my experience, I would highly recommend anyone joining information security to have the following:

- **Solid basic knowledge**: Always remember that knowledge is power. Solid basic knowledge is a must. Networking skills are essential for any information security professional. This knowledge includes TCP/IP, subnets, DNS, DHCP, routers, switches, and other networking general concepts. Completing the CompTIA Network+ and CompTIA Security+ certification and then moving to the CISCO CCNA Certification (CISCO Certified Network Associate) or equivalent knowledge is very highly recommended.

  The next step would be learning basic web security and penetration testing techniques and life cycles, which gives added value. I would recommend at this stage something such as eLearnsecurity JPT (Junior Penetration Testing). This is an online certification with practical hands-on experience and online labs geared toward junior and fresh information security candidates.

- **Soft skills**: Technical knowledge is not the only prerequisite, but soft and personal skills are crucial to success in information security. Complex situations or weird unknown problems that need real problem management and strong troubleshooting skills will frequently be faced. This will require patience and complete dedication until the problem is fixed or resolved. Other situations will require inquiring and interviewing key personnel, which requires a professional to be very analytical and organized. There are several workshops dealing with group thinking and decision-making techniques, as well as professional technical writing and presentation skills.

- **Focus on a specific specialty (your strength)**: Information security spans several areas, such as networks, the cloud, identity, mobiles, the web, applications, analytics, hacking, and so on. A career-oriented professional needs to pick one or two areas that they can master comfortably and focus on them. Nobody can ever cover all areas with the same level of expertise. Maximizing strong points is imperative. Always remember: *Jack of all trades, master of none.*

- **Linux versus Windows knowledge**: Any security professional needs to have basic knowledge of Linux. Most of the available hacking and penetration testing tools are based on a Linux distribution, such as Offensive Security's Kali Linux. Nobody will ever be a good security professional without learning Linux and understanding its main commands. It is advisable to go ahead and download a Linux distribution on a virtual machine and start playing with it. It can also be installed along with a Windows OS (dual boot) or run directly from a live CD. There are several resources and user forums on the internet that can help build your knowledge with Linux. Regarding basic Linux courses, you are highly advised to take the CompTIA Linux+ course as a start.

- **Programming and scripting**: Similar to Linux knowledge, all security professionals need to have basic programming and scripting skills. From time to time, some kind of written code will be needed. Python will be a very good start for any security professional. It is a very powerful tool and well-documented, with several sites and free resources. When getting more involved with software security, databases, and web exploits, you might consider other deep programming languages.

  Also, PowerShell would be an excellent start if you want to write small scripts and functions to manage your system and automate several tasks. Several free and online courses are available.

- **Professional courses**: All the aforementioned steps will lay down a solid career foundation. To move on to the next step, an in-depth professional information security course is needed. I would highly recommend going with CISSP from ISC2; this is a very in-depth, solid course covering most information security areas, and at the same time, it's a highly valuable badge when added to your resumé.

  Another different track that is considered a real professional practical hacking course is the Offensive Security OSCP (pen testing with Kali Linux). This is an online course where students can study on their own and practice online on the Offensive Security labs. To gain this certificate, a given number of systems need to be hacked within a specific amount of time.

- **Practice on your own**: Time and effort must be invested to gain experience. It is all about how much you are willing to spend learning and exploring new tools and techniques. Virtualization makes this easy. Now, a couple of machines can be created and used to simulate and attack a victim with different OSes and start applying the attack and pen-testing tools on the victim's VM. At any point, the old snapshot from the virtual machine can be restored and the hacker can start all over again.

My journey into cybersecurity

More than 25 years ago, I dreamed of learning and studying computer science and information technology; perhaps because I was the gaming expert in the family or the computer geek who could magically assemble a computer, format it, and build it from scratch. But my father had another vision, that computers and technology were still in their infancy and it would be better to study a traditional engineering degree to better secure my career. Accordingly, I picked electrical and electronics engineering as the closest path to technology that would allow me to switch later if this new green field turned out to be promising.

I joined the university and excelled in the electrical engineering field. I was top of my class and tried to relate everything to computers, picking most of the projects that required programming, or the ones with computer simulation and analytics, which is, of course, done through a computer.

During my fourth year at university, I got to know the world of information technology certificates and all the acronyms, and Microsoft MCSE was a dream and a kind of a passport that opened every closed door. I bought my first book (which I still have, somewhere in my library) and started the first step to get my MCSE (Microsoft Certified System Engineer) with Networking Essentials. In those days, you wouldn't go directly to Windows servers and networking/infrastructure configurations, but would first learn the network fundamentals and the underlying layers, through to the physical layer with all the cables and connections.

I graduated in the year 2000, with honors, and was hired as an electrical engineer in my current organization. Although I progressed smoothly in my job, I never really felt I was in the right position, being able to identify and unleash my full capabilities. Therefore, I took the decision to continue studying and working on my dream. So, in the first year of my career, I worked during the weekends (Fridays and Saturdays), studying and attending IT courses by CISCO and Microsoft, either at home or at the office, and attending courses after hours and during weekends. In doing so, I came across several challenging and interesting technologies. I passed all the necessary exams and I was an MCSE, finally. That is a moment I will never forget, especially when I received my certificate signed by Bill Gates!

The hard work paid off when, luckily, two members from the IT group in our company left and they were looking for a replacement, and my direct manager called me for a meeting and asked whether I was interested. This was my chance; I immediately accepted the offer and shifted my career to IT that very day. That is a decision I will never regret; it triggered my passion and energy, and even now, I am glad that I followed my instinct.

I progressed through all IT positions and technologies: from service desk; to networking; to system and application administration, including security, which was part of system administration at that time. If you were managing your domain, networks, and infrastructure, then you would normally handle the firewall and endpoint protection as well. There was no clear, fine line between IT and IS until computer attacks and hackers' actions started to impact the business around the world. I still remember the massive **Distributed Denial of Service (DDoS)** attacks that hit most of the domain names around 2003 and the world began to realize the threats posed by internet attacks and the possibility of getting disconnected from the world.

All organizations, especially the ones dependent on communication and collaboration, started to invest in security. That was the peak time for firewalls and concepts such as DMZ and endpoint protection/management, and again I was lucky enough to be on top of those efforts, managing, administering, and getting trained on the latest technologies to protect and safeguard our data and applications.

Hacking, internet attacks, viruses, and more significant methodologies continued to evolve, especially with the move to online transactions and online business websites, and companies started to invest more in web filters and advanced firewalls. I attended my first hacking/security course, which was CEH (EC-Council), which opened another door to the security and hacking environment. CEH will provide you with a basic foundation in different ethical hacking areas, which can be a good starting point.

I took all EC-Council courses covering forensics and penetration testing, and then I switched to the famous elite information security certificate CISSP, which again provided me with broad coverage of all information security domains.

During the 2012/2013 time frame, and with a lot of new regulations, laws, and governance programs, in addition to the new digital transformation initiatives, organizations started to have a dedicated **Chief Information Security Officer (CISO)**, and sometimes it was a mandate, especially in organizations dealing with public sectors. Based on my previous experience and certifications, I was the perfect nominee to handle and manage the information security efforts and digital transformation initiative.

I never thought I would get attracted to such a career and track. It's very challenging, dynamic, and rewarding at the same time. Feeling that people have confidence to ensure their data and main assets are protected and secured under your custody is the best reward. Being constantly exposed to the latest security trends and technologies always keeps you challenged. If I could summarize my journey up till now, I would simply say *"follow your passion."*

Who is Ahmed Nabil Mahmoud?

Ahmed Nabil has more than 20 years of experience in the field of information technology, infrastructure, systems administration/engineering, security systems, and IT management, and holds several professional IT certifications from Microsoft, Cisco, PMI, CWNP, and EC-Council.

Ahmed Nabil graduated from the Arab Academy for Science and Technology, Egypt, in 2000 with a BS in Electrical and Control Engineering. He completed his graduate education and earned an MSc in Business Information Technology from the School of Computer Science, Middlesex University, UK, in 2007, and an MBA from the International Business School of Scandinavia, Denmark in 2016.

Ahmed's real passion is infrastructure, cloud, and security. Ahmed is currently working as a PGESCoas CISO.

Deepayan Chanda

Cybersecurity Architect, Microsoft

Past, present, and future

The concept of information security can be traced back through the history of controlling information, as this has always been paramount. It needs no examples. Since the early days of the computer's existence, the need for securing the information they manage has been brought forward and has gone through an evolutionary process in the way we secure information and the mechanisms that handle and process information. One of the oldest examples that we can look at is the way the Roman dictator Julius Caesar secured his message transmissions. He used a form of transmitting encrypted information to his generals on the battlefield, which was impossible to decode by his enemies at the time. This method would eventually be known as the Caesar cipher, which is possibly the oldest known code. It was a substitution cipher.

During the twentieth century, technologies were born at an unprecedented rate. Even by the start of the twentieth century, the world was already getting flooded with the use of the most important inventions in history, telephones and radios; these two technologies would change the whole world in the coming decades. Suddenly, everyone wanted to make use of the new technologies, including individual citizens, governments, businesses, and especially the military. The telegraph/telephony and radio proved to be the most beneficial pieces of equipment that the military could have, from then until now. Even though these systems solved one of the major gaps in inter-personal communications, they had a major flaw in their design: the communication lines of telegraphs and telephones, and radio communication, could be tapped into and messages intercepted. This gave rise to the need to encrypt lines and radio communication, especially for the military.

At the time of World War II, the military was using methods that were similar to the substitution cipher, and they were easily breakable by cryptanalysts. There was a dire need for a strong mechanism to secure data before, during, and after transmission, so that even if radio signals were intercepted, which was a very common thing for the opposition to do, it couldn't be decrypted. This dire need then gave rise to the most complex data security method, with the help of available technology during the war. This machine was known as **Enigma**.

Enigma was a physical machine that was used to perform data encryption while typing a message, and used an electromechanical rotary mechanism to encrypt and decrypt messages before and after transmission; originally, these were devices for banks to perform the secure transfer of financial data, but the Germans started using it for all their war-time communications to send encrypted messages to their troops in the field. Just to give you a scale, Enigma had about 150 trillion possible combinations with a poly-alphabetic substitution cipher, meaning that a single alphabet would go through substitution multiple times to finally arrive at a substitution alphabet, and the same had to be reversed to get the original alphabet. This technology was literally causing the allies a lot of trouble to keep up with the war, and they were desperate to break the Enigma code. There were various attempts and various research done at the time to break the code. But eventually, it was broken by Alan Turing, in 1941, which shortened the war by 2 years. Alan Turing is also known as *the Father of Artificial Intelligence*.

During the last quarter of the 20th century, many new technologies emerged, and so did security concerns; at that time, security was only focused on physical systems and making sure no unauthorized personnel had access to them. Basically, locking down physical devices and systems, and only allowing certain authorized persons to access them physically was more important. But this scenario soon changed with changes in the technology landscape. Our early computers were single-user systems, and later, computers became multi-user systems that could be remotely accessed, which made security professionals rethink the approach toward the overall security of access to applications and networks by users. This gave birth to the concept of authentication—to access files based on the user and their need. This concept led to the possibility of a shared system. But this concept had a flaw, because it needed to be configured properly to give the right permissions to the right person, otherwise information leakage could occur.

This scenario became more serious with further advancements in personal computers. With the introduction of **Transmission Control Protocol** (**TCP**) and **Internet Protocol** (**IP**), the entire technology landscape was revolutionized and the computer industry was taken to a new level. And due to the existence of TCP/IP and other, newer client-server models, it was obvious that these systems were getting connected over the telephone network. This connectivity requirement was one of the main reasons why ARPANET, our early internet, came into existence in 1973. Even though, in the beginning, it only connected just a few universities, it evolved into today's internet. This primary requirement of interconnectivity to share data across networks brought new applications into existence.

As technology kept progressing at an unprecedented rate, it also gave birth to two important innovations, **Hyper Text Transfer Protocol** (**HTTP**) and the **World Wide Web** (**WWW**). After this, there was an explosion of new and innovative things. The internet became an essential tool for every business for information sharing. People were buying and selling things over the internet, and they were performing banking and other business operations. Even governments started communicating over this network, as it was now convenient. There was no limit to how much and what you could share, but again, one thing did not change: the sharing and processing of data—what changed over this period was the type of data and information. People started sharing audio, video, and images, and that became a part of our lives in the twenty-first century. This constitutes the new-age data, which is the fodder for cybercriminals.

The latter part of the twentieth century and the beginning of the twenty-first century was an interesting time. During that time, something new was introduced every day. While it was interesting to move at a fast pace, it also brought security concerns, which was struggling to keep pace with the rate of change. Applications and systems were appearing so fast that sometimes developers and engineers overlooked, or perhaps underestimated, the need to build them secure from the beginning. A whole new community of enthusiasts, individuals with good and bad intentions, started to come into existence, and they started breaking applications and systems where they could find any gaps or flaws, sometimes to prove their point that applications were weak, or sometimes just for personal financial gain by misusing a system or the data captured. The requirement to secure information systems was realized by governments too during the latter part of the twentieth century, and they started to come up with laws and regulations related to computer fraud and crime.

In 1983, after ARPANET was made available for public use with no restrictions and moved to new protocols such as TCP/IP, it brought a tsunami of technological changes that led to the emergence of new architectures. But this also brought its own perimeter security challenges. Suddenly, it was also evident that there was a gap in security architectures and that information could be exposed. Once again, military concepts helped, building virtual boundaries with a certain set of rules built into systems guarding the boundaries; whom to allow, whom not to allow. Basically, the focus was to position a gatekeeper around a corporate network boundary and interact via that gatekeeper with other outside organizations. This was named a firewall. These devices were simple packet-filtering appliances. The earliest firewalls, commonly known as first-generation firewalls, would often block or allow traffic by inspecting TCP/IP packets, based on the filtering rules defined on the firewalls.

These filtering rules can be applied in many ways, such as screening the source and destination IP addresses, the type of protocol, or even based on source and destination port numbers; it could even be a combination of those together. Slowly, firewalls made progress and evolved generation by generation. The following generations of firewalls brought in features such as application layer filtering; application-level firewalls will typically examine the stream of data rather than just the TCP/IP packets. These allowed the making of advanced-level decisions to act on packets when they were passing through these devices. Because first-generation firewalls never inspected application-level data streams, they were vulnerable to certain attacks and backdoors. Application firewalls can now be configured to inspect some known vulnerabilities and stop them.

With advancements in computers and networked systems, the need for identity-based access also increased. Because more and more web-based applications started popping up all around, this raised a never-ending need for the use of identity and access management systems to access applications over the internet. Early IAM was extremely complex, costly, and a maintenance nightmare. In the early years of 2000, as the need to secure online systems rose, this required IAM systems to become part of computer security. Slowly and steadily, IAM frameworks also started improving; the expectation from any IAM system was now to provide assurance about any identity with proper rightful access to resources, applications, and networks. By and large, all legacy and modern IAM systems depend on certain policies and principles:

- The way you identify resources
- What roles you assign to resources
- User management
- How IAM controls security and the access of data, applications, and location-specific access
- An IAM system should be able to enforce user rights and access rights
- Must be able to track user activity
- User activity logging capabilities for audit purposes, in real time and historically

With the boom in networked systems and applications getting connected all over the internet, the attack surface also increased. Perimeter security devices and mechanisms were not enough anymore. The industry now needed a system that allowed us to secure our systems, applications, and network proactively, in real time. We needed monitoring systems to keep an eye on attacks against our infrastructure. Implementing a monitoring system could be quite complex, as we needed to know what exactly we should be monitoring, where should we be monitoring, and which application logs we needed to ingest for the proper monitoring of anomalous behavior by applying log analysis or correlation techniques against known bad factors.

Security monitoring as we know it is one of the integral processes in the whole story of cybersecurity. Security monitoring provides any organization with the ability to detect and analyze events from the enterprise network, applications, endpoints, and user activities. This capability is core to the **Security Operations Center (SOC)**. Typically, the SOC has three elements to it: people process, and technology. While the technology helps drive the monitoring of assets such as networks, applications, endpoints, servers, web applications, and various other systems, and generates alerts through automatic correlation and analysis, people in SOCs focus on validating these alerts manually and try to make sense out of them, to further carry out the response process to identify threats and provide detailed information to remediation teams. All modern SOCs these days also tend to integrate the digital forensics process and malware reverse engineering too. Any SOC will have seasoned security analysts as one of its important assets.

The range of cyber attacks and their sophistication is on the rise today. All recent attacks have been successful in bypassing existing security solutions, traditional or advanced. These attacks were successful because they were able to hide within the legitimate realm of our network and infrastructure. Our current security solutions are designed to detect threats based on scanning for known issues, filtering, or dropping bad actors, or even trying to monitor identity and user habits, and so on, but these things are not able to deter attacks. The primary reason is that these are still focused on reacting to a security event, responding to the security findings of security events that have happened, and lastly, planning for how to recover from them. In other words, its a **reactive security response**. A reactive response is good, but does not hold ground to a level where it can compete with the advanced attacks of today. We need to redirect our focus toward a **proactive security response**, and the industry today is moving from a reactive to proactive security response already. This is a paradigm shift in security frameworks and methodologies on how we predict, analyze, and respond to threats. Unlike in a reactive form of security response, proactive methodologies provide greater in-depth visibility into the attack infrastructure. Simply put, a proactive method is to approach from an attacker's view of the attack surface and try to predict attacks in advance and apply proper measures.

As the logic goes, a reactive security response model is the mindset of *"if and when there is an attack, the systems and security analysts will respond to it."* It's about laying a trap with known attack parameters and methods and waiting for the monitoring and detection systems to react to it. In a reactive form, the attention is always given to form a strong perimeter defense to thwart attacks that attempt to penetrate the network. This form of security is very much localized to the business unit and its activities, and it does not take advantage of attacks of a similar nature, against another business or industry verticals. Reactive security does not provide a 360° view of the threat landscape but a reactive way of achieving security operations is always simpler, faster to bring up, and has lower operational costs. Reactive security monitoring can be further enhanced with data feeds from antivirus detection systems, vulnerability scanners, and, at times, DLP systems. The flip side of such a model is that it will always react to security detection after a breach or compromise has occurred.

But proactive security monitoring and responses win over this scenario. It is an intelligence-driven model, where the system is enriched with actionable intelligence data, from multiple internal and external sources, working in line with existing real-time monitoring systems. This proactive method will have visibility of the entire threat landscape and all phases of the cyber kill chain, and not just focus on one or partial phases of the kill chain. One of the key aspects of proactive security is threat hunting, which allows analysts to get more insights into the network and systems by trying to uncover any anomalies, or any abnormal changes in network behavior, any presence of known bad files in the systems, or maybe there are some registry entries that can be found from previously known attacks. As an analyst, you can also look for known **indicators of compromise** (**IOCs**) in the network. Threat hunting is a continuous process and will always involve trying to look for a new set of information as received from threat intelligence sources. Threat hunting can also be done automatically by looking into network behavior, system anomalies, timeline analysis of certain events, looking into the baseline data of the network and the system for a period, and so on.

Today, every organization is extremely worried about the data it holds and how to secure it. Sensitiveness toward data is at an all-time high. In our efforts to keep data safe and be proactive in detecting any threats toward it, we must have proper and effective threat intelligence in place. Threat intelligence can be achieved by acquiring specific threat information (intelligence) about various systems, processes, networks, applications, perimeter defense mechanisms, and other IT assets. This data is then collected, analyzed, and enriched to provide proactive and actionable threat intelligence. One of the reasons threat intelligence is so important is because current threats are highly sophisticated and difficult to detect. We must acquire very specific information and perform a search for signs of compromise with actionable content from any threat intel source. To stay ahead of advanced threats, it is essential that we feed our analytic and correlation systems with proper threat data.

Any effective and mature threat intelligence system must be able to collect and categorize threat information in real time to produce actionable threat intelligence for the SIEM and incident response systems to analyze and correlate the collected threat information with the security alerts and events it is monitoring. These threat alerts from the threat intel system will also empower SOC professionals to create custom signatures for further detection. Threat intelligence systems gather various pieces of information related to incidents, events, logs, security vulnerabilities, recent and past known attack data, detection data from the security and network devices of the organization, along with information from external threat feeds. You can also set up a honey pot system to collect attack information and use it as threat data. All data collection needs to be focused and meaningful for the organization that intends to use it, because every business is different, with distinct needs and types of infrastructure. For threat intelligence to be effective, the collection of intelligence data must be done in a centralized manner, as systems collect threats and vulnerability information from a wide range of locations and devices to correlate data. You must collect data from both internal and external sources, as both combined will provide more detailed information on threats and attack vectors, specific to your industry or organization. Also, focus on collecting information about any ongoing global attack and its attack vectors, related mitigation instructions and detection parameters from agencies such as government CERT, NIST, ENISA, and so on, along with industry sources, Cisco, Symantec, McAfee, Microsoft, RSA, and other major vendors. You may also focus on open source threat intel such as OSINT, SANS Internet Storm Center, and Open Threat Exchange. All this collected threat information needs to be properly categorized and segregated based on threat types, and its importance to the business entity and function; it could be, for example, based on the geolocation of the business unit, the business applications you are using, and IT infrastructures. Geolocation is important from the perspective of identifying where the threat actually originated so that you can have more of a focus on those business locations of yours as a priority, as they may have been affected; this could also help establish whether it is a targeted attack toward your organization, or maybe a country. This scenario can help you pinpoint the most effected business function, application, or unit, and gives you room for remediation in advance, or at least on time, before it's too late. It will also help in defining proper mitigation and a detection strategy to focus on the proper utilization of resources since it is always limited, irrespective of the size of the organization.

A successful threat intelligence system must be able to generate and distribute reports about all of its findings and related investigations to help others involved in the security protection, investigation, and monitoring process to carry out their necessary work at various levels of operations, engineering, and strategic decision-making by governance bodies. Reporting can be via any real-time methods or publishing online advisories. Security threat intelligence advisory might also be shared among industry peers via threat exchange mechanisms such as STIX or the Traffic Light Protocol, for everyone to take advantage of and stay ahead of any attacks.

Since we have witnessed a rise in cyber attacks in the past few years, we are all convinced that prevention and monitoring are just the initial steps of being prepared against any cybersecurity attacks. What we should do is develop more threat hunting capabilities and internal threat intelligence, and strong incident responses empowered by digital forensics investigation.

Most organizations in the industry today are already using SIEM as their primary and central monitoring platform. Traditionally, we have always used SIEM as a platform that receives information from the rest of the network, as we mentioned earlier in this chapter, to correlate and identify threats and security incidents. In essence, SIEM has always acted like a device that listens but doesn't say a word. However, with today's cybersecurity scenarios, it is prudent for SIEM to take a much larger part in the whole process, to say things and collaborate in taking action. One prominent activity that SIEM can be tasked with is integrating with digital forensic platforms to receive more rich and tactical information in real time. Digital evidence, by nature, is extremely volatile, and this also drives the response time for any security incident. This fragile and crucial nature of digital evidence in any cybersecurity incident forces us to approach the problem in a fully automated way. This calls for an automated way of collecting digital evidence from a suspected device, and we should do it right on time and integrate this telemetry with SIEM to trigger the collection of evidence from endpoints, just like a security camera starts recording the actions of a criminal with the help of a motion sensor. This, in turn, provides us with detailed information about what took place and also provides us with more accurate evidence that is collected at the right time—*the time when the incident took place, and not later*. By capturing the state of a compromised machine right after it provides shell access to cyber criminals, providing an initial analysis of the collected evidence, and making everything ready for a deep dive investigation, will help us turn the tables on the bad guys. Actually, this is only the beginning; we should also develop systems/platforms that will automatically analyze collected evidence and enrich this with threat intelligence to gain speed and accuracy.

In the present-day scenario, cybersecurity is gaining more importance than we could ever imagine with the ever-increasing threats and attacks on our information technology assets. This sudden shift in the industry has raised another important question and concern: is our workforce skilled enough to fight this battle? Do we have enough talent that can help secure our networks, applications, infrastructures, and, most importantly, our business and personal data? The talent gap is growing day by day, and as per research from many analysis firms, the gap could be as high as over one million.

Today, it is a fact that this shortage is no longer just a statistic, but a reality. And because of this fact, it is our responsibility to bridge that gap by increasing cybersecurity skills to fill this huge gap over a period. This brings us to the point where we can ask what skills are needed to start in cybersecurity or to switch to a cybersecurity career from an existing career? What do employers look for when they set out to hire cybersecurity talent? But this shortage of skills, talent, and experienced candidates is not stopping cyber criminals from stepping back; in fact, they know that most organizations may not have an adequate work force to defend attacks. It's, in a sense, working in their favor.

To some extent, our rapid growth and innovation in information technology is also responsible for this gap increasing each day. Today, if I look back into the past, technologies were not so diverse and did not change so rapidly either. It was easy to fix security issues, as they were all so steady. But in the current situation, technology is moving faster than ever, and we in the security profession are always playing catch-up. By the time we do catch up with the latest technology and understand how to secure it, the technology moves on again. This scenario is not going to change; rather, this will become the norm for the future. To some extent, as per many industry experts and analysts, who track changes in the industry, this gap in cybersecurity is also because of the gender gap. It is estimated that the ratio between the male and female workforce in the cybersecurity industry could be 8.5: 1.5. Filling the gender gap could certainly help fulfill the need of the hour, but this is not the only area that can solve this issue. We also need to involve more and more ex-military personnel. Veterans don't need to be taught the essence and importance of security; its hardwired into them already, by design, and cybersecurity concepts are still being driven from military terms and best practices. Also, the gap could be filled to some extent by retraining professionals from fields other than IT.

Everyone who wants to start in cybersecurity needs to have some basic information technology skills, know how the web works, how applications work, how system administration is done, and what the security standards are that govern security policies (at a very basic level). I often hear that, if someone wants to start in cybersecurity, then they need to have very strong technical skills in certain areas, but given the situation today with the skills and the talent gap, I think it's illogical not to ramp up others, too. Security is not just one person's, or one group of security specialists' job; it's the job of everyone to know about cybersecurity and to contribute in whatever way they can. So, the skills required for cybersecurity can be built over a period of time. I am not saying that someone can become an expert in a few weeks, or months, but if someone chooses to be in the domain, or make this their career, then they can start at the level they are currently at and grow from there. Gradually, they will become experts over a period of time.

You may think that cybersecurity is very technical, but it's not always the case; anyone who wishes to work in this domain should also possess or develop some soft and other non-technical skills too, such as being very meticulous about how they plan activities related to the security of an infrastructure or design it. Think and act in detail; think about all the possible ways to secure a system, data, or infrastructure; know about the business you are in; and properly define a strategy to make sure the business is not impacted on because you just want to implement security very robustly. You also need to develop strong analytical skills, so that you can find the actual root cause and not just be superficial about coming to a conclusion. Some of the skills that follow are the most sought-after in the industry today:

- **Network security:** As a network security engineer, you need to develop or possess skills on how to maintain and design LAN, WAN, and complex network architectures. Having knowledge of a scripting language and how to develop custom scripts for automating certain network-level tasks will be an added advantage, as networks today are vast and complex, and if you are able to automate tasks that are repetitive and time-consuming, it will be a great advantage. Experience around network protocols is essential if you plan to pursue a career as a network engineer and you are from a different domain; it will be helpful and advantageous to add additional knowledge about network protocols and their working principles. Network security professionals also need to be aware of the regulatory norms, policies, and controls, which will help them maintain IT security compliance and legal aspects. You can focus on the knowledge and skills mentioned here to ramp up a network security engineer profile:
  - Firewalls and switches
  - Routers and WAN equipment
  - Knowledge of subnetting, DNS, VPN, and VLANs
  - An understanding of network- and web-related protocols
  - Encryption technologies
  - Threat modeling for network design
  - Virtualization experience would be an added advantage in today's cloud world
  - Scripting language proficiency
  - The ability to solve complex problems
  - Network design and architecture related skills and techniques
  - Understanding security regulations and compliance
  - Knowledge about antivirus systems

- **Application security:** More than ever, the industry needs many application security engineers as the need for applicants has increased manyfold. This is because of the adoption of digitization in all areas of the industry today. Application security engineers and architects are very important to any application development teams and organizations. Progression toward becoming an application security engineer is also a long journey. This is because people who want to work in this area of security need to understand how any software application works in depth, and how to design a better and more efficient working application. It's possible that engineers who have spent a considerable amount of time developing applications will smoothly transition to become an application security engineer over a period of time, with proper planning, to develop the additional skills required. Also, there is much more training and many other certifications that are available to speed up the process; we will talk about those in Chapter 9, *Knowledge Check and Certifications*. From a skill development perspective, you can plan to acquire experience in the areas mentioned here:
    - Strong knowledge about **Secure Development Life Cycle** methodologies (**SDLC**)
    - Application threat modeling
    - Working knowledge of APIs and their functionalities
    - Web server and database-related skills
    - Strong knowledge about application protocols
    - Encryption technologies and how to use them to secure application and data handling
    - Secure coding methodologies
    - The ability to perform secure code reviews (automated and manual)
    - Standards and capabilities for authentication/authorization mechanisms and related technologies
    - Strong knowledge about web services
    - Knowledge about software threats and vulnerabilities, and how they get exploited
    - Knowledge about software security standards and controls
    - Application penetration testing skills
    - Security architecture skills and how to develop them
    - Skills related to secure software designs and frameworks

- **Vulnerability assessment and penetration testing**: Vulnerability assessment and penetration testing, known as VA/PT in the industry, is one of the important key verticals of the cybersecurity ecosystem. The process of VA/PT assures organizations and security researchers that their information systems are up to date and are not exposed to any critical security risks. VA/PT also helps you to be proactive in finding security threats and risks before attackers do. The VA/PT stream is very exciting and is a highly hands-on field. Apart from security consulting firms and big corporations, currently, many product development organizations also have their own teams for VA/PT as part of their product security teams. VA/PT researchers use various scanning tools to scan the network, applications, and/or other IT assets, such as servers during these scanning activities and try to find as many vulnerabilities as possible that could be exploited by attackers. Scripting knowledge can be very useful here, because, as a researcher, you can then develop your own custom scripts to test information technology assets.

If you are from a software development and quality assurance background, then VA/PT would be the logical choice. Your in-depth knowledge about software functionality could be extremely beneficial in understanding why certain vulnerabilities exist. Similarly, if there is someone from a network background, their knowledge and experience about networks would be crucial to understanding network-related vulnerabilities. In a sense, almost everyone who has hands-on experience in information technology could choose this domain as their next career step. Today, VA/PT by itself is much in demand. Some of the skills that you can rely upon or plan to learn if you choose this as your next career step are as follows:

- Static analysis, fuzzing, and manual and automated testing of networks, applications, and other IT assets.
- **SAST**: **Static Application Security Testing**.
- **DAST**: **Dynamic Application Security Testing**.
- Black, grey, and white box testing to conduct both VA and PT.
- Adequate knowledge about how to measure security risk and exposure.
- Ramp up on security regulations and laws (such as PHI, PII, SOX, PCI, HIPAA, ISO, GDPR, and others). This is important when you have to do VA/PT for a customer or for your own organization.
- Develop in-depth knowledge about security protocols and network protocols (TCP/IP, HTTP, HTTPS, IPSEC, VPN, and so on).

- Learn how network devices such as firewalls, IDS, IPS, switches, and routers work. This will help when performing network-related VA/PT.
- Learn scripting languages such as Python, Ruby, PowerShell, Perl, JavaScript, and Bash, among many others.
- Learn popular VA/PT tools such as Metasploit, Nessus, Kali Linux, Burp Suite, OpenVAS, Qualys Guard, Core Impact, Acunetix, AppScan, Nmap, and PSTools.
- Keep track of SANS Top 20 and OWASP top 10.
- Learn techniques such as SQL injection, XSS, remote file inclusion, PHP/ASP, and code injection.
- Sound operating system knowledge would be an added advantage.

- **Security Operations and Incident Response**: All organizations need security monitoring and incident response capabilities. The security analyst's job in a SOC or a CSIRT is to analyze and investigate each threat that comes toward the organization. They must also work toward providing a detailed incident response, contain the damage to a minimum, and at the same time provide enough threat intelligence to ensure that similar threats and issues are not repeated in future. A SOC will have **Security Information and Event Management (SIEM)** software to detect, investigate, and respond to any security alert/incident, and malicious activities. SIEM generates alerts by correlating logs, alerts, security event logs, and other telemetry from a wide variety of systems and network devices. SIEM is the most important tool that security analysts use in a SOC.

Organizations are constantly on the lookout for skilled and seasoned analysts and incident responders for their security monitoring efforts. Professionals from network operations, system administrators, and other security service areas can look forward to becoming security analysts or incident responders, and this is one of the most technical and hands-on roles, where the analyst needs to know common and advanced attacker techniques, how to detect various incidents, what to look for in those incidents, and how to analyze them. At the same time, they need to be aware of security regulations, laws, policies, and protocols when handling any security incident in SOC, as well as an incident response. Both roles—SOC and IR—have gone through a complete transformation in the way we work in these areas today.

It now involves a diverse skill set, such as collaboration with analysts, log analysis skills, expertise around digital forensics, malware analysis or knowledge about the working mechanisms of any malware in depth, a very keen eye to detect and pinpoint anomalies in network communications, application and user behavior, and also how certain servers and security devices work. SOC in the present day is evolving as CDOC, or centralized security centers with every capability, such as governance, legal, infosec, incident responders, digital forensics, security engineering, and security QAs, besides traditional security analysts, and it will continue to transform further. If you are planning to choose SOC and/or IR as your next career move, then the first thing you need to focus on is serious discipline in regards to how you work, what you work on, how you execute your tasks, what and how you communicate, and more importantly with whom. Let's discuss the list of skills that you will need:

- **Communication skills**: Knowing how to communicate effectively in SOC/CDOC/IR work is crucial. You must be able to get to the facts, find as many details as possible, and include them in your communication. More importantly, knowing who to talk to and what to discuss, and being able to control the flow and content of information, are key factors. Communication in SOC/CDOC/IR includes your responses to emails, providing accuracy and not giving away anything that is not required, the documentation of incidents and related technical details, notifications to appropriate teams or individuals through the proper channels, learning how to communicate with external parties, such as law enforcement or legal entities, and more. You also must have insight into your escalation tree and protocols of escalation. It is essential to maintain an updated list of incidents as well.

- **Following standards**: You must focus on acquiring knowledge about policies and procedures about the organization you work with, or industry standard best practices. Adhering to policies and procedures is very important for the type of work carried out in an SOC and IR environment. Procedures and policies also ensure consistency in the response toward an incident or the event analysis.

- **Integrity**: This is another key skill that you need to develop when it comes to security operations. This is because you will always be dealing with sensitive information. Any untimely leak or release of information may cause serious and costly damage to the organization. You need to be very discrete in handling and communicating information and incidents.

- Learning security principles, such as authentication, access control, and non-repudiation can be useful.

- Knowledge about security vulnerabilities and risks about systems, applications, network resources, endpoints, and operating systems.
- Learning protocols and related flaws that could be exploited for malicious use, such as spoofing attacks or DOS attacks, overflow attacks, flood attacks, and others.
- If you are from an IT and network admin background, then your knowledge about configurations could be very useful, as you may be able to use your experience to detect configuration flaws and weaknesses. For others who are new to this, you may have to spend time learning about it.
- All SOC personnel must have a strong understanding of assessing and analyzing security risks.
- You must also focus on gaining some experience or skills to understand network devices and how they work to a moderate level as you must know what **demilitarized zones (DMZs)** are.
- Learn about how routers secure a network and how packet filtering and packet monitoring devices/applications work.
- Gain knowledge about firewalls and how they protect a network.
- Strong knowledge and understanding of endpoint and operating system-level security risks and issues: how hardening works, how systems get compromised, how and what system logs need to be reviewed, and how to keep data safe in systems and endpoints using various technologies.
- One of the most crucial skills is the understanding of malicious code, viruses, Trojans, and advanced malware. You must enhance your skills to know how they work, what their behaviors are, and how you can detect those activities. Anyone from a malware reverse engineering background will be able to better utilize their skills as a security analyst in SOC and IR work.
- Having programming skills or people from a programming background can be very useful. They can help the SOC team to develop custom tools and scripts to detect threats. On the other hand, they will have a very good hold on software vulnerabilities, which certainly will come in handy while averting threats.
- Developing an incident analysis mindset so that you can quickly analyze an incident by looking into facts such as why the incident happened, who is or might be involved, timeline analysis, and which system/application could have caused the incident.

- **Malware analysis and reverse engineering**: Malware analysis is highly technical and a fully hands-on role in cybersecurity. Reverse engineering plays the role of breaking apart malicious software, malware, viruses, and any other software packages to understand the inner workings of the mechanism. Reverse engineering, commonly known as RE, can reveal a great deal of information about any malicious package—when it was created, what code was used to achieve certain goals, what systems, processes, or applications it impacts, and which other files or processes it calls to stay stealthy or fulfill its motive. Reverse malware engineers use a variety of tools to unpack and disassemble malware files. They also need to be experienced in how files are packaged and packed and know about encryption, compression, and other technologies related to file systems. Engineers will have to use tools such as disassemblers, debuggers, and network traffic analyzers, file behavior analyzers, log monitoring, sandbox technologies, and other tools. As a malware analyst, you will also have to perform tasks on potential samples that the organization has detected from its incident response or other security processes. You will need to establish the impact the malware may be having on the business or the organization. While performing malware analysis, you will also have to tackle the problem of finding out the **Indicator of Compromise (IOCs)**-related information. IOC-related threat intelligence is extremely crucial to create a proactive defense against any future attacks.

If you are planning to be part of this highly agile, dynamic, and engaging career, then you may want to focus on some of the skills described here:

- First and foremost, it is important to become a quick learner with keen observations skills, attention to detail, and the ability to follow proper processes as defined by the organization.
- Unlike other areas of security, for this one, you also need to possess a strong understanding of operating system concepts.
- Learn a few low-level languages, such as an assembly language. You can start with the basics first rather than trying to be an expert to start with in this field. You will gain expertise over a period of time.
- Acquire skills around Perl, Python, Shell, PowerShell, Bash, Java, and other scripting languages.
- Learn application security and network security concepts.
- Learn how to use tools such as OllyDbg, WinDbg, IDAPro, process monitor, process explorer, Wireshark, PEID, PE Explorer, and other commercial, as well as open source, tools related to reverse engineering.

- Learn about malware, viruses, Trojans, APTs, and their working principles.
- Learn how to identify vulnerabilities and exploit tactics.
- Learn PE file formatting and about analyzing files after unpacking them.

- **Digital forensics (DF)** is a very interesting and engaging stream of cybersecurity; if you are planning to get started in digital forensics, then I am sure you will not be disappointed. Digital forensics is based on recovering lost data, investigations, and the collection of evidence and materials found on digital devices. DF is done in most cases where computer crime is involved, and you must prove a crime or theft. DF can be done on any computer assets, such as workstations, servers, mobile devices, and network devices. You need to be extremely careful while performing DF, as you not only have to find evidence but must also ensure its safekeeping, integrity, and sensitiveness, as this evidence may be used in a court of law by the appropriate body or legal team. The current industry standard is to have dedicated digital forensics team or analysts. During DF, proper instructions or orders are followed to acquire evidence from a machine or from the cloud. If you are planning to be a forensic investigator in the digital world, one of the skills that you have to focus on is the process of transferring and preserving artifacts after you have collected them. It's very important to maintain a chain of custody to ensure that evidence is not tampered with; otherwise, it will prove no use in a court of law. Some of the skill sets that you can bank upon to become a digital forensic investigator are listed here:
  - Learn how to imagine the target system, as it will allow you to analyze it without impacting the original digital media under investigation
  - Cryptography and encryption technology skills will certainly add value to digital forensics, as often you will find that data is encrypted and you may have to decrypt it for your investigation
  - Finding and recovering deleted files
  - Knowledge of a file's metadata and how to extract that information for investigation
  - A keen understanding of international as well as local cybercrime and criminal laws, especially for the region you are going to work in, because every country has its own specific laws, on top of international laws
  - In-depth knowledge of cybersecurity and attack methodologies will always be key to your investigation and your analysis
  - A very good understanding of operating systems and networking technologies

- Attention to detail and presentation skills
- Knowledge of forensic tools and software such as EnCase, FTK, Cellebrite, and Volatility
- Knowledge of virtualization technologies will also come in handy

Who is Deepayan Chanda?

Deepayan Chanda has an MBA in IT, is a GIAC Certified Intrusion Analyst, a computer hacking forensics investigator, and a certified ethical hacker with over 23 years of experience in the IT and defense sectors (Indian Air Force), over 18 years' specifically in computer security and software development. He has a lot of experience and skills in technologies related to security operation centers, anti-malware operations, penetration testing, vulnerability assessment, web application security, network traffic analysis, security incident response, security event analysis, and log analysis. He is also an effective communicator with strong people management skills and analytical and relationship management skills, coordinating and executing the design and implementation of large-scale **Security Information and Event Management (SIEM)** solutions, security process automation, security architecture planning, network vulnerability testing, web application vulnerability testing, network security project management, security methodology, pentesting methodology, and security operation automation.

Gary Duffield

Alliances Director

Getting a foot on the cybersecurity ladder

Twenty years ago, if you said you wanted to work in security, you would be issued with a walkie-talkie, a hat, and your own shopping mall to patrol. If you had said you wanted to work in cybersecurity, you probably would have received a nice smile and a change of subject. Times have very much changed since then; those tasked with working security *"front of house"* in those shopping malls are invisibly supported by those working in cybersecurity *"back of house"*. This ensures that the shops and services are as protected from the casual shoplifter as they are to the professional cybercriminal. The infamous case of the retailer Target being hacked in 2013 resulted in a reported loss of $148 million, and nothing compared to the damage it did to their reputation.

Imagine if it were your job that just cost your employer $148 million. I assume Target quickly re-evaluated its cyber security workforce, polices, and processes after this. A quick check of LinkedIn reveals that Target's Senior Vice President of Information Security joined them shortly after this incident (https://www.linkedin.com/in/rich-agostino/).

You tend not to see too many Senior Vice President roles in the 'situations vacant' section of your local newspaper. However, that sort of role sits at the top of a huge pyramid of opportunities for those with a passion for cybersecurity.

The elephant in the room

If you are reading this book, you are likely interested in getting started with cybersecurity. However, maybe you are feeling insecure about your aptitude or your ability. Perhaps you think you need to be a propeller head mathematical genius with a passion for *Star Trek* to succeed. Of course, all of those attributes help, but many of the technical and compliancy skills can be learnt. Perhaps the question to ask to yourself is not *do I have or can I get the skills I need?* but *do I have the aptitude?*

Ask yourself: am I able to think like a potential hacker; do I understand social engineering? Could I throw my aptitude and skills in front of a speeding train filled with professional and amateur hackers driven to deface a public website or empty bank accounts? By doing this, can I also help colleagues to not fall for phishing attacks that let the website be defaced or the bank accounts be emptied? The picture I am painting is one of a need for an individual with both technical ability, street smarts, agility, change management and even business analytical competencies. The elephant in the room? There is no *one* path to enlightenment. Doing a Certified Hacker Course will not alone give you super powers. Plan bigger.

Hacking is easy

We have all seen it on TV or the movies: the super villain hacker - with their banks of equipment, flashing lights, and network cables - plugs in a USB stick. Some command windows open and random technical words appear, alongside a progress bar. Meanwhile, inside the organization being hacked, the victims turn to the aforementioned propeller head, he or she slips on their tank top of choice, and opens a laptop that is immediately available for action... There is probably a map on the screen, with various sections of it turning red as the hacker progresses. Cut to a shot of the progress bar: back to the white knight, the defensive hacker. They randomly mash the keyboard until the map is back to green. The nuclear weapon is disarmed, the list of British agents in the field deleted, or the personal details of 5 million customers of a 5th Avenue New York retailer - attached by cybercrime syndicate Fin7 - are no longer at risk. Unfortunately, in the case of Target, 5 million people had to be contacted and advised their details were out there (`https://mashable.com/2018/04/04/every-store-retailer-hacked/#T_rdfTf4fPqT`).

Still want to work in cybersecurity?

Working for DDLS, Australia's largest provider of technical training, provides me with some fantastic insights into what corporate Australia is training its workforce for. You will not be surprised to learn that courses such as EC Councils Certified Ethical hacker are top sellers. We will come back to talk about specific courses and certifications shortly.

Who knows what the demographics of the readers of this book will be? From the mentoring work I have done with Australian children's charity, The Smith Family, I know that preparing for a career should start early. If you are reading this as and still at school, or maybe a parent thinking about how you can support your son or daughter's journey after they finish school, go and speak with your local universities and colleges about your aspirations. They have worked out that there is a huge need for cybersecurity skills, and money to be made, and they will potentially have diplomas and degrees in cybersecurity available for you to join. Universities across the world already offer a Master of Science in Cybersecurity.

Roles within roles

There is no one size fits all job title, no one set of skills, and I would argue, not one skill set that makes up a cybersecurity job. A quick look at Seek, a popular employment website in Australia, revealed 15 different security job titles on the first few pages. **Analyst** and **Specialist** being particularly popular. These roles require skills such as *"delivering defensive cyber security services across the bank and providing security insights and expertise using the latest security technologies."* So that's pretty clear: change the locks and the job is done. The criteria for a Cybersecurity Analyst for a government department suggested that *"this job requires you to identify and asses key cyber security threats and trends. Tell us about a time you have identified an issue."*

I am not filled with confidence that roles recruited on the above criteria will be disarming those nuclear weapons any time soon.

What I do see are two streams of cybersecurity opportunities. I will describe them as **hands on** and **hands off**

In the hands on stream, I see cybersecurity not just being limited to cybersecurity products, but as the very fabric on which every organization builds its technology. DDLS is a training partner with Microsoft, Google Cloud, AWS, and Red Hat; all of these vendors build fantastic, secure products, which someone has to design, deploy, and manage securely. The point here is that cybersecurity isn't separate from business. It is business as usual.

An Azure administrator will have a level of responsibility for delivering secure cloud services to their business. It is way beyond the scope of this section to dive into developing secure code, but clearly no one wants an application that is easy to compromise. Of course, that hands on stream includes security appliances such as Checkpoint, end point security such as Trend, and network security built into Cisco products. Only after we have thought about the proper opportunity to manage security can we start to think about the more generic cybersecurity training, such as the Ethical hacker programs from EC Council.

I have just mentioned a hands off stream, and these are roles less wrapped up in curly brackets. For example, an Incident Manager is the one after whom the company runs when the company database hits the internet. I see these roles as ones not engaging in the technical aspects of implementing cybersecurity. Consider them as an analyst role, perhaps tasked with analyzing and assessing vulnerabilities in the infrastructure. This investigates tools and countermeasures to remedy the detected vulnerabilities, and recommends solutions and best practices. They also test for compliance with security policies and procedures. The infrastructure in this example includes software, hardware, networks, and people. Therefore, it is easy to see that it would be hard to have domain level expertise across every discipline. You would need the support of someone with hands on skills in Cisco or AWS. Hopefully it's clear that providing a prescriptive view of who is who in the cybersecurity zoo isn't possible. Therefore, here is some homework for you: use tools such as LinkedIn and job seeking websites of choice and check out roles such as Security Analyst, Security Engineer, Security Architect, Security Software Developer, Chief Information Security officer, Security Specialist, Penetration Tester, Forensic Investigator, Disaster Recovery Analyst, and so on.

 Top tip: If you are not currently working in cybersecurity, research your role before you invest in training, as each role has a different path of training required to master it.

Getting the skills you need to be recognized as a cybersecurity expert is a minefield. If you just want to manage a secure hybrid cloud environment, a Masters in cybersecurity is nice, but it won't help you with your day to day job. You actually would be better placed looking at the vendor certifications for AWS, Google Cloud, Microsoft Azure, or your Cloud platform of choice. Following this advice will save you four years and about $70,000 of student debt.

The example above illustrates an interesting perspective. In a secure world there are training courses and certifications that are mapped to a product. A Checkpoint Security certification is really valuable if you support Checkpoint devices; the same rules apply to cloud platforms and networking hardware. You can bet on Cisco as it's very dominate, but if your dream job is for an organization that has built its networking on top of Huawei hardware, Cisco skills are suddenly less relevant . However, they are still usable and concepts tend not to change, just the way the technology deals with it does. There are of course other training courses and certifications that are not vendor-specific. These courses tend to be more portable. The concept of what a denial of service attack is is the same irrespective of your choices of IT vendor.

It would be wrong for me to prescriptively list the courses YOU must take to become a security professional, simply because I don't know what type of security professional you want to be, or will end up being. I can, however, share with you some of the market leaders in this space. Being armed with aligned skills from some of these vendors will help you get a secure foot on the ladder, help you take the next step in your career, or more importantly, help your employer sleep better at night, safe in the knowledge you are one step ahead of the hackers, probably.

Start here

If you are still in education, consider checking out what is on offer at local universities and colleges. Talk to them about what roles students who have completed the courses have gone on to achieve.

If you are not currently working in IT, or perhaps are a first line support and looking for a broad baptism of cybersecurity knowledge, have a look at courses in security from CompTIA. Their Security+ certification *"validates the baseline skills you need to perform core security functions and pursue an IT security career."* This is an ideal starting point.

See yourself as an IT person securely managing complex infrastructures? Check out the vendor certifications for your platform of choice. Currently there are lots to choose from, from the Cisco CCNA Security to Architect level certifications from vendors.

Navigating the options is a consultative exercise in itself. Working with a learning partner, such as DDLS in Australia, can help you navigate the courses and certifications, to get you market specific data—if CompTIA is not a thing in your market, do not take it.

Already have a background in IT and looking to focus on security?

There are three vendors that immediately spring to mind: EC Council, ISC2 and ISACA. There are others too, and all have their fans and their haters. Part of the guidance I would love for you to take from this piece is it's not just about finding the right content from an intellectual perspective, but also from a geographic or organizational perspective. At the time of writing, here in Australia, a quick review of CEH, CISSP, and CISM cybersecurity jobs revealed a similar number of vacancies. There are around 50 more jobs with CISSP as a desirable certification; more than CISM and 70 more than CEH. The level playing field is slightly titled towards CISSP.

Clearly cybersecurity involves a lot of acronyms, including CEH, CISSP, ISACA, and ISC2. But what do all of these mean? Let's just try and make sense of this:

- **CEH – Certified Ethical Hacker**: A very well regarded certification, this is an intermediate-level credential, part of a suite from EC Council. It is well suited to those at the start of their move from IT into cybersecurity; expected experience is lower than that of CISM or CISSP. Quoting the vendor, CEH credential holders possess skills and knowledge on hacking practices in areas such as footprinting and reconnaissance, scanning networks, enumeration, system hacking, Trojans, worms and viruses, sniffers, denial-of-service attacks, social engineering, session hijacking, hacking web servers, wireless networks and web applications, SQL injection, cryptography, penetration testing, evading IDS, firewalls, and honeypots. CEH is a vendor neutral certification.
- **CISM – Certified Information Security Manager**: This is also well regarded. It is an advanced level certification, part of a suite from ISACA. ISACA are focused on governance. CISM requires at least 5 years experience so it's not suited to those wanting to move to a career in cybersecurity. Credential holders possess advanced and proven skills in security risk management, program development and management, governance, incident management, and response.

- **CISSP - Certified Information Systems Security Professional:** In my market, this is curently the most in-demand certification. It is an advanced level certification, which again assumes around 5 years of experience. CISSP is part of a suite of courses from ISC2 (pronounced *ISC squared*). To quote the vendor, CISSP credential holders are decision-makers who possess expert knowledge and technical skills necessary to develop, guide and then manage security standards, policies, and procedures within their organizations.

Many cybersecurity credentials require the renewal of certifications to stay current. This is not a huge surprise as hackers learn new vulnerabilities, and therefore those tasked with staying one step ahead must evolve their skills.

So what did you just tell me?

Cybersecurity is a very rewarding career, both financially and intellectually. There are multiple entry points. Brand new to cybersecurity? Look at CompTIA. Working in 2nd or third line support? Look at Certified Ethical Hacker. Love governance and auditing? Research ISACA. Ready to be the decision maker in your business? Look at CISSP. All of the vendors mentioned have credible, high quality solutions and operate with integrity. Working with a local learning partner is a sure fire way to get something relevant based on your needs, current background and market conditions. All of these vendors have a suite of security offerings, some of which compete. As you move up the career ladder, your training options evolve, but that is a story for the next book.

Who is Gary Duffield?

The day that I realized that learning and development has the power to change lives was the day I was dismissed from McDonalds, 18 and unqualified. Studying to become a Television Engineer helped me fall in love with learning. Television engineers became micro computer engineers; PC engineers became trainers. The die was cast, I was a Learning and Development Professional.

In 2009 I decided I wanted to disrupt my life. I wanted to leave my perfect job of 25 years at QA Training, one of the world's largest training businesses, and move to Australia. My wife, not keen on the idea, set the rules. It had to be Perth. The Australian government set the rule: get in before I was over 45 or the door slammed shut.

I formulated a plan, I did a degree at Manchester Met to help with the visa (it didn't), I asked key vendors who I should work for. They had one name: DDLS. I spent a year trying to contact them, stalking them at global conferences, building relationships with their staff, suppliers and clients.

I had moved - albeit on a temporary visa - to Australia, and I made a real mess of it. I was selling nothing. As a result, I had one of *those* conversations with the boss. I realized my approach was wrong. I realized I knew vendor land. I'm forever grateful to Alan Watts of Microsoft and Sally Adams at Data3. Both took the time to help this pom integrate. I didn't look back. 14 months in sales, and they let a Manchester lad in Perth lead the Microsoft business. A year later I joined the senior leadership team.

Right now, I'm helping lead DDLS through a digital disruption as we on-board new vendors, forge new partnerships and seek to better service the needs of our clients.

I actively mentor under-privileged children for The Smith Family and am a passionate advocate of Women in IT and Leadership. I am after all, a dad with a daughter, who is now a passionate Australian. Without learning and certification, where would I be?

Dr. Erdal Ozkaya

Head of Information and Cybersecuirty, Managing Director, Standard Chartered bank

Cybersecurity: The Beginner's Guide—**a comprehensive guide to getting started in cybersecurity.**

I am so used to hearing questions such as the following:

"How can I start my career in cybersecurity?"

"How can I switch to cyber?"

"What are your recommendations for us to be successful?"

If not every day, it must be at least a few times every week that, those questions are asked of me. Regardless of whether I am in Australia, Asia, Africa, America—you name it—I receive the same questions again and again. I wrote a few blog posts about the topic on LinkedIn and `https://www.erdalozkaya.com/`, but they are not detailed enough to help beginners or career-switchers as they don't provide in-depth help.

It's not a secret; everyone is talking about the huge talent gap in the cybersecurity industry: *Forbes Magazine, Tech Republic, CSO Online, DarkReading, SC Magazine*, and others, as well as, Fortune CEOs such as Satya Nadella, McAfee's CEO Chris Young, Cisco's CIO Colin Seward, and others.

Organizations such as ISSA and research firms such as Gartner are also discussing this. So, nearly everyone is talking about this topic.

Working closely with Microsoft's Cybersecurity Solution Group's Corporate Vice President Ann Johnson, knowing her passion for working closely with cybersecurity talent and closing the diversity gap has always encouraged me. With her tweets and her talks, in our one-to-ones and through her public speeches, she has influenced me to do more in this area.

And, finally, while I was delivering a cybersecurity workshop in India for a group of IT experts, when I received similar questions on how they could become experts specifically in cybersecurity and AI, I noticed it was time to do something; while chatting to Deepayan, who was also an instructor at the same workshop, he shared with me his experience on the same topic.

There are possibly endless resources and information already available on the internet today, which talk about how to start in a particular area of cybersecurity. Even so, if many people are reaching out to people in the industry with the same questions and seeking basic guidance to kickstart a career in security, then it must be a general problem and could be a very simple one to solve. After analyzing the case, I found out that the information available on the internet is either overwhelming for someone to process or is too fragmented, so individuals are unable to see the forest view of the cybersecurity world and then pick a tree for themselves.

With the final push being the course attendees and Deepayan, I decided to reach out to Heramb, the **Acquisition Editor** (**AE**) from Packt Publishing and shared my idea. And, of course, Packt was also aware of the same issue.

And finally, here is the book; after completing it, we reached out to some close friends who have spent years in cybersecurity, and we asked them to share their experience with *you*, our readers, as well.

I hope it will help many individuals and organizations.

References:

- *The Cybersecurity Talent Gap is an Industry Crisis*: https://www.forbes.com/sites/forbestechcouncil/2018/08/09/the-cybersecurity-talent-gap-is-an-industry-crisis/#3dbc6a0ca6b3
- *Cybersecurity Skills Shortage*: https://www.csoonline.com/article/3258994/cybersecurity-skills-shortage.html
- *McAfee CEO Calls for Rethink on Cybersecurity Talent Shortage*: https://www.scmagazineuk.com/mcafee-ceo-calls-rethink-cyber-security-talent-shortage/article/1473725
- *How to Fight the Cybersecurity Talent Shortage*: https://www.verizon.com/about/our-company/fourth-industrial-revolution/how-fight-cybersecurity-talent-shortage
- *Confront the Cybersecurity Talent Shortage*, (Gartner): https://www.gartner.com/smarterwithgartner/solve-the-cybersecurity-talent-shortage/
- *The Cybersecurity Talent Gap*: https://www.pwc.com/us/en/services/consulting/cybersecurity/library/broader-perspectives/cybersecurity-talent-gap.html
- *Bridging the Cybersecurity Talent Gap*: https://www.darkreading.com/careers-and-people/bridging-the-cybersecurity-talent-gap/a/d-id/1331858
- *Recruiting in the Age of the Cybersecurity Skills Gap: Challenges to Overcome*: https://www.information-age.com/recruiting-in-the-age-of-the-cyber-security-skills-gap-123476988/
- *Microsoft's Ann Johnson Wants to Close Cybersecurity's Talent Gap*: https://www.cnbc.com/2019/03/12/microsofts-ann-johnson-wants-to-close-cybersecuritys-talent-gap.html
- Satya Nadella , Microsoft CEO's tweet: https://twitter.com/satyanadella/status/1105558119961133056
- *Infographic: How to Solve the Cybersecurity Talent Gap in Your Organization*: https://www.techrepublic.com/article/infographic-how-to-solve-the-cybersecurity-talent-gap-in-your-organization/
- *Is the Future of Talent Recruitment about Leadership?* https://www.cisco.com/c/en_uk/solutions/executive-perspectives/skills-gap/future-of-skills-and-talent.html

How did I become involved in information security?

My first hack (!) happened when I was 9 years old. My brother received a James Bond-style three-digit manual bag as a birthday gift. He used to hide his secret stuff inside the bag, and one day I realized he had something really interesting in his bag, and I wanted to get access to it. Of course, my brother was not that keen on me having access to his bag. So, to cut a long story short, after running a manual password attack, which, of course, took me a while since I had to write every single combination down, within weeks I was able to open his bag. My reward was his magazines; as a nine-year-old boy, having access to those kinds of magazines made me the most popular boy in my primary school.

Starting my career as a network administrator, then moving on to infrastructure engineering with every project I completed, the security gaps that I have found have always frustrated me, researching every single issue that I have faced, reading many staff comments on the net, and doing many hands-on exercises. Then, moving on to IT consulting and sharing my insight with my clients from all organizations showed me the biggest gaps in IT departments. So, I decided to move toward information security and build my skills and knowledge in the field to be able to pass them on to everyone else around me.

A very long time ago, when I was still a teenager in Germany, I used to work part-time in a small computer shop where I had to teach customers how to fix minor issues. Back in those days, computers were not in every house, and I used to teach friends how to operate them. Then, in university, I completed a teaching degree as my secondary degree.

When I moved to Australia, I started a part-time side-business from my garage, selling computers and providing networking, implementation, and security services. In the meantime, I was still studying network engineering and getting Microsoft certifications.

My MCT training career started in 2002; I got multiple MCP/MCSE certifications, and there was a huge IT boom. I became extremely busy, running between training centers as a part-time tutor, teaching many Microsoft and security courses. That led to me opening my own training company, where I had only one room, and at the same time I was still working somewhere else as a full-time IT professional. Finally, in 2006, I quit my full-time job and started to work for myself, where I grew the business into a multi-branch training company. Within a few years, the business grew from a one-room training center to a multi-million dollar business with branches all across Australia.

SPOT LIGHT ON OUR MEMBERS

Erdal Ozakaya
A Conscientious Achiever

Great achievements are not attained by impulse. Achievement is the culmination of many feats, experience, education and acquired knowledge that are all brought together. Erdal Ozakaya, a NSW ATBC member, is a testament to this statement. He has conscientiously studied and passionately worked at his career to enable him to attain some very prestigious awards from Microsoft.

Erdal was born and educated in Germany, however moved to Turkey to complete his University studies to attain his, Bachelor of German Literature. His love of literature and language is apparent by the fact that he can speak four languages: English, Turkish, German and Arabic.

After completing his tertiary education in Turkey, Erdal met his future wife Arzu. Eager to make his mark in the world, Erdal had to confront the fact that his future wife had no desire to move to Germany, so Erdal made the move to Australia. During their courtship Erdal spent many hours on the computer conversing with his future wife, which sparked off his interest in Computers.

Upon arriving in Australia, Erdal immediately enrolled himself into Tertiary courses where he attained his *Diploma of Networking Engineering* and then his *Bachelor of IT support*. Erdal completed these courses whilst working in the field of Information Technology.

Erdal has only been in Australia for nine years. He is a co-founder and Senior Microsoft Instructor at CEO IT Training & Solutions Pty Ltd, one of Australia's Gold certified Microsoft Learning Partners. Erdal travels across Australia teaching IT workshops and has served as Project Manager/Engineer for several large organizations in Australia, China, Philippines and the USA.

Erdal also actively participates in worldwide events as a technical lead and speaker. He was selected "Best Technical Learning Guide" and "Best Speaker" in Microsoft Technical Education Seminars (Tech Ed) Australia. He specializes in Windows 2003, Active Directory, Windows Client O/S's, Security/Exchange, Windows 2008/R2, Sharepoint, Windows 7, EC-Council, ISO 27001.

The passion and commitment that Erdal has shown to his work has been recognized by Microsoft. In 2009 and 2010 Erdal Ozakaya was awarded the Microsoft Most Valuable Professional award.

Recently, in April 2010, Microsoft went one step further and announced Erdal Ozkaya as the FIRST **Microsoft Certified Leaning Consultant** in Australia. There are only 16 recipients of this award in the world, with only one recipient in Australia, and that is Erdal Ozkaya.

The 'Microsoft Learning Consultant certification' recognizes trainers who have frequent consultations with their customers. Their role is more that of a technology trainer, they are also

required to diagnose current and desired business performance and design learning solutions to bridge the gap.

To attain this degree of certification from Microsoft is not an easy feat. The technical instructor must have exceptional technical knowledge and have great communicating skills. They must also be passionate about sharing their deep, real-world knowledge about Microsoft technologies with others.

The ATBC would like to congratulate Erdal for attaining certification as a Microsoft Learning Consultant.

If you would like to benefit from Erdal Ozkaya's inexhaustible IT knowledge, you may contact him at CEO IT Training & Solutions. Telephone: 1 300 424 446 or by email-eozkaya@ceotraining.com.au

ATBC in Australia sharing my profile with their members

In 2012, the success of my company gained the attention of another company, who offered me a deal to buy the business, which I could not resist. The handover of the business took a year; in that time, I continued to deliver security assessments and security/ethical hacking classes:

PenTestMarket   **CONFERENCES' SPEAKER**

Interview with

Erdal Ozkaya

Erdal Ozkaya is the founder and Senior Microsoft Instructor of CEO IT Training,

Erdal travels across Australia teaching IT workshops and has served as Project Manager/Engineer for several large organisations in Australia, China, Philippines and the USA.

Erdal actively participates in worldwide events as a Technical Lead and Speaker. He was awarded "Best Technical Learning Guide" and "Best Speaker" in Microsoft Technical Education Seminars (TechEd) Australia. He specialises in Active Directory; Windows Client and Server O/S's; Security/Exchange 2007/2010; Sharepoint2007/2010; EC-Council Security and ISO 27001/27002/ 27005.

The passion and commitment that Erdal has shown to his work has been recognized by Microsoft. In 2009, 2010, 2011 Erdal Ozkaya was awarded the Microsoft Most Valuable Professional (Windows Expert -IT Pro) award. Erdal is also a Security Consultant and Certified Ethical Hacker Trainer.

Recently, in April 2010, Microsoft went one step further and announced Erdal Ozkaya as the FIRST Microsoft Certified Leaning Consultant in Australia. There are only 16 recipients of this award in the world, with only one recipient in Australia.

PenTest Magazine Issue 1 (2012) interview with me

In the meantime, I was still working toward my goals and dreams of *"making cyberspace more secure;"* my contributions caught the attention of Microsoft and I was given the Microsoft Most Valuable Professional award (I was awarded an MVP from 2008 until I joined Microsoft in January 2016):

Microsoft Corporation   Tel 425 882 8080
One Microsoft Way   Fax 425 936 7329
Redmond, WA 98052-6399   http://www.microsoft.com

 Microsoft

Thursday, January 01, 2015

Re: Erdal Ozkaya, Most Valuable Professional, Windows Expert-IT Pro

To whom it may concern,

It is with great pride we announce that Tim Barrett has been awarded as a Microsoft® Most Valuable Professional (MVP) for 1/1/2015 - 1/1/2016. The Microsoft MVP Award is an annual award that recognizes exceptional technology community leaders worldwide who actively share their high quality, real world expertise with users and Microsoft. All of us at Microsoft recognize and appreciate Tim's extraordinary contributions and want to take this opportunity to share our appreciation with you.

With fewer than 4,000 awardees worldwide, Microsoft MVPs represent a highly select group of experts. MVPs share a deep commitment to community and a willingness to help others. They represent the diversity of today's technical communities. MVPs are present in over 90 countries, spanning more than 30 languages, and over 70 Microsoft technologies. MVPs share a passion for technology, a willingness to help others, and a commitment to community. These are the qualities that make MVPs exceptional community leaders. MVPs' efforts enhance people's lives and contribute to our industry's success in many ways. By sharing their knowledge and experiences, and providing objective feedback, they help people solve problems and discover new capabilities every day. MVPs are technology's best and brightest, and we are honored to welcome Tim as one of them.

To recognize the contributions they make, MVPs from around the world have the opportunity to meet Microsoft executives, network with peers, and position themselves as technical community leaders. This is accomplished through speaking engagements, one on one customer event participation and technical content development. MVPs also receive early access to technology through a variety of programs offered by Microsoft, which keeps them on the cutting edge of the software and hardware industry.

As a recipient of this year's Microsoft MVP award, Tim joins an exceptional group of individuals from around the world who have demonstrated a willingness to reach out, share their technical expertise with others and help individuals maximize their use of technology.

Sincerely,

Steven Guggenheimer
Corporate Vice President
Developer Experience & Evangelism
Microsoft Corporation

Microsoft Most Valuable Award letter from the Corporate Vice President

In the meantime, I have also finished a Bachelor of IT degree at the University of Western Sydney, and have spoken at many conferences as a Subject Matter Expert. In 2008, I was selected as Speaker of the Year at Microsoft TechEd (now, it's called Microsoft Ignite). I was also selected as Best Microsoft Certified Trainer in Australia, and I received the Global Instructor of the Year award by EC-Council for getting excellent feedback from my ethical hacking, forensics, and penetrating testing classes:

Microsoft Tech Ed 2008, Gold Coast Australia, Speaker of the Year

This award helped me to speak at even bigger conferences with a few thousand attendees. The more time I invested in developing myself and sharing my experience with communities helped me meet many people, which gave me a lot of international exposure. This is what I tried to explain to you in Chapter 7, *Networking, Mentoring, and Shadowing*. Networking, mentoring, and finding the right coach can help you excel in your career:

Hacker Halted Miami 2011, Global Instructor of the year, together with the CEO of EC-Council Jay Bavisi

Microsoft Ignite North America, more then 2,000 attendees are listening

In 2012, while I was handing over my business at one of those conferences, I met Martin Hale, the CEO of IT Masters (as you read in the *Experts' advice* section). Let's read the rest of the story from Martin:

> *"I first met Erdal back in 2012 when he was Chief Technology Officer for an IT infrastructure design company called Fastlane. Erdal's enthusiasm and vitality was infectious, and I couldn't help but suggest he channel it into postgraduate study. Erdal soon went on to enrol on one of our cybersecurity master's degrees, later taught some of the subjects, published several best-selling books on cybersecurity and just last year graduated from our Doctor of IT. Today, Erdal travels the world, helping companies that have been hacked and companies who are about to be hacked."*

This example is also a good reference for what we mentioned in Chapter 7, *Networking, Mentoring, and Shadowing*, so make sure to network well, again, as was mentioned in Chapter 4, *Skills We Need for a Cybersecurity Career*; once you choose your path, make sure to gain the right skills and, again, as mentioned in Chapter 9, *Knowledge Check and Certifications*, knowing what you are doing, getting the right certification, and always trying to do your best will always get you moving forward:

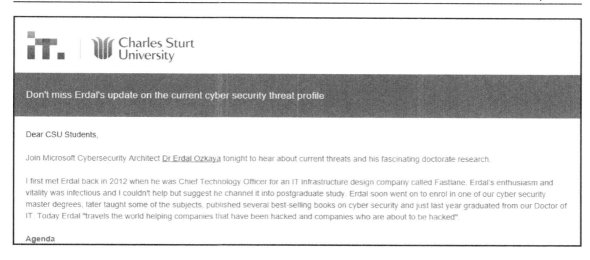

When I started to do my master's, I also got an offer from IT Masters and Charles Sturt University to share my experiences with their students. Since then, I have been lecturing at Charles Sturt University:

In 2013, I joined Kemp Technologies as a regional director for 2 years. I helped Kemp to grow its business in Australia and Asia. While at Kemp, I was still part of the community, and any free time that I could find I invested in building cyber-aware campaigns to raise the security bar against hackers:

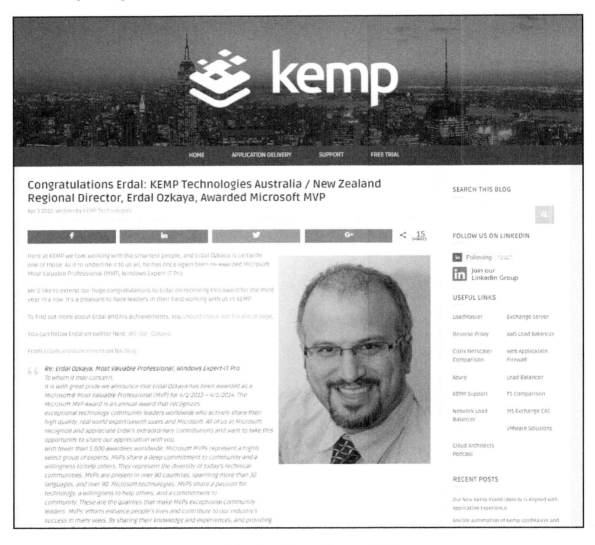

Kemp Technologies' web site, announcing my award (2013)

My full-time work never held me back from working toward my dreams. My hard work also grabbed the attention of newspapers. The following are some screenshots from those news articles:

Entrepreneur Magazine, Philippines 2012

The following is a photo of me making a thank-you speech for my Professional of the Year award in 2014, in Sydney, Australia:

Then, I had a great offer from EMT Holdings. The company offered me the Regional CISO position for the Middle East and Africa and a Vice President status, based in Dubai:

Channel *buzz* Middle East
Channeling ideas

| HOME | NEWS | INTERVIEWS ▾ | BUSINESS ▾ | EVENTS ▾ | NEWS BY PR NEWSWIRE | ABOU |

You are here: Home / Appointments / Business / Distributors / News / Press Releases / Vendors / IT Security Guru, Erdal Ozkaya Joins emt

IT Security Guru, Erdal Ozkaya Joins emt

📅 12 February, 2015   💬 Comment Off   👁 4 Views

emt Distribution, the specialty IT security products distributor announced the expansion of its team with the appointment of Erdal Ozkaya as Chief Information Security Officer (CISO).

Erdal is an IT Security Guru with business development and management skills, and is armed with world class qualifications, such as Master of Information Systems Security (M.I.S), Bachelor of Information Technology (B.I.T.), MVP, Microsoft Certified Trainer, Microsoft Certified Leaning Consultant, ISO27001 Consultant, Certified Ethical Hacker (CEH), Certified Ethical Instructor, and Licenced Penetration Tester. He is also completing his Doctor of Philosophy (Ph.D.) in IT Security.

He is also a globally recognised award winning speaker and technical expert and has been part of several major conferences such as; Microsoft TechEd, Hacker Halted, Microsoft Management Summit, AusCERT, trade shows and have featured in webcasts for Microsoft and EC-Council and many other vendors. He was awarded "Best Speaker" in TechEd Australia and won the "Circle of Excellence Award" from EC Council. His proven success deployments especially in the areas of Microsoft workloads in real life has become subject to IT magazines across Australia and New Zealand.

Dubai, United Arab Emirates was a brand new market for me; yes, I was born in Germany, and I have also lived in Turkey, then Australia, traveling around Asia, but none of those places can be compared to the Middle East. I had to start from the beginning, as I didn't know too many people, so I followed all the recommendations that I have made to you.

Me and my family moved to Dubai in December 2014, and within a year I came second in the Top 50 Security Professionals by *Channel MEA* magazine for my contribution to helping the community to be cyber-aware:

Channel Middle East Magazine, Channel Champions (2015) in Security

Next is Erdal Ozkaya, the chief information security officer and vice president of emt Distribution, based in Dubai. A prolific speaker and security specialist, it's clear why his presentations are popular in the cyber community. His language and personality are supercharged when discussing security. Each answer comes as if it's been shot out of an electric socket.

"The first thing that comes to mind when these events happen is that it's a cyber attack from China," says Ozkaya.

2015: Modern Trader Magazine, USA

I started from scratch and just repeated what I knew was going to work, and it did. Events started to catch the attention of the journalists all across that region. The following is an example from a newspaper in Bahrain:

This caught the attention of Microsoft, and I found myself joining Microsoft as a cybersecurity architect responsible for Europe, the Middle East, and Africa. For 3 and a half years, I reached out to customers all around the world.

Not just with our customers, but internally I was also volunteering to deliver advanced cybersecurity classes, as well as cyber classes for CxP levels. I was awarded membership of the Platinum Club, which is the highest level of achievement in Microsoft that an employee can achieve:

2017 Microsoft Circle of Excellence Platinum Club award, Microsoft CEO Satya Nadella, Microsoft Executives, and other award winners.

Some newspaper examples from South Africa, Nigeria, Turkey, and the Gulf

All of this never killed my desire to learn; in 2018, I was able to finish my doctorate degree remotely from the Charles Sturt University in Australia:

I loved my work at Microsoft, but I was traveling way too much, and at the beginning of 2019, I decided to move to another great global company, the Standard Chartered bank, as Head of Information and Cybersecurity (Managing Director).

What advice would you give to someone who is considering a career in IT? How can they get started?

As I've explained throughout this book, anybody who sees themselves in IT has to keep one thing in mind: the learning curve will never, ever end, so you have to love learning, researching, and being up to date. The IT industry will not appreciate the past; being current and being ready for tomorrow with the experience from the past is the best piece of advice I can give you.

Technology is moving so quickly, and it is it difficult to stay up to date, so if you don't like to read and learn, your knowledge will become outdated very quickly. We are in an era where knowledge can be gained much easier than 20 years ago; back then, for us to be able to learn, we had to go to libraries, borrow books (if we were lucky, as not too many IT books are in libraries), but, today, blogs, computer-based training, YouTube, and classroom-based training is much easier to reach and much more affordable. So, to keep it short, even if you cannot attend conferences, today, most of them are broadcast live, so watch them; follow technology leaders on Twitter; subscribe to a couple of valuable email lists; and read, learn, and, of course, practice.

Looking back at my career, from a small business owner to a multi-million dollar company, then moving to Kemp Technologies, Secunia (EMT Holdings), and Microsoft, I have worked with many governments and Fortune 100 companies in the financial and medical sectors:

An award from NATO, Center of Excellence Fight Against Terrorism

Selling hardware and implementing services can be repetitive, but being a Trusted Security Advisor working with Tier-1 Security issues can be unique. You might visit an organization that has 30,000 computers wiped out. Being able to work with customers in bad times is very special. Being able to help them resume services as soon as possible is indescribable for me.

At the same time, when I teach workshops or when I speak at conferences, sharing the real-life experience that have I gained in the field, helping students/attendees to be better makes me happy, and seeing my customers being able to fight sophisticated attacks makes me proud. Reading feedback via email—or you name it—makes me feel the best; mission accomplished—until the next challenge, which could be in the next hour.

Get feedback, listen to feedback, and keep improving yourself

Being awarded a doctorate in your career after two master's and two university degrees might sound like the pinnacle, but it isn't. I know I am still as I was on the first day of my career. My biggest mission is to make cyberspace more secure for everyone. Having a doctorate or working in a C-level job has no direct impact on my mission. I will probably still take the time to write books, speak at free events and webinars, as well as Tier-1 conferences, in order to share my experiences, findings, and recommendations with as many people as I can. Knowing humans, and how vulnerable we are, having the mission of helping to make every person and every organization more aware of cyber threats is not an easy task.

As my final word, I would like to share my speech from my doctorate graduation with you. If I can do it, so can you, and please don't forget that the highlight of my career happened in my late 20s, when I was married and had children:

> *"I had a dream, a dream that was not easy to reach; I **planned**.*
> *I had to take the necessary steps to achieve my goal; I **act**ed.*
> *There were times when I felt alone, when I thought I would never go through with it; I had some negative feedback that I needed to address; there were times when I fell.*
> *I learned from all those to move forward, **learn**ed from my mistakes.*
> *Finally, in the end, I am a doctor; **I made it**.*
> *Today, when I look back, I know nothing happens without **dream**ing, without taking the first step, without checking your progress and learning from your mistakes."*

Today, from my speech, if you wanted to walk away with one thought, I would say *"never give up,"* regardless of how tired you are or how many times you fail. **Stick to your ambition, to your goals, and ACHIEVE them.** **I know you can, because I just did it**, and I just shared my *"secret recipe."*

Good luck!

Dr. Erdal Ozkaya

12
How to Get Hired in Cybersecurity, Regardless of Your Background

In this chapter, we are going to cover the tips and tricks on getting into cybersecurity as well as helping you to find the right job, with common interview questions based on job skills.

Keep in mind, regardless of how many certifications you have, or how good your honors degree in university was, you will start your new job most probably from the bottom and you need to work your way up. There is no shortcut. The first step toward choosing any career must be identifying your core strength. If you are not a developer and you don't like coding, for example, don't force yourself to become one. This chapter will give you a holistic overview of how to secure a cybersecurity job from scratch. You will be equipped with knowledge of how you should proceed with your job search.

This chapter will take you through the various skill sets needed to kick start your cybersecurity career. And to that end, the following topics will be covered:

- Cybersecurity talent gap
- Cybersecurity jobs that you can fulfill
- Getting into cybersecurity from a technical background
- Getting started in cybersecurity with a non-technical background
- Transitioning from your current technical role
- Your journey from first contact to day one at work

The following chart from ISACA shows statistics and facts about the skills gap in cybersecurity:

ISACA cybersecurity skills gap (http://www.isaca.org/)

Getting into cybersecurity from a technical background

Having prior IT knowledge and skills will be always a plus when trying to get in to cybersecurity. If you can write a code, reverse engineer a piece of software, or at least understand the basics of networking, OSI layers, and so on, that will surely be an added advantage.

Having a technical background does not mean you should have an official degree or certification, but could instead mean that you have a few basic skills that you gained from your hobbies.

If you don't have those skills now, you should atleast know how to gain those skills since you've read every single chapter of this book.

Cybersecurity jobs to target

Technical cybersecurity jobs require a detailed level of computer knowledge; however, here's the good part: much of the work you do will be learned on the job. Therefore, don't let a desired skill (outlined in the job description) deter you from applying to certain jobs. As you'll read later, there's a difference between required skills and desired skills.

Just as for non-technical cybersecurity jobs, there are a variety of different technical cybersecurity jobs. Some job titles include the following:

- **Chief Information Security Officer (CISO)**: CISOs have a whole range of responsibilities, ranging from hiring IT experts to support their work, to providing leadership and training to those less skilled than them. They will also manage individuals, ensuring they are focusing on the right areas of strategy at the right time.
- **Security engineer:** In this role, you would test the network for vulnerabilities, monitor for security breaches, and develop security plans and policies. You would also mount an incident response in the event of any security breaches.
- **Incident responder:** An incident responder's job will require them to immediately respond to any new security threats, intrusions, or exploits, as they occur. Part of the job may also involve control of change management, ensuring orderly transitions during software, or hardware fixes, upgrades, and patches.
- **Cryptographer:** As a cryptographer, you would analyze, decipher, and perhaps even develop encryption algorithms. The goal of these encryption algorithms is to secure data. The idea is that even if a hacker steals data, they wouldn't be able to read it due to the encryption lock.
- **Computer forensic analyst:** People in this role combine their computer science background with their forensic skills to recover information from computers and storage devices. Analysts are responsible for assisting law enforcement officers with cyber crimes and retrieving evidence.
- **Malware analyst:** Here, you would stay up to date on the latest viruses found in the wild. Your job would also be to help develop software that would fight or defend against these new viruses.

- **Penetration tester**: This is the ultimate security job if you associate cybersecurity with hacking. As a penetration tester, you become a hacker; however, you will be an ethical one who must follow strict rules governed by the agreements your company has with a client company. Every action you execute will be documented. Companies hire penetration testers because they want to make sure malicious hackers cannot exploit their networks.
- **Security consultant**: Security consultant's are responsible for identifying, developing, and implementing security solutions to meet their client's needs.
- **Security architect**: A security architect is responsible for securing enterprise information by determining security requirements; planning, implementing, and testing security systems; preparing security standards, policies, and procedures; and mentoring team members.
- **Information security officer:** This person is responsible for establishing and maintaining a corporate-wide information security management program to ensure that information assets are adequately protected. Their responsibilities include developing, implementing, and monitoring the strategic and comprehensive enterprise information security and IT risk management program.
- **Computer security specialist:** The responsibilities of such professionals include designing and implementing safety measures and controls, monitoring network activity to identify vulnerable points, and acting on privacy breaches and malware threats.
- **Risk manager**: A risk manager designs and implements an overall risk management process for the organization, which includes an analysis of the financial impact on the company when risks occur.

Hard versus soft skills

Regardless of which industry you work in, you will need some basic soft and hard skills.

Hard skills are what are in your CV; if you have a technical background, and if you are a programmer, then you might know how to use C++ as a penetration tester and Kali Linux. If you're a web developer, you may already know how to defend against SQL injection attacks, which is essential as a cybersecurity developer.

On the other hand, soft skills are typically intangible and difficult to quantify. As we covered in Chapter 7, *Networking, Mentoring, and Shadowing*, the ability to connect with people or communicate technical topics to a non-technical person can be classified as a soft skill.

As a job seeker, I am sure you are already keeping an eye on LinkedIn or other global job search websites. Once you find a job that you think you will be happy to do, go ahead and apply, or if you think there are some skills missing in you, with this book, now you know how to gain them. In any case, try meeting the hiring manager or recruiter. Even if they don't hire you in your first interview, they might guide you in the right direction. Taking the effort and reaching out to them is already proof to them that you are keen to learn new skills; as we will cover later in interview tips, you might be able to find a common connection point and get hired.

You can read more about Forbes' recommendations for starting a cybersecurity career here: `https://www.forbes.com/sites/laurencebradford/2017/02/27/how-to-start-a-lucrative-career-in-cybersecurity/#5896cca71066`.

Getting started in cybersecurity with a non-technical background

Don't worry if you have a non-technical background. You don't even need to find a technical position if you want to work in the industry. Having a non-technical background means you probably won't have coding and development skills; however, it's possible that certain coding or development skills aren't even necessary to be hired.

Cyber risk analyst and technical writer are just two examples of non-technical cybersecurity jobs. These are positions you could obtain with skills you might already have. For example, a college degree may be the only thing required for an entry-level policy analyst position. If you're an avid writer and have a grasp of grammar, starting as a technical writer isn't a bad idea to get your foot in the door.

As discussed before in Chapter 9, *Knowledge Check and Certifications*, gaining certifications such as a Logical Operations CFR or EC Councils CEH can put you on the fast track with getting a technical cybersecurity position. These certifications can be obtained much faster than a university degree.

Once you get your foot in the door, you will start to gain experience at work, and if you take time to improve yourself through self-training, you can reach to your desired position faster. You should be keen to learn, read, and research. The industry has a huge talent crunch, and the more you learn, the more you will be welcomed.

Transitioning from your current technical role

If you are currently working, say as a Microsoft Exchange administrator, focusing on email security could be a good start for your cybersecurity career. Or if you are a system administrator and you have good know-how of operating systems, digital forensics could be your next job, after gaining the required skills, though.

Based on LinkedIn, 89% of surveyed professionals would be interested in hearing from a recruiter, and with this in mind, transition from your current role should not be too tricky. Again, based on LinkedIn, there are roughly half a million cybersecurity job openings in the United States, with a projected need of 1.8 million additional cybersecurity professionals to fill the workface gap by 2022.

When we look at the Asia-Pacific region, there is a shortage of 2.14 million, and Europe, the Middle East, and Africa have a shortage of 140,000 skilled workers, which is projected to be in the millions by 2022.

Demonstrate your worth – before you apply

Don't forget, most probably, you will be not the only one who will apply for a job. While there are many openings for qualified candidates, job seekers still need to demonstrate that they are not only qualified, but also the best person for the role. Demonstrating value starts years before filling out a job application. Know your stuff, plan your next move, and set yourself apart from others. Don't forget that being skilled is not essential but being dedicated is. You are worth hiring if the following apply:

- You have thirst for knowledge
- You are willing to ask questions and learn
- You learn from your mistakes
- You enjoy your work
- You can communicate empathetically
- You know how to say *no*
- You have the desire to help people

After now having learned how to secure a cybersecurity job, let's explore further and see how you can expand your knowledge base. As you can see in the following diagram, it's really important to learn what is required to make you a cybersecurity professional, and apply your knowledge, and develop an action plan to help you move on:

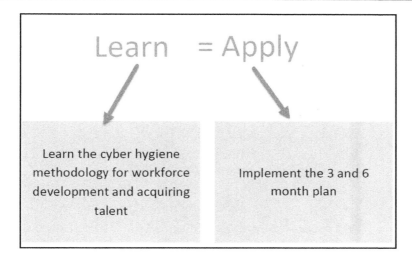

In the next section, we will discuss how to nurture your cybersecurity knowledge and skill set.

Read, listen, watch, and talk

Read as much as you can. Packt Publishing has great books on cybersecurity and offers various subscription options. Keep an eye on security websites and blogs. Follow the industry leaders on Twitter/LinkedIn and surround yourself with cybersecurity experts as discussed in Chapter 7, *Networking, Mentoring, and Shadowing*. Community meetups also are immensely helpful in ramping up your cybersecurity knowledge base.

What should be in your CV?

The first step in a job hunt is preparing your CV, and when you're exploring the avenues of cybersecurity, you need to have a CV that packs a punch. In this section, we will walk through the various aspects of CV making and will find out what its must-have elements are:

- **Education history**: Although it's not 100% necessary, having a solid education history can be good proof that you are a good learner. Schools/colleges teach you important skills in communication, writing, business, and project management. A university qualification will ease your way to management positions. Some employers now demand proof of a bachelor's degree before they consider candidates.

- **Relevant job experience:** List any previous IT positions plus any other work related to IT security. This can also include volunteer work, internships, and apprenticeships. For government jobs, hiring committees will be interested in any military or law enforcement experience
- **Hard IT skills**: While you're building your cybersecurity resume, work on developing hard IT skills such as the ones listed next. These are often in high demand by employers:
    - **Operating systems and database management**: Depending on the job you are applying for, showcasing your skills on Windows or macOS can help improve your CV:
        - Windows, UNIX, and Linux operating systems
        - MySQL/SQLite environments
    - **Programming and coding**: If you are a programmer, be sure to list what you know and the projects that you have worked on. If this is your first job as a programmer, the path that you want to take can give you some extra points:
        - C, C++, C#, and Java
        - Python, Ruby, PHP, Perl, and/or Shell
        - Assembly language and disassemblers
        - **Regular Expression** (**regex**) skills
        - Linux/macOS Bash shell scripting
    - **Networks**: Do you want work as a network engineer? Then showcase your skills in networking; here are some examples:
        - System/network configuration
        - TCP/IP, computer networking, routing, and switching
        - Network protocols and packet analysis tools
        - Firewall and intrusion detection/prevention protocols
        - Packet shaper, load balancer, and proxy server knowledge
        - VPNs

- **Specializations**: Thanks to the nature of their job and industry, security experts usually end up specializing in a specific area of interest such as one of the following:
    - Cisco networks
    - Cloud computing
    - Microsoft technologies
    - Wireless
    - Database modeling
    - Open source applications
    - Cryptography

    There are others. To gain extra experience in these areas, you can volunteer for tasks at work, collaborate with a mentor, and/or invest in self-directed learning and guided training.

- **Certifications:** Industry certifications are usually the best way to showcase what you know. So, the following are some certifications that you might like to thing about. If you are not sure which certification you want to take, please refer to `Chapter 9`, *Knowledge Check and Certifications*:
    - **Non-security certifications:**
        - Cisco CCNA
        - CompTIA A+, Server +, Network +, and others
        - ITIL, COBAT, and others
        - Microsoft certifications
        - VMware certifications
    - **Security certifications:**
        - SANS
        - Logical operations
        - OWASP
        - EC-Council and others

Don't forget that certifications are usually the best way to prove what you know. And they can be important during prescreening.

Checklist for what to include in a CV

In a nutshell, your CV must be able to stand out from others. To that end, you can learn from the pointers discussed previously and imbue that X-factor in your CV. Let's end this section with a checklist that will help you structure your CV in an effective way:

- Stand out. Your CV should demonstrate your unique blend of skills and experience
- Keep your CV simple
- Check your CV for any errors, and ensure you have zero mistakes
- Keep your CV updated
- Keep your CV real
- Tailor it and make it look good

Your journey from first contact to day one at work

Candidates think about their next career destination or alternatives for a career. To that end, discussions with family, suggestions from friends, and acquaintances are very important. Candidates search for information about career opportunities and potential employers on the web, at career fairs, at company presentations, or other information days. This is just the beginning of the entire job-hunt journey. There are many milestones that a candidate can cross while looking for jobs and the entire process demands a lot of work and perseverance. The following diagram is a good illustration from Kinesis on how a candidate's journey looks:

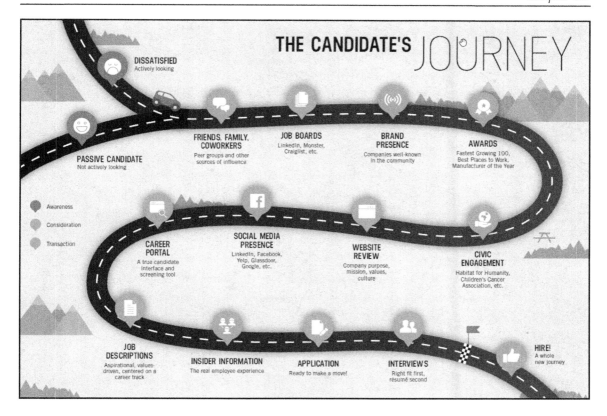

This diagram provides us with an overview of your journey from day one to the first day of new job, courtesy of Kinesis Inc. You can download the poster version free from its website: `https://www.kinesisinc.com/talent/`.

Now let's shift our focus to the types of job interviews in the cybersecurity domain.

Job interview types

A job interview is a formal meeting in which an applicant is asked questions to determine their suitability for a particular job. Job interviews can be conducted face to face, or via phone or video, and could be one-on-one, in a panel, or as a group interview. But no matter what the format, every job interview can be structured in three different ways.

Structured interviews

In structured interviews, the questions are planned and created in advance, which means that all candidates are asked the same questions in the same order. This will make it easy for a recruiter to compare candidates answers and hire the right talent.

This is what a structured interview comprises:

- Set of questions
- A scale
- Grading and comparing the talent to the other candidates

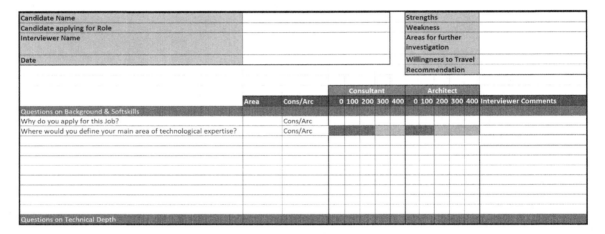

A sample Excel worksheet of a structured interview

Unstructured interviews

This is a type of interview where the interviewer will ask questions that are not prepared in advance. This type of interview is also known as an informal or casual interview:

- Unstructured interviews are more personalized
- Unstructured interviews are a free conversation, which can help to showcase your hidden skills

This is what will be in an unstructured interview:

- The recruiters will look into your day-to-day interactions; this can be a perfect opportunity to showcase your soft skills
- The recruiters will look to see whether you can stay focused, and whether you are flexible enough to talk about anything
- Your body language will also be taken into consideration

Semi-structured interviews

Semi-structured interviews are a type of interview where the interviewer asks only a few predetermined questions while the rest of the questions are not planned in advance. This is a hybrid interview style.

This is what will be in a semi-structured interview:

- The recruiters will structure their questions based on your responses
- The recruiters will see whether you can follow the natural flow of conversation

Common cybersecurity interview questions

The interview process is tough, not only for the candidates but also for the interviewers. The process is tough because well-looked-after talent will not move from their companies. Keep in mind that people will go where they are invited, but they stay only where they are welcomed. Besides, hiring skilled professionals comes with a cost.

The general interview process

The following pointers summarize what a general interview process entails:

- Resume shortlisting
- Basic HR interview (for external hires)
- Technical interviews
- HR interview and job offer (hopefully)

Commonly asked cybersecurity interview questions

These are just some sample questions; questions differ from role to role.

The following are some sample questions for entry-level jobs:

- Explain the difference between a risk, a vulnerability, and a threat?

  It's important to back up your answer to this one with an easy-to-understand example.

- What is the difference between asymmetric and symmetric encryption, and which one is better?

  Keep the answer simple, as this is a vast topic.

- What is an IPS, and how does it differ from an IDS?
- What is a firewall?

  Be simple with the answer, as this can get complex and lead to looped questions.

- How do you keep yourself up to date with the latest information security news?

  Just in case you don't follow any, here is a brief list: Hacker News, Threatpost, and Pentestmag.

- What is CIA ?

  CIA is the main reason why cybersecurity exists.

The following are some sample questions for junior roles:

- What is port scanning?
- What is compliance?
- What are the various response codes from a web application?
- Explain the objects of a basic web architecture.

 Different organizations follow different models and networks. Be generic.

- When do you use `tracert`/`traceroute`?
- What is the difference between VA and PT?

The following are some sample questions for experienced professionals:

- What is the difference between policies, processes, and guidelines?
- What is *pass the hash*?
- What is data leakage? How will you detect and prevent it?
- Explain the least-privilege principle.
- Provide some examples for mitigation against lateral movement.
- What do you understand about privilege escalation?

The following are some sample questions for master roles:

- What are the different levels of data classification and why are they required?
- What are the various ways by which the employees are made aware about information security policies and procedures?
- What should be included in a CEO-level report from a security standpoint?
- What are the defenses against CSFR?
- Reverse-engineer this code
- What do you think about security convergence and its effect on our company?

Personal questions

The following questions deal with your personal ambitions, goals, and thoughts about yourself, and are not strictly asked for cyberseurity positions only:

- Why are you looking for a new position?
- Tell us about your personal achievements or certifications.
- What are your greatest strengths and accomplishments?
- What are your greatest weaknesses?
- How do you envision your first 90 days on the job?
- Where do you see yourself in five years?
- Why are you changing your current role to cybersecurity? (If you are currently in a different role, that is.)

Communication skills

The following questions are set to test your communication skills and how well you can communicate your thoughts:

- Tell us about a time you found it hard to communicate with a customer or coworker. How did you resolve the situation?
- Tell us about your favorite manager or coworker to date. What made them so great to work with?
- What do you find yourself grateful for?
- Do you think your coworkers appreciate you more for your directness, or your ability to smooth things out?

Problem solving and judgement skills

The following questions are a test of judgement and how you approach a problem:

- Tell us about a time something didn't work the way you wanted it to. What would you do differently next time?
- How do you measure success at work?
- When you look back at your work experience to date, what makes you the most proud?
- Tell us about a time you were confronted with a situation for which you didn't have an answer in a policy or manual. What did you do?

Motivation and passion

The following questions gauge your motivation to work:

- What motivates you to come to work every day?
- Why do you want to become part of our company?
- Tell us about a time you went above and beyond for a customer.
- Tell us about something you are passionate about outside work.

Common tips

The following are some tips to keep in mind while appearing for an interview:

- Be precise in what you say, listen carefully, and think before you answer.
- Keep your answers simple (unless needed). If asked, provide details.
- Be confident (as much as possible).
- Be aware of security news.
- Learn about the company, and check whether they have had any incidents.
- Keep a positive attitude.
- Be a team member. Don't think that you are more important than others.
- Be responsible if you make a mistake—no excuses!
- Grow with the company and keep learning or get left behind.

Consider these points before accepting a job

The following points need to be kept in mind if you have a job offer in hand and are considering whether or not you should accept it:

- **Benefits and perks:** Make sure to question the details.
- **Work/life balance**: This should be one of your considerations if you are a person who likes to maintain a balance between work and your personal life.
- **Opportunity to learn and grow**: This will show whether the company is ready to invest in you.
- **A manager invested in your growth**: While choosing a new job, you should also evaluate whether the manager/leader you are going to work for is someone who will help you grow in your career. A bad manager can make you really unhappy; regardless of your success in the company, they can force you to leave.
- **Salary transparency**.

The view from a hiring manger or recruiter

So far, I have covered how you can improve your chances of getting a job. To make this chapter more valuable, I wanted also to add the recruiter's views on talent. You can also check out Chapter 11, *Expert Opinions on Getting Started with Cybersecurity*, where we asked some questions that can help you to learn from some known industry experts. Being a recruiter might look easy to you, but they have many tasks to do, such as finding talent like *you* in a short time frame, while there is a huge skills shortage in the market:

How to Obtain Talent in 60 Days

- Identify common language projects and tasks for the role

- Identify amount of time individual will spend on each task and project

- Identify correct salary for desired role

- Understand and share need and growth strategy of this role with perspective candidates

- Have a quick and efficient interview process

- Expect applicant is passive and has many people courting them.

- Make offers quickly

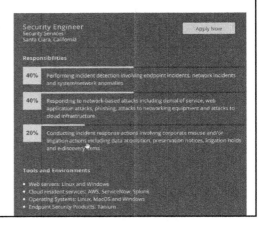

As you can see, they have a pre-defined score card, so make sure to read the job description carefully and try to find common ground with it to prove that you are the right candidate.

Based on the *McKinsey Global Survey*, 82% of Fortune 500 executives don't believe that their companies recruit the most talented people. If you follow the right tips, you can train yourself to be the right talent and sign the contract of your dream job:

A whopping 82 percent of Fortune 500 executives don't believe that their companies recruit highly talented people.

% of Fortune 500 executives who agree that their organizations ...

... recruit highly talented people — 18
... know who are high and low performers — 14
... retain high performers — 7
... develop people quickly and effectively — 3
... quickly remove low performers — 3

McKinsey&Company   **Source:** "McKinsey Global Survey: War for talent 2000," refreshed in 2012

Some recruiters use some additional tools, such as **My Dream Employee**, that help them to identify a remarkable employee:

In the preceding screenshot, you can see how the My Dream Employee worksheet looks, which should help you to build the right strategy for your interviews.

What is the hiring process for recruiters?

If you are wondering how the hiring process works, please have a look at the following diagram carefully; it should give you an indication as to what recruiters do in the background and perhaps why the process takes more time than you expect:

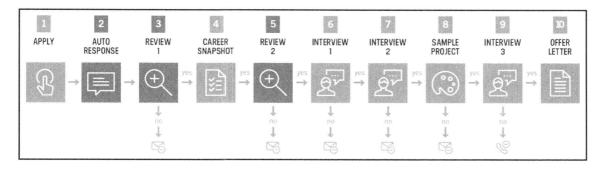

How to get hired at Microsoft

The Microsoft Careers website offers really great resources and help for free. I would highly recommend you have a look at it. In `Chapter 11`, *Expert Opinions on Getting Started with Cybersecurity*, you read stories and recommendations from Microsoft employees:

Microsoft recommends that anyone who wants to work for them should do the following:

- Apply for a job that they're interested in
- Understand the position and Microsoft as business
- Know their career path and how they want to grow
- Be aware of how to work with others
- Showcase a desire to learn, a passion for technology, and a willingness to work hard
- Be prepared to solve job-specific issues

For more information, you can visit the Microsoft Careers website: `https://careers.microsoft.com/us/en/interviewtips`.

How to get hired at Cisco

Cisco recommends the following tips for people who want to work for them:

- Be prepared. Be unique. Be yourself.
- Understand the business.
- Understand the job.
- Reflect on your strengths and growth areas.
- Think about your skills and achievements.
- Stay calm and take your time.
- Be curious and ask questions.

Please keep in mind that Cisco has three types of interviews: telephone, competence, and panel interviews. The recruiter should tell you what you should expect.

For more information, check out the following: `https://www.cisco.com/c/en/us/about/careers/working-at-cisco/students-and-new-graduate-programs/interview-tips.html`.

How to get hired at Google

Google has two rounds of interviews, and between each round it gathers feedback from the interviews and determines the next steps.

Google conducts interviews over the phone, on Google Hangouts, or in on-site interviews, and it recommends the following:

- Be prepared
- Be able to predict the future (yes, you read it right)
- Have a plan
- Be data-driven, and try to answer each question with a story that demonstrates your knowledge
- Be hands-on

For more details on getting hired in Google, check out the following: `https://careers.google.com/how-we-hire/interview/#interviews-for-all-roles`.

How Google's CEO did his interview when he was first hired in 2004!

Sundar Pichai, CEO of Google LLC, said the following when visiting a university:

> *"So, I remember doing my interviews during the day and people kept asking me 'what do you think of Gmail?' But I hadn't had the chance to use it. I thought it was an April Fools' joke. So, in my first three interviews, I couldn't answer it well because I hadn't used the product. It was only in the fourth interview when someone asked me: 'Have you seen Gmail?' that I said 'no.' He actually showed it to me. And then the fifth interviewer asked 'What do you think of Gmail?' And I was able to start answering it then. And in the final four interviews, I actually told them about what I thought of Gmail and how to improve Gmail. And that's my interview experience."*

According to CNBC, Sundar Pichai was able to succeed at interview as he was able to display intellectual humility, give a reason with a story behind it, and redirect the conversation. You can read more about the story here: https://www.cnbc.com/2019/02/01/how-google-ceos-brilliant-answer-in-a-job-interview-helped-him-get-hired.html.

How to get hired at Exxon

Exxon is one of the biggest companies in the world according to Fortune. It hires based on background and location. Like other Fortune companies, its careers website has examples on how to shape your CV. If a job requires assessment, the company gives you information on what is needed. The website also has some tips on what to expect in an interview and even on what to expect in an offer. So, please go ahead and browse its website to find the right job for you.

More information about Exxon hiring can be found here: `https://careers.exxonmobil.com/en/how-we-hire/our-hiring-process.`

Popular job search websites you should know

As I cannot list all the Fortune 500 companies' career websites, I highly recommend you keep a close track on the companies that you want to work for. If it has alerts on new job openings, be sure to sign up. If you are not sure which company you want to work for, you can keep an eye on the following websites:

- **Glassdoor**: `https://www.glassdoor.ie/index.htm`
- **LinkedIn**: `https://www.linkedin.com`
- **CareerBuilder**: `https://www.careerbuilder.com`

In summary, to find a job, you have to look for it, or you have to have an advocate/referrer who will recommend you to the hiring manager or HR. If you follow the recommendations in this book and get the right lessons from our experts, you will get a new job very soon.

Good luck!

Summary

There is a big talent gap in the cybersecurity job market. Recruiters are having difficulties finding the right talent, and the talent gap is opening new doors for anyone who wants to be a cybersecurity professional, regardless of their background.

This chapter has gone through the current needs of the industry; it covered what people need to do to find their desired job. The chapter also covered the recruiters' perspective and what they do when they hire talent, and it gave recommendations on how to get hired, from writing the best CV to passing the interviews. It ended by covering how to get hired in some top companies.

Other Books You May Enjoy

If you enjoyed this book, you may be interested in these other books by Packt:

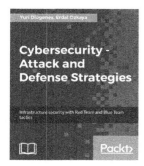

Cybersecurity - Attack and Defense Strategies
Yuri Diogenes, Dr. Erdal Ozkaya

ISBN: 9781788475297

- Learn the importance of having a solid foundation for your security posture
- Understand the attack strategy using cyber security kill chain
- Learn how to enhance your defense strategy by improving your security policies, hardening your network, implementing active sensors, and leveraging threat intelligence
- Learn how to perform an incident investigation
- Get an in-depth understanding of the recovery process
- Understand continuous security monitoring and how to implement a vulnerability management strategy
- Learn how to perform log analysis to identify suspicious activities

Hands-On Cybersecurity for Architects

Neil Rerup, Milad Aslaner

ISBN: 9781788830263

- Understand different security architecture layers and their integration with all solutions
- Study SWOT analysis and dig into your organization's requirements to drive the strategy
- Design and implement a secure email service approach
- Monitor the age and capacity of security tools and architecture
- Explore growth projections and architecture strategy
- Identify trends, as well as what a security architect should take into consideration

Leave a review - let other readers know what you think

Please share your thoughts on this book with others by leaving a review on the site that you bought it from. If you purchased the book from Amazon, please leave us an honest review on this book's Amazon page. This is vital so that other potential readers can see and use your unbiased opinion to make purchasing decisions, we can understand what our customers think about our products, and our authors can see your feedback on the title that they have worked with Packt to create. It will only take a few minutes of your time, but is valuable to other potential customers, our authors, and Packt. Thank you!

Index

Printed in Great Britain
by Amazon

79308958R00228